DAMNED IF WE DO

Contradictions in women's health care

Dorothy H. Broom

ALLEN & UNWIN

© Dorothy H Broom, 1991
This book is copyright under the Berne Convention.
No reproduction without permission.

First published in 1991
Allen & Unwin Pty Ltd
8 Napier Street, North Sydney, NSW 2059 Australia

National Library of Australia
Cataloguing-in-Publication entry:

Broom, Dorothy H.
    Damned if we do: Contradictions in women's health care

    Bibliography.
    ISBN 1 86373 054 0.

    1. Women's health services—Australia. 2. Women—Health and hygiene—
    Australia. I. Title.
362.1082

Set in 10/11pt Sabon by Adtype Graphics, Australia
Printed by Chong Moh Offset Printing, Singapore

Contents

Figures and Table

Figures

Table

Abbreviations

AMA	Australian Medical Association
BSE	Breast self-examination
CEP	Commonwealth Employment Program
CHP	Community Health Program
CR groups	Consciousness-raising groups
FPA	Family Planning Association
IWY	International Women's Year
NGO	Non-government organisation
NHS	National Health Service
SAHC	South Australian Health Commission
STDs	Sexually-transmitted diseases
WHIRCCA	Women's Health, Information, Resources and Crisis Centres Association
WICH	Women in Industry, Contraception and Health

For my kin network, fictive as well as formal,
in two hemispheres,
especially Inez, half a world away,
yet always right here

Preface

One great gift of the women's movement has been its insistence that there is no neutral, genderless, objective position from which to view the world or speak about it. Feminism has contributed to the awareness that we each occupy a unique 'subject position' that shapes our understanding of events and how we subsequently represent those events to ourselves and to others. Consequently, a writer is obliged—as far as possible—to identify the subject position from which a statement is produced, and to take responsibility for the distinctive character of her statement. That strikes me as a good use for a preface.

I make my living as an academic, teaching women's studies. Because university academics are supposed to do research as well as teach, and because I am committed to the women's movement, I want to identify research projects that involve and may ultimately serve women. Having studied women's consultations with their general practitioners, I was eager to learn more about the ways women are confronting the problems they experience as a result of traditional medical care. Australian women's health centres fulfilled those criteria, presenting me with two challenges: first, undertaking research that might shed light on women's efforts to claim more control over the knowledge, procedures, and institutions involved in health and healing; and second, conducting and reporting that research in a form that would make it accessible and useful to the women whose lives are at issue. In the work discussed here I try to do both those things.

This book is not, however, an authorised biography. It makes no claim to be the history of Australia's women's health centres. It is *a* story, a story researched and told by a white middle-aged American-born academic feminist, trained in the liberal arts and in sociology. Like many women my age, I have often been troubled by my treatment—both medical and social—when I sought health care. As with many more women, pregnancy and childbirth marked turning points in my experience of my own body and in my understanding of the importance of reproductive health to women's autonomy. Despite my privileged education, it has always required great energy to obtain the information and other resources I need to build and protect my own health, and to obtain appropriate care for myself and members of my family. These 'lived experiences' have shaped my thinking about women's health and women's health centres, sometimes in ways of which I am not aware. Nevertheless, the experiences have also contributed to my determination to learn as much as I could about this unique and innovative movement of women, and to make the information available to those women and to others who might learn from their story. Ultimately, I believe women's health centres are a powerful force for women's resistance and a crucial element in the gradual, sometimes painful transformation of a patriarchal social order.

In writing this book, I have been troubled with a pronoun problem. No, not *that* pronoun problem. At the best of times, I don't hold with use of the masculine in place of the generic, which is correctly labelled 'he-man' language. Anyway, the actors in this story are nearly all women, so in describing the work of an unnamed women's health activist, the default option singular pronoun is appropriately 'she' or, because of its collective character, 'they'. My pronoun problem is whether to use first person 'we' or third person 'they'. It often makes me uncomfortable to read a book by a woman about women framed in the third person, as if the author were not herself one of the women about whom she writes. Simone de Beauvoir excluded herself linguistically from *The Second Sex*, for example, and although she was exempt from many of the circumstances she described, she was striving to develop a theory of the production and consequences of femininity that would include all of us who are, as she so insightfully put it, not born but rather made into women.

In the case of the subject matter of this book, like all women in the developed west, I am on the receiving end of medicine's ignorance and incompetence where women's bodies are concerned. And having been involved in the women's health movement for nearly two decades, I consider myself in many respects a part of the larger picture. But the account here is not so much of women's health generally, or even of the women's health movement less generally. Rather, it is about Australia's women's health centres, the women who brought them into being, and the women who continue, in a variety of capacities, to invest themselves in those centres. However much affinity I may feel, I cannot take personal credit for direct participation in any of the centres, except to a small extent in the Canberra Women's Health Centre which has been incubating during the same years as this book. It would not be appropriate for me to include myself among those who have been instrumental in instituting and continuing the several dozen women's health centres around the country that are the focus here.

The solution I have adopted is usually to stick to a more impersonal sounding 'they' in order not to claim credit for work in which I maintain a deep interest, but am not a participant. Occasionally, I have reverted to the first person plural, and even to the academically proscribed first person singular. But mostly, I refer to women in the third person. Both linguistically and experientially I am marginal: at once both an insider and an outsider to this story. Some years ago, Dorothy Smith (1974) suggested that women's marginality (both insiders and yet outsiders in male-centred society) made for insightful observation and analysis. I hope that this somewhat awkward position will have its benefits since it results in a certain amount of pronominal oscillation at times.

Another linguistic problem I have is with tense. Insofar as this is a history, it would seem that past tense is the obvious choice, and where I am seeking to describe a sequence of events that took place some time ago (such as a particular group opening a centre), I have made that choice. It becomes a little more difficult to know how to word descriptions of events that are continuing in the present (such as women's discovering the centrality of health to women's liberation), although perhaps in a somewhat altered form and usually with the involvement of different women. Because I am not an historian, I was not previously aware of how evanescent is the distinction between 'past' and 'present'. The 'now' of this writing is not the 'now' of the reader's reading, let alone of any specific events I may have described. Unlike the difficulty with pronouns, I have not been able to devise any succinct decision rule to resolve the question of tense.

A final challenge has been accountability. Ultimately, however much I may want to provide a mechanism for women's health workers to speak, the voice in this book is mine. Some women were understandably reluctant to talk to me, although remarkably few refused outright. In work that is as highly politicised and as chronically embattled as that for women's health centres, it makes sense to be chary when it comes to giving out information. You never know how it will be used. I have tried to be frank with women from whom I was seeking information, acknowledging my own confusions and my commitment to their work. I promised women who talked to me that I would vet with them any quotes or discussion that would identify individuals, and I have also sent parts of the draft manuscript to staff at centres and other informants. The logistics of getting feedback from such a diverse and busy group are daunting, and I found myself torn between burdening them with large piles of typescript (which they probably would not have time to read), and perhaps unwittingly censoring the most vexed material by selecting only segments for their reaction. Nevertheless, their comments, when they could make them, have been revealing and valuable. I readily confess to rising anxiety, as well as excitement, at the prospect of this book becoming public property. Critical documents will doubtless drop into my lap after the manuscript has gone to the printer, as will the (correct) phone numbers of women I should have interviewed.

Anyone who reads contemporary feminist writing knows that texts are as significant for their absences and silences as for who and what they purport to consider. The sources of data available to me have not permitted me to say nearly enough about the clients of women's health centres; I can say nothing about which women find their way to the centres, which ones of them return, and in both cases, why? Nor can I say anything at all about those women who know about the centres but elect to seek health care elsewhere. Although I have done a few interviews with officials of the Commonwealth and State public services, I know very little about their work or their views concerning women's health centres. Class, race and ethnicity are bound to be relevant but my capacity to deal with them is limited. 'The contradictions of class and racial oppression. . .are insistent presences speaking from beyond the text but not yet in it' (Smith, 1987: 8).

Like the women's health movement itself, this book represents the input of many women whose names do not appear—either through their preference to remain anonymous, or because they number in the hundreds and cannot simply be listed, or because my tape recorder or pen failed me at a critical moment and I could not retrace the contact later. They are the first people I must thank. Most of them gave an hour or more (sometimes much more) of their precious time to this project in the faith that it would result in a document of value to the work in which they are or were engaged. I hope they will not be disappointed while at the same time I acknowledge that some of them will be. To those whose names are omitted inadvertently, I offer apologies and the request that they let me know. We can't count on second printings or revisions, but anything is possible. Anne Walton was involved with this project for a short time at the beginning, when she conducted several interviews and brought fresh insight and energy to the project. Rebecca Albury gave me the use of a box of material she had collected on the early years of women's health centres in New South Wales; that box turned out to be a gold mine. Gwen Gray also had papers that filled in some significant gaps in my own collection. John Deeble and Marian Sawer provided information at the last moment. Jill Matthews is a source of personal friendship and intellectual challenge as well as names of participants in this story. Additionally, I thank Jude Abbs, Jocelyn Auer, Anne-Marie Delahunt, Daina Neveraskas, Lyndall Ryan, Meg Smith and Sue Wills for their special help with the process of collecting the information. In particular, Barb McLennan maintained an active involvement in the project for nearly four years, and I owe her a special debt for her friendship and facilitation. Jacqui Woodland assisted with two of the most thankless tasks—proofing and the index.

I ignored quite a bit of good advice in the process of writing this book. Several people read part or all of the manuscript, and it is owing to their good offices that the text is as intelligible as it is. They include Gabriele Bammer, Gretchan Broom, Leonard Broom, Ronelle Brossard, Chris Brown, Nancy Corbett, Areti Devetzidis, Helen Garton, Doris Horvath, Sylvia Kinder, Teresa Lea, David Legge, Richard Lipscombe, Barb McLennan, Silver Moon, Nicola Pilkinton, Lyndall Ryan, Sidney Sax, Stefania Siedlecky, Meg Smith, Di Surgie, Margaret Taylor, Carol Treloar, Jocelyn Vieira and Annie Zon. Their suggestions were, on occasion, mutually contradictory, but that is only to be expected of a book with a title like this one. Robin Darroch and Richard Lipscombe encouraged, facilitated and supported in their own assorted and inimitable ways. Perhaps most significant was their cheerful and unswerving conviction that I would, indeed, complete the book during those moments when I had my doubts. The Faculty of Arts, Australian National University, granted me a semester's blessed release from teaching at a critical moment; and a Visiting Fellowship at the National Centre for Epidemiology and Population Health gave me the opportunity to write practically the entire book during that semester. I have never enjoyed such a facilitating environment in which to write: an office near interesting colleagues, a computer on the desk, and a telephone with a silent number.

DHB
Canberra, January 1991

Introduction

This book is an account of the history and functioning of women's health centres in Australia. It describes the origins of women's health centres in the broader women's movement, and discusses the theoretical and political analysis that informed the founding and operation of the centres, particularly the first women's health centres during the mid-1970s. The movement for women's health centres has been, by and large, an active part of the feminist movement. So this is a history of one element current within the women's movement, an element that throws light on the accomplishments and problems of contemporary feminism.

The work of women's health centres has been highly productive, but it has also been marked by conflict at several levels: industrial conflict between management and workers; interpersonal conflict among the women involved with the centres; political conflict between centres and their funding bodies; and institutional conflict between centres and other community organisations or professional bodies. Some of these strains can be readily explained in terms of power struggles or the distinctive interests of particular actors or groups. Other problems are not so easily understood, and some participants in these struggles account for them in terms of internal political disagreements or personality clashes. However, I believe that most of the conflict within the women's health centre movement is not a matter of the particular personalities involved. Rather the conflict derives from structural contradictions inherent in Australian women's health centres. The main focus of this study is on the contradictions that arise when women in the feminist movement translate their personal and ideological commitment to women's health into the institutional format of a health centre, particularly a state-funded centre. We are, it seems, damned if we do . . .

This book is based on more than six years of research into the women's health centre movement in Australia, including visits to most of the centres currently functioning (there are now around 40) and interviews with more than 120 women, including workers and former workers, members of management bodies and collectives, and state officials. I have also consulted files and archives of the centres, as well as personal documents made available to me by women who have been involved. But my interest in the centres goes back a long way. In research for my PhD, I investigated the relationships between general practitioners and their patients to see whether there was any truth to the feminist claim that women do not receive the same kind of care as men. While I was preoccupied with documenting the way medicine contributed to women's oppression, I was also curious about our resistance to that oppression. I sensed at that time in the 1970s that the growing women's health movement would be important to me later on, and—more through good luck than good management—I spent several days observing at the Collingwood Women's Health Centre and talking with women there. Because that centre was never funded and was closed after nearly four years in 1978, my detailed notes on Collingwood are all the more valuable.

Australia's women's health centres, like women themselves, are varied, differing among themselves and from time to time. That diversity makes them and their work fascinating, but it also complicates this research, and the decisions I have made to select or exclude a particular centre. In general, I have sought to study those centres doing comparatively general work rather than more specialised projects, and I have emphasised several that have been critical in the history of the movement. However, as is often the case, it is easier to indicate what I have not studied.

I have not included organisations that specialise exclusively in services to victims of sexual assault, domestic violence, or incest. The histories of these groups are closely intertwined with women's health centres. Many occupy the same premises, the same women are often involved in their founding and operation, and the first state-funded refuges and women's health centres were financed by the Whitlam government's Community Health Program. Most of the centres I have studied regularly see women who are seeking services because of violence or incest, and some centres have, at times, had a policy of working with them on these issues, as well as on their health needs. I have also omitted centres that specialise in abortion counselling or terminations of pregnancy. There are many similarities between these specialist services and the centres I have studied, but for practical reasons—mainly because there are too many to do justice to them all—they have been excluded. Furthermore, the fact that all the excluded groups are concerned with significant legal as well as health problems raises important additional considerations that are beyond the scope of this study. Residential centres with health services have also been excluded, not because their work is less important, but because the residential element introduces distinctive considerations that deserve more attention than I could give them.

Secondly, I have not studied Family Planning Association clinics directly. I am glad to say that task has been undertaken by others (Siedlecky and Wyndham, 1990). However, several of the centres included have either served as an auspice body for Family Planning, or Family Planning has served as an auspice of the centres. The Family Planning Association (FPA) predates generalist, feminist women's health centres, even though contraceptive services and advice have been fundamental to both. The fact that FPA developed out of the older racial purity and eugenics movements signals its rather distinctive ideological and social base. Although feminism and fertility control have always been linked (feminists have worked within FPA, and indeed a number of activists have moved back and forth between FPA and women's health centres) FPA has never to my knowledge presented itself explicitly as a feminist organisation. Most of the centres in this study are more or less overtly feminist in their vision.

Finally, I have not systematically sought information about private, fee-for-service women's centres except where such groups have been directly involved with a state-funded centre. It has been difficult enough to draw the line around those generalist women's health services that sought government funding, since any one centre may move in and out of that category at different periods of its history. However, when both conventional and alternative therapies are included, the private centres are very numerous. Furthermore, the problems and issues confronted by such groups are in some respects different from the challenges facing those who are committed to rendering a free service, or one well below cost. In the course of my research, however, I have visited a few private women's health centres, and the insights I have gained from them have helped me understand better the work of the centres that are funded by government bodies or are run on volunteer labour.

The distinction between government funding and volunteer is, like all others, a matter of degree. When we think of government funding, we usually think in terms of grant applications and allocations, and that is what I mean here when I use the term 'funding'. However, there are other ways to get money from government. Throughout most of the period covered by this research, the Commonwealth government has made some provision for reimbursing medical practitioners for services if the doctor billed the Commonwealth medical insurance system directly rather than charging the patient. At various times, most of the centres discussed here employed doctors whose services were 'bulk billed', and the rebates were paid to the centre. If the doctor worked as a volunteer and donated her services to the centre, or if she worked for a salary that was lower than the amount rebated from the Commonwealth, the centre was, indirectly, subsidised by government funding even though it did not receive a grant in the usual sense. Thus a centre may at times be a hybrid, run largely on volunteer labour but still with connections with the state. Because they illustrate the complications introduced by relations with the state, and because many centres experienced several incarnations, one of which was such a hybrid stage, I have included these centres.

It is even more difficult to describe the 'sample' of women who appear in these pages. Of the women I interviewed, only a few are named in the text. It is clearly invidious to name some and omit others, and all the women concerned, as well as other readers, deserve some explanation. Precisely because of the collective, non-hierarchical commitments of feminist groups, it is often simply inaccurate to attribute a particular accomplishment to an individual woman, even if her name is on a document or in the newspaper. This presents me with a difficulty, because all the women who have contributed to the work of women's health centres deserve to have their contributions acknowledged, but I do not know who all of them are. In some instances, I can be confident that an individual woman did something, but the events in which she took part provoked conflict and animosities which are better left to heal. There are a few cases where, as far as I could determine, a woman's role was relatively undisputed; I have named a few such women in part to put their contributions on the record, and in the hope that they can, in a sense, represent the thousands who are not named.

Several people have suggested to me that if I cannot name everyone, I should name no one. In the end, I have chosen to reject that wise advice. I have done so for two reasons. First, it implies that a complete census of the relevant women is actually possible, a proposition which, on reflection, I believe is untrue. Most of this story concerns unofficial events for which no full, formal list of participants could be composed. But even in the case of more official actions (such as applying for funding), the lists would be misleadingly complete. For example, once when I located a centre's original submission showing all the women who signed, I subsequently learned that it contained names of women who had not been actively involved (but who were included in the document to make up the numbers). Additionally, I was told of women who, for various reasons, would not appear on the submission even though they contributed work such as research on which the submission was based. In the face of the impossibility of completeness, I am uneasy about the prospect of presenting the story as if it were a project advanced by anonymous women. While in one sense the work of women's health centres *is* accomplished by a great mass of unnamed women, it has also been the product of many extraordinary individuals. Only some of them are named here, but I hope that will enable the reader to have an occasional brief glimpse of a real woman who engages this work as part of her life. I also hope that those who are named can, in a symbolic way, stand for the scores of others who are not named and should be. A list of those I interviewed appears in Appendix 1.

Not only women's health centres, but other feminist women's services face dilemmas similar to the ones described here. I have not undertaken a systematic comparison between the health centres and other community-based women's services, but such a project would yield valuable insights. For example, a brief consideration of the refuge movement acknowledges some of their similarities and points to important differences. More has been written about women's refuges than about other women's services (for example, see Dowse, 1984; Smith, 1985; Morgan, 1981; Tierny, 1982; Ahrens, 1980; Johnson, 1981; Pahl, 1985). Refuges are criticised from both inside and outside the women's movement for numerous alleged sins: political extremism, separatism, excessive radicalism, failure to include a class and ethnic analysis, and imposing a false universalism. They are also accused of playing into the hands of right-wing elements, selling out to state bureaucracies, and being co-opted. Virtually all of these contradictory claims have also been made about one women's health centre or another at some time. However, refuges and women's health centres differ in critical aspects of their political histories.

Most significantly, refuges differ from Australian women's health centres in having more mixed ideological foundations. In Australia and the US, soon after feminist activists had founded the first shelters for battered women and made the problem public, other agencies came into the field. These included churches, The Salvation Army, local councils, and charitable community groups that had little in common with the feminists who had pioneered women's refuges. This shift was less marked in Britain according to Pahl (1985). Until at least the mid-1980s, however, state-funded women's community health centres in Australia have all been explicitly feminist. Other groups and agencies had moved into this work only at the margins. Thus despite their similarities, the stories of women's health centres cannot be subsumed into the history of other women's services.

A book about feminist women's health centres crosses many disciplinary boundaries and risks offending many disciplinarians. A sociologist more interested in health than in women would have changed my emphasis, wanting more sociology and less feminism. A proper historian or political scientist would each construct a story quite differently from the way it is presented here. So would an expert in organisation theory and practice, or a health educator. Still, this material has something to say to all of those people. This book is intended for the women about whom it is written and many others as well. It should be of value to people interested in women's health generally, in community health, the sociology of health and illness, the politics of social movements, alternative organisations, and the relationship between feminist theory and practical interventions. But first of all, it is intended for the women who establish and run feminist women's health centres. It is their story, and it is past time it was told.

Readers who are familiar with the workings of non-government organisations (NGOs) will find much that is familiar here; others may appreciate a brief introduction to the typical structure of such groups. Most women's health centres and other NGOs consist of three basic working parts: the *staff* who do the day-to-day work of providing services to women and who are normally but not always paid; the voluntary management group or *board* (which may include members of staff) who meet regularly to determine policy, hire staff, and make major management decisions; and the *association*, a larger group of members who meet at least annually to elect the members of the management group and to discuss the long-term directions and concerns of the centre. In many cases, one or all of these groups is organised along *collective* lines, minimising the identification of formal office-bearers and other distinctions, rotating or sharing responsibilities, and maximising the extent to which decisions are made by consensus. Women's health centres usually encourage clients of the centre to join the association and become involved with the management group. In the event, few centres conform strictly to this tri-cameral description. In particular, the lines between these three components of a women's health centre are often quite blurred, and it is not always a simple matter to determine which 'women's health collective' took a particular action. Especially in the early days, the same women were often the association, the board, and the staff.

The situation in the mid- to late-1980s, when most of my research was conducted was very different from the radical, tumultuous, optimistic mid- to late-1970s, when the first dozen centres opened. As Susan Ryan remarked at the 1990 National Women's Conference, 'the way ahead is. . .not as exciting as it was in 1972'. Although there is much more superficial legitimacy for women's health services now than there was in the 1970s, some of them have 'lost their radical feminist edge, and have moved closer to the bureaucracy' (Auer and Shuttleworth, 1990: 7). Many of the women who were involved with the first centres have gone into other kinds of work, some have moved to other States or overseas. Despite remarkable feminist networks, several important informants were never contacted, or were located too late to include their accounts. A few have died. Because of the nature of the centres and their work, the records, particularly from the early days, are informal, scanty and often dispersed. These women were fully occupied doing the work; there was little time to document it. As I have travelled around the country listening to women talk about the work, I have developed a sense of urgency to record this story and make it public. Some materials and memories have been lovingly preserved. For example, the archival

'First Ten Years' collection, housed personally by Sue Wills in Sydney, contains valuable documents covering the period up to the end of the 1970s, including vital information about women's health centres. A similar collection is held in Adelaide in the Women's Studies Resource Centre, and Karin Hoffman has developed the Lespar Library of feminist material in Darlington, Western Australia. But these collections are the exception rather than the rule. Much of the written material is in suitcases and boxes in somebody's shed or at the back of a wardrobe. Much more has been lost in the course of successive moves, fires, floods, divorces, and other crises. In explaining that she had, unaccountably, discarded her files about Leichhardt, Lyndall Ryan (an historian, no less!) told me, abashed, 'We had no idea we were making history'. Those of us who admire and want records of the activities and accomplishments of this wave of Australian feminism have no time to waste.

As new generations of women are recruited to work in women's health, I have felt an obligation to document as much of this story as I could, and to give it back to the women of Australia. I do not imagine that women thinking of starting a women's health centre or going to work in one can somehow be spared from all difficulty if they know what happened before. Although many of the underlying problems are the same, the political, social and economic environment of the 1990s is very different from the 1970s, when, as one woman put it, the plan was to 'smash patriarchy...by Christmas'. It is now clear that the work of the women's movement is not a matter of months or years, but of generations. So the work itself must be geared to lifetimes rather than a brief burst of idealistic zeal.

Still less do I imagine that all the women whose work is described here will feel themselves affirmed by my account. Sometimes, the stories I have been told directly contradict one another, and it is rare that I have found it possible to verify accounts in a way that would convince me I had understood exactly what happened. Where I am aware of such discrepancies, I have tried to describe them. There are surely instances where I have not succeeded, and other instances where I was simply unaware of other versions of events. These gaps and imbalances will, I hope, prompt the women who have been too busy doing the work of women's health centres to remember and react, perhaps in some cases to set the record straight. In all cases, I trust they will see themselves reflected with care, respect and admiration.

The book begins with a verbal photo album. Chapter 1 contains a portrait of the beginnings of the Leichhardt Women's Community Health Centre in 1974, and goes on to give somewhat less detailed pictures of the other first dozen women's health centres in Australia. Much smaller snapshots follow of the centres that opened during the 1980s. Each centre deserves a book of its own; in this Chapter I have sought to introduce the reader to something of the distinctive profile of each individual centre, and, through the composite, to cover the various qualities, experiences, and activities that distinguish and characterise Australia's feminist health centres.

The next two Chapters present the two main elements—the feminist movement, and the state—that constitute the sociopolitical context of women's health centres. Chapter 2 discusses the theoretical and political links between women's health and the broader women's movement. The feminist analysis of health and illness emphasises the importance of women's social position in the production of their ill health. This understanding, more recently labelled the 'social view of health', underlies the twin aims of the women's health movement: to change the overall social structure which is sickening to women, while at the same time providing improved individual services, health information and health education to women whose personal health is compromised.

The problem of the relationship between women and 'the state' had been a perennial issue in feminist debate. In Chapter 3, we see how the issues are spelled out in the context of the movement for women's health centres seeking funding from government sources. The Chapter describes the origins and aims of the Commonwealth's Community Health Program, initiated under the Whitlam government, as this was the source of initial funding for most of the first dozen centres. It shows that during the 1970s, with certain lag effects, the prospects for starting women's health centres more or less followed the prospects of the Community Health Program itself. By the time of the revival of the Program under Hawke in 1983, the women's health centres had connected with a wider range of sources of funding.

Many women's health centres appear to have gone through a more or less similar cycle of establishment, crisis, and reformation. That cycle is described in Chapter 4, drawing extensively on case analysis from several different centres. Concentrating particularly on the (now closed) Hindmarsh Women's Health Centre in Adelaide, the discussion indicates a sequence of 'phases' through which nearly all centres seem to pass, sometimes ending in a successful new form of operation, sometimes in the dissolution of the centre. This cycle is an illustration of what sociologists have called the 'problem of institutionalisation'.

Chapter 5 is the analytical heart of the book. It develops the argument that the situation of Australian women's health centres is inherently contradictory. In its most basic sense, their fundamental contradiction is *using the system to change the system*. The women's health movement arises out of the feminist analysis of women's health discussed in Chapter 2, and hence involves an explicit and radical critique of society and social institutions, including medicine. But Australian women's health centres have been funded by the state; thus they are intimately connected to, and to some extent dependent on, two of western capitalism's most patriarchal institutions: the state and medicine. After discussing these central contradictions, I consider briefly a variety of more immediate conflicts arising out of them. Chapters 4 and 5 together explore in detail the expressions of the contradictions.

The women's health centres of the 1970s and early 1980s were all products of women's initiatives, coming from the community. Subsequently—in part as a result of effective advocacy by women's health centre staff—South Australia, New South Wales, Victoria, and the Commonwealth itself have all developed women's health policies, some of which include provision for women's health centres. Some activists are worried that women's health centres are being co-opted when the impetus for their establishment comes from the state rather than the community. The book concludes (Chapter 6) with questions: What are the circumstances of women's health centres in the 1990s? Can community-based feminism survive 'top-down' initiatives? Can the women's health movement survive this particular form of success?

The story of the clients of women's health centres is yet to be told. That is an even larger project than the one described here, but it forms the vital other side of this coin. Most of the workers I interviewed were convinced of the value of their work to the women who come to the centres, and some went to work in centres after having been clients there. But they were usually careful, even diffident, about making claims concerning the impact of the centres. 'Evaluation' is an 'in' word in contemporary bureaucracies, and there have been several efforts to evaluate the work of women's health centres as individual projects and as a group of related projects. The results are, to my knowledge, largely favourable, and I have been told that some reviews have been suppressed because they were *too* favourable for the commissioning government, which had different results in mind. But I doubt that such evaluations do more than scratch the surface, and some of the women from the centres would probably argue that they do not tell us very much about what these centres really do. In my judgment, it will require very subtle, sophisticated and long-term research to do justice to the accomplishments of women's health centres. Some of their impact, perhaps their most important results, will not be evident for years or even decades. Furthermore, what women's health centres accomplish is inextricably linked to the efforts of many other social movement organisations and agents of social change. Insofar as they are able to approach their deeper goals—which involve nothing less than the transformation of the patriarchal social order—we will never be able to disentangle the work of the women's health movement from other feminist initiatives because it is part of the large agenda of the women's movement.

1 The first of their kind

One Thursday evening shortly before Christmas in 1973, Lyndall Ryan came home from the Mitchell Library to her house in the Sydney suburb of Annandale, collecting the mail from the letter box on the way inside. The day's delivery contained one item that came as a complete surprise: a cheque for $33 000 from the Commonwealth of Australia's Hospitals and Health Services Commission. The funds were to establish and equip a women's health centre, with $55 000 per year for operating costs promised for the next two years. Lyndall was the nominal convener of *Control*, a women's health collective which had applied for funding to open a community health centre, by women for women. Not expecting their application to succeed, the collective was unprepared for the organising and management tasks the grant now presented. They had an idea, a dream perhaps, but little in the way of practical preparation for what they were now about to do.

Over the next three months, the collective was to find and rent premises, advertise for and hire staff (two doctors, two nurses, an administrator/secretary, a health educator, and a research officer), equip the facility, and form a committee of management. On International Women's Day, 8 March 1974, the doors were officially opened at the Leichhardt Community Women's Health Centre located at 164 Flood Street. When Leichhardt was formally opened by Bridget Gilling, Australia Party candidate for the Senate, the Centre had already been operating since 29 January, offering medical, counselling, and health education services.

The first cheque was a breakthrough, marking the beginning of what would, over the next decade and a half, become a significant new feature in the Australian primary care landscape: state-funded feminist women's health centres, run by women for women. In another sense, however, the advent of funding was not the beginning, but simply one important step in a long and continuing process of struggle by women for control over a fundamental aspect of their lives: their own bodies. As early as the late 1960s, women in New South Wales had been campaigning for abortions to be provided in public hospitals. Following a forum called the Women's Commission, which celebrated International Women's Day in March 1973, a group of Sydney women set up an abortion referral service called *Control*. Their leaflet proclaimed 'Abortion . . . a woman's right to choose . . . a child's right to be wanted'. The women in the group contacted Sydney doctors who were known to do terminations of pregnancy, and negotiated with some of them to make the procedure accessible to more women by performing abortions at lower cost. Between August 1973 and August 1974, *Control* was contacted by 335 women seeking abortion counselling and referral. Of those women, 82 percent were single, divorced or separated (Members of the Centre, 1978:142). They 'acted as an advocacy and surveillance agency . . . set up a referral network of sympathetic doctors . . . and kept a close watch on the way women were treated' (Siedlecky and Wyndham, 1990: 87).

The collective also co-operated with other feminist groups in Adelaide and Canberra as well as Sydney to produce and distribute a booklet of sexual health and birth control information called *What Every Woman Should Know*. Distribution of the booklet to teenagers outside high schools provoked a backlash of opponents who sought to have the publication banned and the perpetrators silenced, signalling the sort of discordance that was to characterise relations between the women's health movement and certain other sectors of the community.

Although their initial emphasis was on birth control and particularly abortion, members of *Control* soon broadened their perspective as they became aware of widespread and deep dissatisfactions with existing health services in general. They realised that lack of access to safe termination of pregnancy was not 'the problem': it was symptomatic of the fact that the large, powerful medical system was failing to meet women's needs; and that failure was not an occasional accident, but a structural characteristic of western medicine itself. In the middle of 1973, a group of about a dozen women acting on their concern about inadequate and inappropriate health services for women in Sydney, and particularly the lack of facilities for safe, first-trimester abortions, decided to try to establish a women's health centre—the first of its kind in Australia.

Initially they hoped they could establish the centre with voluntary staff. In July they wrote to the Commonwealth Minister for Health, Dr Doug Everingham, explaining their concerns and their idea for a women's health centre. The collective thought they were being brushed off when the Minister's Secretary replied in August that they should present a submission and budget to the Hospitals and Health Services Commission for a grant under the Community Health Program. Like many community-based groups before and since, the members of the collective lacked the technical knowledge and discursive tools on which to base such documents. Some of them went to see George Palmer, Professor of Health Administration at the University of New South Wales, who helped them prepare the documents, requesting a budget of $55 000 a year (Sandall, 1974). The collaboration with Professor Palmer is an example of the way resources were borrowed, gathered and variously acquired by women who had little idea of what they had got themselves into.

Getting Leichhardt Centre off the ground required the collective to develop a new set of political, intellectual and management skills far beyond anything they had expected. Not that these women were inexperienced: they had all been in the workforce, some for many years, and most of them were well educated. For example, Lorraine Osborne had trained as a nurse, Beverly Garlick was an architect working for a private firm, Betty Pybus was an accountant, and Lyndall Ryan was working on a PhD in history. But Leichhardt was something new: a state-funded, collectively-managed, community-based women's health service, and nobody knew how to develop and run one of those. They had to invent what they were doing as they went along, setting the precedents themselves.

Despite many unanticipated challenges, the collective had considered the basics of an ideal women's health centre, so they were able to reach conclusions quickly about several aspects of the facility. For example, the Flood Street premises never looked like a 'proper' medical facility, nor was it meant to. The collective had declined a proposal from the Leichhardt City Council to construct a special-purpose building, feeling that an informal suburban house was a more appropriate setting for the kind of service they had in mind. They were convinced that women who had experienced degrading or inadequate treatment in traditional clinics would be more at ease in an environment that looked decidedly *un*like a hospital or medical clinic. Fortunately, they had little difficulty finding a suitable house at a favourable rent. A Kings Cross abortionist who was enthusiastic about their project owned a rental property in Leichhardt, and he went out of his way to make sure the collective got the lease. The Centre had a garden where children could play, and was convenient to public transport. The sign at the front identified the Centre in Greek and Italian as well as English.

The choice of Leichhardt as the suburb for the Centre was carefully made. One highly practical consideration was that the local council was thought to be approachable. More important, the area had a high proportion of non-English speaking residents, households on low incomes, and families headed by women. If articulate middle-class, well-educated women like those in the *Control* collective found the medical establishment unsupportive, how much more daunting were the obstacles to good care facing women from the Leichhardt area. From the Women's

Commission and public meetings on the abortion question, it had become evident that access was a special problem to such women. Thus, the collective established the precedent of providing a free, sympathetic service first of all to women whose need was likely to be most urgent. The intention was, however, worlds away from traditional philanthropy. The services at Leichhardt, like those at the other feminist women's health centres, were designed to empower women, to facilitate self-determination rather than to provide charity for the needy. The collective believed that women would be eager to come.

They were right. The first client arrived, desperate and frightened, before the Centre had even been furnished, and 'had to be examined on the desktop' (Siedlecky and Wyndham, 1990: 87). There was some surprise at the numbers of women coming from the eastern suburbs 'which have the city's highest ratio of doctors to patients' (Commonwealth Department of Health, 1975: 10). Six months after the official opening, the Administrator Judy McLean reported that an average of 35 clients a day were coming into the Centre, with appointments booked out ten days in advance. The staff were 'only just coping', and they were struggling to reserve time for women in crisis who came in without appointments. They had already asked for and received extra funding (a top-up of over $26 000 was paid in June), but even so, the first funding crisis was just around the corner. In the first nine months, around 3500 women sought the services offered at Leichhardt.

Although the provision of first-trimester abortions had been an impetus behind Leichhardt's founding, it quickly became apparent that terminations could become the Centre's only work unless other provision was made. The staff saw the need for other activities, including health education and advocacy work, rather than to specialise in abortions and contraception. A free-standing abortion clinic, Preterm, was opened in June 1974, and 'after the establishment of Preterm and the feminist abortion centres in Sydney, Leichhardt ceased doing abortions' (Siedlecky and Wyndham, 1990:89). One of Leichhardt's first major community development projects was to support the founding of other women's health facilities: the Liverpool Women's Health Centre (see below) was one, and the Bessie Smyth feminist abortion clinic was another. Two workers from Leichhardt were effectively seconded to establish Bessie Smyth, which opened in 1977. These initiatives established a pattern which was to be repeated many times over—existing centres providing a variety of assistance for the founding and development of new women's services.

Before the Leichhardt Centre had even been officially opened, opposition began to appear, and many of the sources of antagonism remain almost unaltered a decade and a half later. In the 1970s in Australia, abortion was a provocation to single-issue lobby groups. Despite the fact that the Centre offered first-trimester abortions to only some clients, and

4

only as part of a much more general array of health services, the press initially concentrated on terminations of pregnancy. Both the *Australian* and the *Sydney Morning Herald* published articles on 23 February 1974 carrying headlines announcing that Leichhardt was doing abortions; the Right to Life and Festival of Light immediately went on the attack, demanding that funding be withdrawn even though abortions were not unlawful in New South Wales if the mental or physical health of the mother would be jeopardised by the pregnancy. On more general grounds, elements in the medical establishment agitated against the Centre. For example, the Australian Medical Association (AMA) wrote to the NSW Health Commission to complain that the Centre was 'unethical' (*National Times*, 3–7 June 1974). Conservative paediatrician Clair Isbister mounted a campaign against Leichhardt, claiming that treatment at the Centre was 'degrading' and 'questionable', and complaining that staff were 'anti-male and anti-doctor'. Even the fact that everyone (doctors included) at Leichhardt was addressed by their given name was cause for concern. Isbister and others objected to explicit illustrations and cartoons contained in some of the Centre's leaflets, which the AMA claimed were 'pornographic' (Milio, 1984). Figures 1.1 and 1.2 show examples of offending material. 'Local churches warned women against the centre and unwittingly acted as publicity agents' (Siedlecky and Wyndham, 1990:87).

The *Medical Journal of Australia* published a remarkably sympathetic editorial on 1 November 1975 (page 698), explaining how Leichhardt had been set up, describing the services and staffing of the Centre, and referring to the staff as a 'group of devoted and intelligent women'. It acknowledged that 'the response of the local medical practitioners has been mixed. Hostility and suspicion have in some cases given way to acceptance and cooperation'. However, it also raised the spectre of standards being eroded by the use of untrained staff. The next issue of the *Journal* (6 December 1975: 887–8) contained a letter from G. S. Rieger, President of the NSW Branch of the AMA. Rieger was much less sympathetic, castigating the *Journal* for its 'thinly disguised approbation' of a group who sought to undermine medical authority, restating the hazards of allowing staff without medical training to perform 'medical' tasks, and accusing the Centre of bringing about 'the substitution of modern medicine by second rate first aid for reasons of prejudice alone'. In 1976, a group of five women doctors functioning as the 'Medical Women's Society to Prime Minister Fraser' called for funding to be withdrawn from the Leichhardt and Liverpool Centres, and from the NSW Family Planning Association (Siedlecky and Wyndham, 1990: 88).

A group of ten first-year medical students (two of them women) prepared a group project on Leichhardt in 1975, based on two visits to the Centre and interviews with 'a number of people' who had attended the Centre. This study concluded that the staff were 'aggressive' and the

pap smears & cervical cancer

from Leichhardt Womens
Community Health Centre
164 flood St Leichhardt
NSW 2041 ☎ 560 3011
a free womens health
centre funded by the
Australian & N.S.W.
governments.

The cancer smear test (or Papanicolau, Pap for short) is the simplest and most effective method for detecting cancer of the cervix in its earliest and most curable stages. But, most importantly, it can pick up danger signals five or ten years before any cancer become obvious. Cancer of the cervix (mouth of the uterus) used to be a major cause of cancer deaths in women, simply becuase by the time there were any symptoms, it was usually too late to do anything about it. For example, there is no pain in the early stages to signal trouble ahead. The dramatic drop in the number of deaths from this disease since the cancer smear test came into use has made many health workers believe that if every woman had regular cancer smears, death from cancer of the cervix could be eliminated almost entirely.

how cancer smears are done

The test takes only a few seconds, is easy to do and is painless.

You can learn how to do it yourself on a friend as women in self help groups have done.

Family Planning centres, womens health centres, clinics offering gynaecological services will also do them. If your doctor won't do one, ask to be referred to one who will.

A speculum is inserted in your vagina so your cervix can be seen.

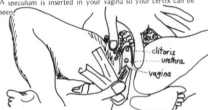

clitoris
urethra
vagina

Then! a small wooden or plastic stick is inserted into the opening of the cervix and gently rotated to pick up some of the cells that are constantly being shed from the cervix.

(opening to cervix)   spatula

These are spread on a glass slide, fixed by adding a chemical and sent off to a cytologist for examination.

MARY BLOW

Ask what happens to the results. If it is normal, many clinics wont do anything with the result except file it away in your file.

You should be notified if it is class 2, 2R, 3, 4 or 5 (see below). If you know when the result will be back you can ring the doctor/clinic to make sure you get the result or if you dont want folks at home to find out about your personal medical history.

Figure 1.1   The Leichhardt Pap smears and cervical cancer leaflet

the leichhardt womens community health centre* guide to CONDOMS

★ 🏠 164 flood st. leichhardt 2040
☎ 560 3011
a free womens health centre funded by the Australian & NSW governments

frangers   rubbers   wetcheck   frenchies
french letters
english mackintoshes

If you're thinking of an alternative to the pill or an IUD, and have only thought about diaphragms, then think some more — about condoms. Condoms (rubbers, frenchies, french letters, frangers), have been used for centuries, though only in the last century when rubber was produced did they become available on a mass scale. They are used as a favourite form of contraception in countries like Sweden, where they are sold everywhere, not just at chemists.

One of the difficulties with condoms is getting used to the idea of using them as a regular contraceptive — so many myths and prejudices surround them. A lot of people try them as a first contraceptive, when they are often not very relaxed about sex, and are not in a regular relationship. Consequently, they are often associated with 'bad' sex, when it mightn't be the condoms fault at all. Popularity depends a lot on how you use them, so give them a good try first!

You can buy lubricated or dry ones — we recommend the lubricated kind, as the vagina is less likely to react to rubber if it has lubrication on it. Don't use any other petroleum-based lubricants with condoms — they will deteriorate the rubber (like vaseline).

Shortly after the man comes, his penis becomes smaller and softer. Make sure that the penis doesn't move around much in the vagina after it becomes smaller, and that it is removed soon after — the condom should be held tightly against the base of the penis when it is being removed, to make sure that no sperm is leaked from the condom back into the vagina. Condoms aren't reuseable, they should be thrown away after each ejaculation, so have a supply handy.

DONT LITTER LOVERS LANE

how to use them

At present, condoms are sold mainly at chemists, though there are some vending machines in railway stations that sell them. They only come in one size, although you can buy single ones or packets of them. They cost around $1.50 a dozen (our price is at cost, chemists will charge more).

LARGE   SUPER LARGE   OUTSIZE   NORMAL

Condoms should be put on the erect (hard) penis before the penis enters the woman's vagina. This is because there is some evidence to show that there may be some sperm on the tip of the penis before the man ejaculates (comes). Anyway, controlling when you ejaculate isn't easy or foolproof, so it's better to be cautious.

So before actual intercourse, either of you should roll on the condom, making sure that about ½" space is left near the tip of the penis, to allow the sperm to collect there after the man comes. Most condoms have a tip for this use, but if you buy ones that don't, just allow the ½". Condoms are pretty strong (read about the tests done on them later), but still watch out that neither of you snags the condom with fingernails or rings etc.

how effective are they?

Effectiveness is hard to test, as it depends on how condoms are used. If they're used properly (ie put on before intercourse and tightly held against the penis while withdrawing soon after ejaculation), the failure rate should be as low as 2-5%. This means that if 100 women used condoms as contraception every day for 1 year, between 2 to 5 women would get pregnant. This is about the same risk as an IUD or diaphragm, but a greater risk than taking the pill.

But this is only true if they are used properly — careless use increases your risk to about 15%. Condoms mainly fail because of the way they are used, not because they break or burst.

PILL	IUD	CONDOM	DIAPHRAGM
1	1-2	2-5	2-5

pregnancies per year if 100 women used each method

Some condoms are now tested in Australia and will soon be packaged with the Australian Standards Association stamp on them. To pass the ASA test, less than 0.1% of a batch of condoms are allowed to burst during testing. Testing consists of blowing-up the condom to about 500 times its size, and leaving it for 3 minutes filled with 300 mls of liquid — both these tests put far more strain on a condom than they would have in normal useage. Brands that pass these tests are — Wetchex and Checker, and Durex Gossemer.

Figure 1.2 The Leichhardt Women's Community Health Centre guide to condoms

services 'useless'. Like Isbister, they were shocked by the 'extreme ideas' purveyed at Leichhardt, and especially by the portrayal of doctors in the pamphlets. Two pages of their report were devoted to the leaflets which were said to represent doctors as ignorant, insensitive and cruel, indifferent to women's problems, moralising and imposing their own values on women, and scientifically 'impotent'. They were also dismayed by the 'glorification of the female genitalia' in Leichhardt's literature which they feared 'verges on a lesbianic [sic] preoccupation'. These students concluded that because of their fanaticism, Leichhardt women would have 'only themselves to blame if the problems persist'.

Another early complaint was that the Centre was 'expensive.' An article by Glennys Bell in the *National Times* (15–20 December 1975) quoted an unnamed woman doctor who claimed that Leichhardt had spent $300 000 treating 5000 women. Even with the increased allocations ($123 000 for financial years 1975–76), it is difficult to know the source of the $300 000 figure, but all such attacks required responses from the collective or staff who felt they had to set the record straight. They were the first, a model, and hence their public image was of vital importance to their future and the future possibilities for other women's health centres. In the first few years, women were often busy responding to allegations in the press and Parliament. One document in the Centre's files chronicles thirteen letters and articles attacking the Centre published between October 1975 and February 1976: under such onslaughts, the women of the Centre felt at times that they were under siege. Because there was no point of comparison, it is impossible to know how the negative publicity affected the prospective clientele.

But if there was opposition, there was also strong support: Leichhardt addressed an obvious need. Staff from the Centre were in constant demand as speakers, groups and individuals wanted copies of Leichhardt's leaflets on such topics as contraception, menopause, monilia and painful periods, and many organisations and institutions sent students to observe and train at the Centre. And most immediately important, women from all over Sydney sought the Centre's services. Clients voted with their feet: some women came because they had no access to other sources of primary health care. Some women came for what were at that time unusual health education groups, and to get information they could not find elsewhere. But even if medical facilities were available in their local areas, some women were willing to travel great distances to receive care from women staff whom they knew would be sympathetic to them, as women.

By the end of 1974, the staff included two nurses, an administrator, a counsellor, a researcher, a health educator, and a receptionist/phone counsellor. These full-time workers were all paid the same salaries ($7500 per year, well over the minimum wage at the time). In addition, four doctors were employed on a sessional basis, and the Centre employed three part-time workers: a psychotherapist, a cleaner, and a gardener. Only the doctors were paid more than other members of the staff. Leichhardt was about to be joined by other women's health centres: by the end of 1974, sister centres had opened in Collingwood (Melbourne) and Perth, and more were in the planning stages. By the mid-1980s more than twenty were in operation, although some of the original centres had disappeared. In addition, major State policies on women's health had been developed in South Australia, New South Wales and Victoria. In the late 1980s, most other States had or were developing a women's health policy. A national women's health policy was released in April 1989 followed by funding for implementation. Around 40 women's health centres were by then operating with government funding, and new ones were seeking support. Leichhardt signalled the start of something big.

The bulk of this Chapter is devoted to a sketch of the other eleven of the first dozen 'founder' centres. After each of these centres has been introduced, I outline the variety of work undertaken at the centres, showing how diverse has been the implementation of the shared vision of community health centres run by women, for women.

HOT ON THEIR HEELS

The group in Sydney were not the only ones concerned about women's health care. All over the country, women felt the need for a different kind of health care for women, and more centres were soon established. After the first three opened in 1974, another nine opened between 1975 and 1977: Liverpool, Brisbane, Mayfield (Newcastle), Darwin, Hindmarsh (in South Australia), Gosford, Alice Springs, Bankstown, and Women in Industry, Contraception and Health (WICH, in Carlton). Most of these had received initial funding, as had Leichhardt, under the aegis of the Community Health Program, with co-operation from the relevant State health authority, and in the expectation that the State would gradually take over increasing responsibility. However, Collingwood never received government funding from either the Commonwealth or the State. Despite several applications, the Central Coast Women's Health Centre in Gosford did not succeed in obtaining funding until late in the 1970s, while Bankstown was not to receive substantial funding until 1985.

The comparative ease with which Leichhardt and several other original centres obtained Commonwealth government support should not give the impression that funding was a simple matter. From the beginning, Commonwealth–State conflicts and other difficulties complicated the process of obtaining resources, and battles broke out within the women's health movement over the politics of money. (These problems are discussed in detail in Chapters 4 and 5.) For example, other factions of the Sydney women's movement demanded that the Leichhardt collective hand over the grant which they defined as belonging to women as a whole, not just to the Leichhardt collective who were accused of being elitist. By 1977, the grant to the Brisbane Centre in Roma Street had been withdrawn, and funding for the Women's Health and Community Centre in Perth had been 'suspended'. Thus the fortunes of the various centres, while linked at some points, have always followed individual paths. As a result, the profile of women's health centres in Australia has always been a varied one. While they share important features, each centre has had a distinctive history and personality. What follows is a series of 'snapshots'.

Liverpool

Once Leichhardt opened, it quickly became apparent that there was much more demand than anyone had anticipated. Women within Leichhardt decided to start another centre 'based on the Leichhardt plan' in another area of need (Liverpool funding submission, 1974: 1). Chronologically, Liverpool was not the next Australian women's health centre to open after Leichhardt, but it was the next in metropolitan Sydney, and—at least initially—it was the most direct descendant of Leichhardt. The application for funding for Liverpool observed that 17 percent of the women who attended Leichhardt during its first month of operation had travelled from the outer western suburbs, indicating that the services in their local region were not meeting their needs. *Control* had established an incorporated body, the Women's Health and Resources Foundation, to serve as an umbrella organisation for founding and administering new women's health centres. After some delays, the Liverpool Community Women's Health Centre opened, approximately a year after Leichhardt.

Nola Cooper, one of the Centre's first employees, still works at Liverpool more than fifteen years later. It is rare for a woman to remain at one centre for such a long time, and her experience of Liverpool illustrates important features of its origins and development. Nola had worked on organising the 1973 Women's Commission where health had been such an important concern, so in some ways, she was indirectly involved in the founding of Leichhardt. She was originally hired at Liverpool to work as a receptionist and to set up a 'community file' of services and professionals in the area to whom women might be referred. However, once at Liverpool, she found that instead of working as an individual employee on a specialised task, she had become involved in a collective process.

In February 1975 nine staff began painting the centre and acquiring the furniture to get the premises ready for business. Trainers from the

Family Planning Association and other agencies helped to get the staff ready. Some of the new staff already had health and medical backgrounds (for example, several had done courses at Leichhardt), but everybody participated in training. As a result of the shared training and the commitment to collectivity, everyone became involved in delivering services, even though they had been employed to do other things. Nola was soon seeing women who came in for contraceptive advice, information and advice about pregnancy and pregnancy tests, and basic counselling. Functioning as a collective did not require everyone to do exactly the same range of tasks, but there was a core of work in which all staff participated at different levels, depending on their level of experience and skills. All the staff worked at the reception desk greeting clients and answering the phone, all did paramedical work at the level of their ability, and acted as counsellors. Some also took on the role of health educators. Staff were frequently called upon to go into the community to talk about the Centre and its services, as well as to discuss specific areas of women's health. Administrative tasks tended to be divided up according to interests, skills, and previous experience. Except for the doctors, all staff received the same salary.

Collective meetings were held weekly to discuss the daily work of the Centre and to sort out policies and directions. Policy was also discussed with the 'support group', a sub-group from the Women's Health and Resources Foundation. Several directors from the Foundation and some local women who had been involved in helping establish Liverpool met monthly with staff to discuss directions of the Centre. The support group operated for about eighteen months, and then gradually fell away, perhaps because it was felt to have achieved its purpose. The Foundation continued to function, and staff from Liverpool had meetings with directors as required by the constitution, but effectively the Foundation directors handed over power to run the Centre, which became basically self-managing.

Two years after it opened, Liverpool staff had seen over 3000 women for individual consultations, conducted dozens of sessions with groups, had run cervical cancer clinics outside the centre, and developed a considerable clientele among Spanish-speaking women. Indeed, their migrant health worker was obliged to restrict her contact with the local South American community because so many women were contacting her with emotional and social problems rather than strictly medical ones. The widespread need for the Centre's services was evident from a sample of 100 clients seen during the first three months of operation, which showed that nearly 20 percent came from a distance of 10 or more miles away (Cooper and Spencer, 1978). By the mid-1980s, they were also seeking to address the needs of local Aboriginal women, and they had expanded the health education and health promotion activities (Edwards, 1984).

Melbourne Women's Health Collective,[1] Collingwood

This Centre's story exemplifies the difficulties that a community group can experience when it gets caught in crossfire between Commonwealth and State. Like Leichhardt, the women in Collingwood began as an abortion referral group whose agenda grew. Although the Hospitals and Health Services Commission approved funding for Collingwood, the Centre never received the money which was to have been administered and 'topped up' by the State intermediary, the Victorian Hospitals and Charities Commission. Consequently, when the centre opened in 1974, it furnished clinical services and health education with support only from donations, volunteers, and fees from clients who could recover the money from a health insurance fund. Once Medibank came into operation, the Centre relied on Medibank rebates. It functioned on this basis for two years, and for another two years providing only health education groups.

Some of the women believe that the Hospitals and Charities Commission was right-wing and opposed to their project. Other informants suggest that the problems originated in the Victorian Health Department rather than with the Commission. In any event, the Hospitals and Charities Commission was the body with whom they dealt, and communication with that Commission was bewildering. Bureaucratic barriers were placed in their way: they were told they would have to treat men as well as women, include men in the Collective, pay doctors on a fee-for-service basis, and employ only professional staff (Hull, 1986). Information and instructions changed abruptly: the women were instructed to establish themselves as a benevolent society, then that their constitution did not conform to the requirements of a benevolent society (although no specific objections were supplied). Subsequently they were advised to register as a co-operative, but this turned out to be an impediment rather than a solution (McKenzie, 1979: 41). The Hospitals and Charities Commission refused to turn over the funding because the service would be free to clients, because staff were involved in the Centre's management, and because doctors were to be paid salaries (equal to other members of staff) instead of fees-for-service. Inspections of the building led to false claims about inadequate standards of hygiene; for example, one said that open buckets of 'dirty linen and dressings' were left in the Centre (McKenzie, 1979: 38). However, the women had no power to dispute such damaging indictments. The Collective tried to get the Commonwealth to fund them directly and fully, but the State agency kept assuring them that they would participate once the technical difficulties were ironed out. Whether it was an intentional anti-feminist strategy, the Hospitals and Charities Commission effectively blocked the transfer of funds that had been granted to the Collective.

Despite the obstructionism, the Collective pieced together a wide array of services, and women came from all over Victoria and from as far away as Tasmania to attend the Centre. Members of the Collective sponsored the establishment costs, supplemented by occasional donations. Women who were covered by health insurance were charged only what they would be rebated, and other women were not charged at all, so the services were always free. Apart from the Hospitals and Charities Commission, the most significant case of official obstruction came from one insurance company, Hospital Benefits Association, which refused to pay rebates for medical services at the Centre because the money 'was not going directly into the doctors' pockets' (McKenzie, 1979: 34–5). All workers always volunteered their labour, so when Medibank began, doctors' rebates largely supported the running costs of the Centre. The Collective concentrated on gynaecological services, and contraceptive counselling and advice. Not only doctors and nurses did Pap smears, swabs and smears for vaginal infections. General women's health workers also did them. This would have been an economy measure if the workers had ever been paid. The nurses in the Collective could also take blood for tests. The Melbourne University Microbiology Diagnostic Laboratory, which was conducting research on bacterial vaginal infections, did the Collective's lab work in return for the information obtained from the specimens. Pap smears went to the Cytology Department at Prince Henry Hospital.

When women arrived at the Centre, they were given their own files to read and write in, keeping records of their menstrual cycles, unwanted effects of medicines, and other information. Abortion counselling and referral was done mostly in groups as was preliminary health education and health promotion. For example, women arriving for a clinic on vaginal infections were involved in a brief discussion of causes and prevention, home remedies, and medical approaches to the treatment of such conditions before they were examined. The Collective also ran education groups on subjects such as stress, nutrition and premenstrual syndrome.

In addition to running the Centre, the Collective met every Saturday, sometimes all day to debate and discuss processes of collective work. They assessed what they were doing, whether women from the community were involved enough, and how to handle the ongoing funding drought. Janet Bacon, a doctor at Collingwood who has worked in women's health centres in four states, told me that the lack of state funding had advantages, in that they were not confined to following guidelines or priorities stipulated by outsiders.

After more than a year of negotiating with various bureaucracies and delivering services free to clients (and virtually free to the State), the Collective decided to close the service because of lack of funding. The decision was carefully considered. The Collective felt that it was vital for local women to become actively involved in the Centre, not simply to come in for services. At the time the services were stopped, there were 2500 women on the Centre's files, there was still demand for what they were providing and commitment from the Collective. Unlike some other volunteer services, this one stopped as a going concern; it did not gradually wither away.

Women's Health and Community Centre, Perth

Like several other centres that opened during the mid-1970s, the Women's Health and Community Centre at Glendower Street in Perth was—as its name implies—more than a health centre. It also included a rape crisis centre and refuge, organised under the umbrella Women's Centre Action Group. Elizabeth Reid, Prime Minister Whitlam's special adviser on women, had visited Perth, and her visit plus an International Women's Year conference had inspired Perth women to seek funding to provide services like those at Leichhardt. A women's centre was already operating on a voluntary basis, offering some child care and consciousness-raising groups; but the prospect of Commonwealth funding was an opportunity to do something more ambitious. The Perth experience is parallelled in several other cities where women found that it was easier to run counselling and information services (such as abortion counselling or rape crisis) on volunteer labour and donations, but individual clinical services were more difficult to sustain without more substantial and reliable support.

Several of the women involved in the original Perth Centre were at pains to point out to me that they had been conventional, middle-class, married women with children when they first became involved with women's health care. By the time a crisis reached its peak and funding was withdrawn about eighteen months after the Centre opened, the women had been fundamentally changed by their experiences. Largely unaware of their own transformation, they found that what they had come to think of as normal and appropriate behaviour was regarded by other women in the community and by government officers as radical. As one woman put it, 'We didn't realise how unrespectable we had become'. Another observed that they had, almost unwittingly, gone 'a little beyond the Pap smear stage'. Although the process may have been more dramatic in Perth than in some other cities, the work of women's health centres undoubtedly makes a profound difference to the lives of the workers as well as to clients.

The precipitating cause for the withdrawal of funds was a move by the collective to dismiss one of the Centre's doctors. This issue represented a profound conflict between worker control and deference to professional authority, but it also condensed deep disagreements over a variety of other issues, including sexual politics. Some of those who opposed the sacking took the brewing struggle to the press, labelling the collective as a lesbian anarchist group. They were charged with improper use of the grant. The Minister's letter discontinuing funding says that 'the expenditure of public funds is unjustified' because the group 'appears to have been unable to maintain suitable staff or to operate a centre which can be seen to fulfil the purpose for which it was created'. The press were informed of the suspension of funding five days before the Centre was given formal notification, and a fortnight before an informal deadline for the management collective to hire another doctor.

Hunter Region Working Women's Centre

Mayfield is an industrial suburb of Newcastle, which is itself an industrial city. Appropriately, the Centre that opened there in 1975 labelled itself as a 'working women's centre'. Unlike centres elsewhere which began in tandem with rape crisis or refuges, this one started as a multipurpose centre. A year after its health centre opened, it had added a child care centre. It is still one of the few centres to own its premises, which were purchased and renovated (under the direction of a woman architect) with funds granted by the Hospitals and Health Services Commission ($25 000), the interim committee of the Children's Commission ($42 000), and the International Women's Year Committee ($41 220). In addition to health services, the Centre also gives legal aid, general counselling and information, services targeted to employed women, health promotion and recreation programs, migrant English classes, and longday child care. Services are not confined to the Centre itself; it also has a caravan that goes to shopping centres and showgrounds to take basic health education and physical examinations directly to women, and health promotion sessions are conducted in factories. From the beginning, ongoing groups were formed to discuss sexuality, obesity, menopause, widowhood, and childbirth (Callcott, 1978:155). Because of the variety of activities undertaken at Mayfield, the Centre has always sought grants from a range of sources. For example, they applied to the Department of Social Security for funding for welfare officers, and to the Attorney-General for a lawyer to provide legal advice to clients of the Centre. Such diversity in the funding base has probably helped it to weather ebbs and flows in funding.

Establishing the Working Women's Centre involved considerable lobbying of Newcastle politicians such as the Lord Mayor and their federal Member of Parliament. Mary Callcott, one of the founders of the Centre, believes that 'the establishment of the National Advisory Committee for International Women's Year . . . was the most important single factor leading to our success' in establishing such an ambitious project with support from a variety of sources (1978: 154). An effort was made in staffing the Centre to hire local women of different ages and ethnic backgrounds, a commitment that has been characteristic (with varying degrees of success) of many women's health centres.

Women's House Health Centre, Brisbane

A group called the Women's Community Aid Association outlined the political analysis underlying their plans for a multipurpose women's centre to the International Women's Year national conference on Women's Health in a Changing Society in 1975 (Masion, 1978, on behalf of the Association). This analysis placed power and social factors at the centre of their understanding of women's problems, and pointed out that women's care is often fragmented as their various difficulties are channelled into specialist services. They announced their intention to provide integrated services 'in the fields of education, the legal service, information and support, counselling, housing and health' (p. 157), and to adopt an approach that would stress self-direction and self-help. They defined health education as 'part of the liberation of women' and promised to 'prove that Sisterhood is indeed powerful!' (ibid.).

The rhetoric was radical. The women involved were drawn from a mixture of 'old left' groups such as the Communist Party of Australia and newly politicised feminists. This informal coalition was a source of strength and diversity, but it also contained an explosive potential that was ignited following the election of the Fraser government in Canberra with its implicit threat to the Community Health Program. The health centre was the most expensive part of the multipurpose women's centre. It was funded in mid-1975, following State–Commonwealth difficulties similar to those in Victoria. Its first co-ordinator was Nancy Peck, who later worked (among other places) at the Women's Health Resources Collective in Carlton and then as the director of Melbourne's Healthsharing Women. The health service staff of the Brisbane Women's House was largely more conservative than those who proclaimed the power of sisterhood. The Roma Street premises also had a child care centre, and served as the first point of contact for women going to the refuge, which was at a different location. From the beginning, there were difficulties recruiting doctors, perhaps in part because of a decision that they should not be paid more than other workers. At times the doctor shortage was so severe that they were forced to employ men in order to continue rendering medical services.

The conflict between radicalism and reformism broke out into open warfare, and the Centre lost its funding after less than two years of operation. To one of the nurses who had been recruited, the radical feminists, many of whom were from the University of Queensland, were 'speaking another language', and when one of the Centre's own factions made charges of misappropriation of funds, they gave State bureaucrats a basis for withdrawing the grant. A relocated health information and support service survived the crisis, but state-sponsored women's clinical services would not be restored to the women of Queensland until after the watershed 1989 election of a Labor government in that State.

Darwin Women's Health Centre

Of all the obstacles to establishing a women's health centre, only the women of the far north had to cope with an act of God. The devastation of Cyclone Tracy delayed the opening of the Darwin Women's Health Centre by six months. A Family Planning clinic had been established in 1973, and members of the Women's Electoral Lobby had prepared a submission for funding to the Community Health Program which included support for a combined refuge and health centre. The submission had been approved, contingent on the Northern Territory government supplying accommodation. But then the cyclone struck on Christmas eve of 1974.

The cyclone drastically influenced everyone's priorities for some time, and many women and children were evacuated to the south until housing and other facilities could be reconstructed. However, as the population began to return, the need returned with it. There were comparatively few general practitioners in Darwin after the cyclone, and the need for contraceptive services was particularly acute. Lynn Reid was the Darwin Centre's first doctor, and for a year its only doctor. She was swimming against the professional current by working at the Centre for a salary. She had been involved in establishing the Centre, and had also worked for Family Planning. When the Centre was established in 1975, its refuge functions influenced the health services. The Centre's house had several bedrooms and a large verandah, but women and children were soon sleeping in the surgery and in offices as well as in the spaces originally allocated for them. In light of the combination of health centre and refuge, it is not surprising that the health services concentrated on minor gynaecological care, domestic violence, and primary care for the children of women clients. Few women's health centres have made medical care available to children, preferring to concentrate on serving the most immediate health needs of adult women. Lynn explained that caring for the children could easily have become a full-time occupation. The lack of other services in Darwin also put pressure on the Centre. For example, the staff had to keep warding off drug addicts who came there looking for a place to sleep, especially during the wet season.

Like both Brisbane and Perth, the Women's Health Centre in Darwin eventually lost its funding in a dramatic crisis that simultaneously revealed and deepened divisions in the women's movement in that city. With the advent of self-government in the Northern Territory, local bureaucrats and politicians came to exercise increasing power and it appeared to many of the women involved in the Centre that they were looking for any excuse to close it. 'In March 1980, the Northern Territory Health Department issued new guidelines for agencies in receipt of grants-in-aid.' Certain elements in the guidelines appeared to be 'designed specifically to limit the political activities of any organisation receiving Health Dept. money' (Zon, 1982: 3). Feminists in Darwin had already made powerful enemies by successfully challenging a local newspaper which had been printing 'girly photos' on the front page, and a local bar which had introduced 'topless' waitresses. The situation was further inflamed by the arrival of numerous visibly radical activists from southern states for the third Territory Women's Festival. These women did not conform to what was expected of the tourist the Northern Territory sought to attract. Some of them had shaved heads and wore overalls, they camped and squatted in unoccupied buildings, they lived on minimal incomes, and provoked outrage from locals. In the public eye, the Centre became identified with these 'undesirables'. When more explicitly radical, collectively organised women took over the health centre, they gave the Northern Territory government the opportunity they had been waiting for, and funding was withdrawn. Housing problems and police harassment (at times violent) drove many activists out of Darwin, and a remnant of committed volunteers struggled for two more years to maintain the service. When the Minister for Community Development (who had been Minister for Health when funding was stopped) discovered that they were still occupying a government supplied house, he abruptly gave them two weeks notice to vacate, after more than seven years of operation.

Central Coast Women's Health Centre, Gosford

Like Collingwood, this Centre's history began in 1976 as a volunteer group; unlike Collingwood, however, after more than two years, they had their first success in obtaining funding (a co-ordinator's position), but they continued to rely mainly on volunteers and donations until 1984 when they finally achieved a dramatic increase in State support. The central coast of New South Wales is an area of high population growth, with poor public transport, and geographically the population is dispersed around a lake. Many residents in the area have moved there from Sydney seeking cheaper accommodation. Many men commute to Sydney for work, leaving women and children, behind often without a car. Gosford also has a number of pensioners and single mothers. These factors create circumstances of isolation and emotional health problems for women of the region, and the Central Coast Women's Health Centre was established and tailored to meet such needs. For some time, the Centre owned a mini bus to transport women to and from sessions at the Centre, but eventually they found the service was not viable for the number of women being transported, and they decided to sell it. Child care is available for women attending the Centre. At one stage, the Centre had the use of two buildings a few kilometres apart, one of which (called 'Jenny's Place') it owned. During 1989–90, they sold that house, bought a new, larger building and consolidated all their work in one location.

Perhaps because of its volunteer history, the Gosford Centre has a highly developed volunteer program. It offers a systematic, graded sequence of training courses for volunteers, introducing them to basic counselling skills and developing the volunteer's abilities and confidence. Volunteers who have had some training are encouraged to co-facilitate groups, and some of them go on to become paid workers. Volunteers do a variety of tasks such as assisting in the small resource collection or answering the phone. The services at Gosford include massage as well as primary gynaecological and contraceptive care. The Centre offers several Family Planning clinics a week, and houses a sexual assault centre.

After such a long period (nearly eight years) with only minimal funding, the transition to living with financial support was not entirely smooth. Although they had wanted money and anticipated the benefits it would confer, the change required major adjustments. Hiring paid workers (most of whom were part time) created some friction between those who were paid and those who continued to work for nothing, a 'them' and 'us' situation that was both amplified and eased when they acquired the second building. Both volunteers and paid workers told me that having the volunteers take more responsibility for managing themselves had improved the situation; while they had Jenny's Place the volunteers were forced to be independent since they were largely separately located. Many volunteers originally came to the Centre when they themselves were in crisis and found help and support. Once their own lives were in better order, they wanted to put energy and resources back into the Centre. I heard similar stories of self-recruitment all over the country.

Hindmarsh Women's Health Centre, Adelaide

Hindmarsh also went through a period when it was staffed by volunteers, but in this case, the main volunteer phase followed rather than preceded a period of funding. The Mary Street premises were officially opened in 1976, but Hindmarsh had been functioning in the Prospect home of one of the doctors, Margaret Taylor, during 1975. The collective (originally called 'The Body Politic') was inspired by a visit Margaret Taylor had made to Leichhardt soon after it opened. The group (mostly young women) prepared a funding submission which was successful in Canberra, but which then got hung up in the South Australian Health Department.

Such obstructions were no surprise in Victoria or Queensland, where the State governments were conservative and ideologically opposed to such initiatives, but in progressive South Australia under Premier Don Dunstan, one might have expected an easier passage. One sticking point was the plan to employ salaried doctors. No other South Australian community health centres funded at that time were organised this way, and the public servants were sceptical. Lyndall Ryan (who conducted a review of the women's health centres for the Commonwealth Department of Health in 1975) suggested to me that the South Australian bureaucracy was used to leading in such matters, and they were taken aback to have a strong community initiative that was more progressive than anything they had devised themselves. One officer from the South Australian Health Department later admitted to a staff member from the Centre that they had deliberately made matters difficult for the women, although once the Centre was up and running, the same officer sent visitors to see the 'success story' that was Hindmarsh. When it was impossible to get the Health Department to release the funding in advance, the women simply went ahead and hired staff, furnished and renovated premises, and later claimed for the money they had spent.

Their intention to serve a disadvantaged clientele was apparently largely fulfilled; the women who came to Hindmarsh had often 'done the rounds' of other services and doctors in Adelaide, and had either found no satisfaction elsewhere or had been defined as 'too hard' by mainstream services. The collective had selected Hindmarsh as the location because of their political commitment to these women.

As far as I am aware, Hindmarsh is the only women's health centre that has ever been subject to a formal takeover by the State. During the late 1970s, factions consolidated who articulated conflicting views of how the Centre should be working. For some, this was a matter of having a different community in mind as the target for the Centre's services. While the original emphasis (and the reason for setting up in Hindmarsh) was to serve working-class and ethnic women, some women came to feel that too many concessions were made in an effort to attract conservative clients. Other lines of division formed among staff members, some of whom had little or no explicit commitment to feminism while others, deeply involved in the Women's Liberation Movement, felt that the Centre was betraying its origins in not maintaining the original vigorous, collectivist and explicitly feminist agenda.

Women who felt the Centre had lost its radical vision and its commitment to community education and community action (specifically included in the Centre's aims) came into conflict with others who believed that pursuing a supposedly extreme ideology would frighten and alienate the women they should be attracting to the Centre. Supplying community health care was also an official aim. When a new constitution was proposed that required members to sign a 'loyalty oath', committing them to oppose uranium mining and to support socialism and feminism, the situation reached a crisis. By the time of the State election and the defeat of the Labor government in September 1979, much of the Adelaide women's movement had become embroiled in the Hindmarsh crisis, and the new conservative government had all the ammunition it needed to move on the Centre. The government demanded that the constitution be changed to remove the more radical clauses, exacerbating internal tensions. In January 1980, the South Australian Health Commissioner formally notified the Co-ordinating Collective that Dr Barbara Orchard, an employee of the Health Commission, had been appointed to manage the Centre, that she would control the accounts, and that she would 'report to the Commission on the administrative and clinical procedures in use at the Centre'. Staff were instructed 'you are responsible to the Commission through Dr. Orchard for the carrying out of your work and that membership of the organisation known as the Women's Community Health Centres Group Inc. in no way governs your duties as a member of the staff of the Centre'. The drama of the takeover and the subsequent events are described in more detail in Chapter 4. When funding to Hindmarsh was withdrawn, collectives of dedicated women were able to continue to offer services on a volunteer basis for nearly four years. The work of these volunteers is full of lessons for women as individuals and for feminism as a social movement.

Alice Springs Women's Centre

If Hindmarsh has the distinction of being the only centre that was officially taken over, Alice Springs is probably unique in being the only one that was bulldozed! The Alice Springs Women's Centre opened in 1975 as a volunteer organisation, providing crisis counselling, referrals to local services, emergency accommodation, and a resource centre. As a result of a subsequent reorganisation and reformulation of direction, funding was obtained in 1977 to include support services related to the shelter, and this enabled them to open a health service in the Centre. The Centre was principally a refuge, but women working from the premises also ran workshops, did lobbying and advocacy, and conducted discussion groups. During its comparatively short life, it offered Family Planning clinics, abortion referral, counselling, and health information.

A city as small and racially divided as Alice Springs can be volatile, and in less than two years the centre of gravity had shifted dramatically to the left, the refuge was accommodating many more women and children, and the Family Planning clinics were discontinued. Women from Alice Springs disagree about whether the proportion of Aboriginal women using the Centre had increased dramatically, but they concur that the numbers of women at the refuge—and *which* women—had become an issue. Women with more radical, more pro-Aboriginal, and more anti-male ideas had joined the group, and a number of the original group had moved away, including one woman who was identified as an important mediator. Over time as increasing numbers of women used the Centre, conditions in the building—marginal at the best of times—began to deteriorate.

The Centre was conceived as being half refuge, half resource centre, but the refuge was taking over the resource centre. The sheer pressure of numbers increased dramatically, since many Aboriginal women were accompanied by a large network of kin. A group consisting of more than a dozen adults and children sought shelter at the home of a woman connected with the Centre, and I gained the impression that this was not unusual. In the final months, many of the refuge residents had little previous experience of town life. They were not used to the appliances or the confinement of a conventional suburban house, and some people felt that—however great the need—the refuge placed them in accommodation that was inappropriate to their needs. Those who defended the Centre's use charged their critics with racism; those expressing reservations accused the Centre of being hostile to men and excluding of non-Aboriginals. The availability of a white-sponsored alternative to traditional Aboriginal norms introduced an element of culture conflict that complicated matters for everyone. A council of Aboriginal women was involved with the Centre, but the problems were monumental. When an Aboriginal teenager fleeing from an arranged marriage to an older man came to the refuge, it exemplified the dilemmas confronting the women who worked in the Centre.

Responding to the growing clientele, the collective applied for a dramatic increase in funding, thereby calling itself to the attention of the Northern Territory government. In a bizarre combination of portfolios, the Minister for Health was also Minister for Mines and Energy. He visited the house and noticed posters and literature opposing uranium mining and US military installations in the Territory, thus confirming the connection between the Women's Centre and other left-wing political activities. By this time, priests were attacking the Centre from the pulpit, accusing it of destroying the family and forcing women to have abortions.

The situation was inflamed by a threatened takeover of the Centre by a right-wing group. At this point, some of the original members returned, and the conflict became dramatically polarised. Feelings ran high, and women from both sides say that there were threats of violence, verbal assaults, and cars were run off the road. The Centre was occupied by members of the more 'moderate' group who locked the collective and residents out of the building. They were issued with a summons to vacate the premises, and a mass public meeting was held outside the house the night the occupation ended. The police were present at this meeting where members of the Right to Life Association and other extreme conservatives called for funding to be stopped and the collective to be evicted. The collective moved back in, but the situation was beyond redemption. Funding was withdrawn, the Centre was closed and the building demolished. Women of Alice Springs had no women's health centre until the Aboriginal Congress Alukura opened seven years later.

Bankstown Women's Health Centre

By now the story is familiar. 'Although the Health Centre did not become a reality until 1978, four years of meetings, submissions and disappointments were encountered by the women who formed a committee in 1974' (Bankstown Women's Health Centre *History of the Centre: 1974–1984*). Janet Wakefield, who played a crucial role in the committee, had been involved with women's issues for over 40 years. The committee encouraged the women of Bankstown to articulate and advocate for their own health needs, and sponsored 'speak-outs' which gave local women a forum where they could 'have their say'. Some members of the committee had also been involved in founding the feminist women's refuge Betsy, and with the help of the Liverpool Women's Health Centre they arranged for a free Pap smear day at the local Fox Clinic. Women doctors saw more than 90 women during the day, confirming the need for women's health services in the area. Although they did not receive any funding until 1978, they began offering regular services in February 1977, operating out of the Fox Clinic and a local baby health centre. Even when minimal funding was granted, they were heavily dependent on voluntary donations until the mid-1980s.

In addition to conventional medical services, Bankstown is explicitly eclectic in its approach to health, and it offers a range of alternative therapies including hypnotherapy, colour therapy, and reflexology. There is a strong emphasis on prevention, community education, and 'holism' in health care. Counselling for migrant women is available in Vietnamese, Cantonese, and Mandarin. From the small beginnings in the late 1970s, they have grown. They now receive referrals from dozens of professionals and agencies in the area, and see thousands of women a year. In 1987, around 5500 women attended the Centre, and by 1989–90, that number had risen to 7500.

Women in Industry, Contraception and Health (WICH), Melbourne

By some definitions, this is not a 'women's health centre' since it does health education, health promotion, and occupational health education at industrial workplaces rather than individual clinical services. Its distinctive approach, however, is a model of how much can be accomplished with small resources. It had its beginnings during 1976 and 1977 when John Leeton and Susan van der Vickt studied use of contraceptives by women from non-English-speaking backgrounds. 'Nearly half of the abortions carried out at [Queen Victoria Hospital] in Melbourne during the 1970s involved married migrant women' (Siedlecky and Wyndham, 1990: 149). Consultations with migrant women revealed their difficulties in gaining access and adequate services from the sources available to English-speaking women.

WICH was founded by a group called Action for Family Planning, formed following a 1977 conference held at Monash University Department of Social and Preventive Medicine. The conference discussed the health and health education needs of migrant women. Delegates were shown a video entitled 'Without Knowledge—Without Choice', which illustrated the problems of unwanted pregnancy encountered by many women from non-English-speaking backgrounds. 'A wide range of health workers and migrant groups were represented. . .[and] resolved that accurate, multi-lingual information on contraception should be made available to women of all ethnic backgrounds' (Caddick and Small, 1982: 10). From the beginning, the aim had been to give information that will enable migrant women to make their own choices and to gain access to existing services rather than to establish additional clinical services.

The main emphasis of WICH is a factory visits program, run in close co-operation with the trade union movement. WICH's factory program co-ordinator liaises with appropriate unions who approach management directly to arrange factory visits. Once a visit has been approved, teams of bilingual health educators go to the factory where they conduct informal health education discussions in the women's lunch break. The exact content and approach to the sessions varies from factory to factory, depending on the number of language groups represented, the needs of the particular group of women, and whether men are present (in which case they may use a minimum of audiovisual material to avoid embarrassing the women). In addition to contraception and reproductive health, WICH also deals with 'occupation safety and health, workers' compensation, equal opportunity, sexual harassment and domestic violence' (Powell, 1986: 39). Usually, the WICH team make four visits of half an hour to each workplace, a bare minimum of time to distribute printed information, hand around anatomical models and samples of contraceptives, explain about Pap smears, teach breast examination, and refer women to other services. Lack of funding, a chronic problem for this organisation, has limited their ability to conduct follow-up evaluation sessions of most of their factory visits.

Despite limited resources, however, they have maintained an active advocacy and lobbying program on issues such as the Dalkon shield. One of their objectives has been to sensitise unions to the concerns of women workers, particularly those from non-English-speaking backgrounds. They have also made the educative process a two-way street, learning about traditional remedies and health practices from migrant women as well as giving information to women in the factories. For example, some middle-class advocates of modern contraception have assumed that only ignorance and lack of access have prevented less educated women from using oral contraceptives or IUDs. However, in light of the unwanted consequences of medical contraceptives, low-technology methods of birth control such as abstinence and withdrawal become more attractive, and migrant women's choices—provided they are indeed choices—of such methods come to be understood as well founded and appropriate.

Women's Health Care House, Perth

The story of this Centre illustrates the problems that beset anyone who tries to enumerate 'all' the women's health centres in Australia. Unless one takes a strict and legalistic approach to definition, it is not easy in several cases to determine exactly when a particular centre began. The Women's Health and Community Centre in Perth (discussed above) was one of the first centres to open, but its funding was discontinued in 1976 after a bitter division among the women connected with the Centre. When the State health department stopped the funding, they invited the women of Perth to regroup and submit new proposals for financial support. The successful group founded Women's Health Care House, originally in West Perth, located in a different building and still functioning more than a decade later. The more radical faction continued to operate without funding for about six months, first at the original Glendower Street premises, later moving to cheaper accommodation. They offered few if any clinical services, concentrating more on education, counselling and referrals, and political action. Without a doctor, its reputation as a radical lesbian group apparently discredited it in the public view.

Women's Health Care House can be seen, in some senses, to have risen from the ashes of Glendower Street, although the two operated in parallel for a while. Women's Health Care House has placed a heavy emphasis on individual gynaecological services and 'consumer education' for women. Members of the staff describe themselves as providing 'an alternative form of traditional health care for women, tailored to fit their expressed needs, ·rather than an alternative *to* traditional health care' (WHCH Staff Members, 1985: 164). Despite efforts by some staff members to enlarge the vision of the House and open it to a wider clientele, during the 1980s it was accused by some local feminists as being limited mainly to middle-class white women, little more than a 'nice women's GP service', having lost its sense of mission. If that is partly true, it is perhaps understandable in light of the history of the Centre. The experience of losing funding appears to have left deep traces in the memories of the women who stayed on, impressing on them the necessity for moderation, and generating a culture of caution. They are dedicated to seeing that the House and its services continue, and they apparently feel that its survival would be jeopardised if they were to press a feminist approach too strongly or to challenge the bureaucratic expectations of their funding bodies. This is a tightrope that all funded centres must walk, but it is all the more hazardous in a nervous or hostile political environment.

In many ways, the events in Perth mark a significant shift in the direction of the women's health movement in Australia. The comparative freedom of the initial period had ended. From 1978 until 1983, no new women's health centres were funded, unless one counts the Adelaide Women's Community Health Centre which opened in 1980, using funding that had previously gone to the centre at Hindmarsh. Instead of openings, the late 1970s and early 1980s were a period of suspensions (Perth), takeovers (Hindmarsh), and closures (Brisbane, Darwin and Alice Springs). The centres that did begin work during this period, including the Blue Mountains, Coffs Harbour, Wagga Wagga and a new centre in Brisbane, all relied on the patchwork of informal sources of support based on volunteer labour, pledges, and fundraising activities.

The difficulties of this period prompted the centres in New South Wales to form an organisation, Women's Health, Information, Resources and Crisis Centres Association (WHIRCCA). WHIRCCA began in 1982, facilitating communication among the various centres, organising quarterly workshops, and co-ordinating relations with the New South Wales Health Department, which by then had become totally responsible for funding. For the first few years of the Association, the organising and communication tasks of WHIRCCA were simply rotated among centres, adding to their existing workloads. They applied for funding repeatedly and unsuccessfully, although they were able to secure a Commonwealth Employment Program (CEP) grant for 1985. In 1987, a virtual freeze on NSW Health Department funding persuaded them that there was little point in continuing to seek State funding for the organisation, so they agreed to levy themselves in order to fund a woman to work two days a week on their behalf.

THE NEXT WAVE

The women's health centre movement began to move forward again in 1983, with the opening of two new regional South Australian centres in Elizabeth and Noarlunga, and the Women's Health Resource Collective in Carlton. In 1984, the third regional South Australian centre opened in Port Adelaide, as did an Aboriginal women's health service in Nowra (called Jilimi at the time, now named Waminda South Coast Women's Health and Welfare Aboriginal Corporation), and Women's Health in

Industry (in Lidcombe, NSW; this group is similar to WICH). Several of these centres, as well as others that relied largely on volunteer labour, availed themselves of a new source of government funding: the Commonwealth Employment Program's (CEP) job creation scheme, which made relatively short-term grants to organisations that would provide unemployed people with job-related skills. A number of women's initiatives turned the adversity of high unemployment among women to advantage, and used the funds to support development work for organisations.[2] The Women's Health Resource Collective and Jilimi both used job creation funds to start their work, and later obtained ongoing grants from health department sources. Although the Brisbane Women's Health Centre would have a much longer wait for upgraded and more stable funding, they also survived for several years on such hand-to-mouth funding sources.

Over a dozen centres began work during the next four years: in 1985 the Illawarra Women's Community Health Centre, the Multicultural Women's Health Centre in Fremantle, and the Shoalhaven Women's Health Centre in Nowra; in 1986 centres opened in Albury-Wodonga and Bathurst; in 1987, Blacktown, Lismore, Penrith, Campbelltown (called W.I.L.M.A.), Hobart, and the Alice Springs Congress Alukura all opened; and in 1988 two new services were initiated in Melbourne— Healthsharing Women, and the Women's Health Service at Footscray, as well as a small shopfront Women's Information and Referral Centre (concentrating on health) in Rockhampton.

It is difficult to draw sharp lines to separate the various periods in the development of Australian women's health centres, but rough divisions can be made between the originating phase in 1974–77, the leanest years from 1978–82, and a period of new growth from 1983–88. However one divides it, this is a dynamic movement, continuing to evolve right up to the present. For practical reasons, this study concludes its systematic coverage at the point of the launching of the Commonwealth Women's Health Policy and National Women's Health Program in 1989, even though several centres opened during 1989 and 1990 that were already 'in the pipeline' . Still, I believe that the Policy marks such a dramatic departure, and creates such a different political environment, that it and its consequences require intensive research attention beyond the scope of this study.

But if the atmosphere changed dramatically in the last years of the 1980s, there are also drastic differences when one compares the centres opening in the mid-1980s with the first wave of the mid- to late-1970s. For one thing, the funding and administrative arrangements were different from those that had prevailed under the Whitlam government. These changes are discussed in more detail in Chapter 3, which considers the relationship between women's health centres and the state. But equally importantly, by the mid-1980s, the women's health centre movement had some experience on which to build. Women in the women's movement had heard stories about the accomplishments and the conflicts at some of the centres. . .perhaps more about the conflicts than about the accomplishments. Women travelled and talked to colleagues in other locations. Some women who had worked in one women's health centre became involved in the founding or operation of another. For example, in the early 1970s, Janet Bacon participated in the volunteer Melbourne Women's Health Centre in Collingwood. She went on to work in the Women's Health and Community Centre in Perth, and then to be active in the founding of the three regional women's health centres in South Australia. At Elizabeth she was the Project Officer who developed the submission for funding, and later a doctor employed at the Centre. She now serves on the board of the Lodden Campaspe Women's Health Centre in Bendigo. Diana (Whitehead) Wild is another doctor who worked in more than one centre (Hindmarsh and Perth). Betty Pybus, who helped found Leichhardt, went on to work at Liverpool. Trish Morgan worked for a time at Leichhardt, and later became co-ordinator at Lismore. Pat Ann worked at both the Perth and Southern Women's Health Centres. There are dozens of similar examples of women who travelled, taking personal experience and feminist political history from one centre to another.

The centres have differed not only in their histories, but also in the kind of work they do. The variation in their activities is, of course, partly a function of the amount, sources and constraints on funding; but it is also a response to the particular interests and talents available in a centre at a given time, the character of the surrounding community, and the ability to attract staff with relevant skills. The combination of a distinctive history and a particular emphasis gives each centre a special 'fingerprint' that distinguishes it from the others, whatever formal and other features they may have in common. The next section reviews briefly the variety of work undertaken by the various centres.

THE WORK OF THE CENTRES

Because women's health centres do such different things, and in such varied combinations, it is no simple matter to summarise their activities. A 'bird's eye' view is provided in Table 1.1. In broad terms, one could separate those with clinical services from others, but even within either of those categories, the centres display diversity. For example, among those with no clinical services, two concentrate exclusively on *health education targeted to specific disadvantaged groups* (Women in Industry and WICH). Both of these centres work with women employed in industrial settings, and provide health education at the workplace. Many centres offer *libraries* available for students and women in the

Table 1.1 The work of women's health centres

Health education
    generalist
    specially targeted
	Counselling
	    crisis
	    long-term

Library or resource room	Primary gynaecological care

Research
    library based
    consumer-based
	General primary care
	    care for other members of a
	    woman's household

Developing health education or training materials	Alternative therapies
Training health workers or educators	Child care

Advocacy and lobbying	Other ('non-health') groups
	    e.g., coffee mornings, reading
	    groups, English as a second

Community development	language
Sponsoring other groups	Other ('non-health') services e.g., legal aid
Referrals to other services	

community to do research, and staff may also develop their own educational material, or encourage women from the community to research and write pamphlets or information kits. These information-oriented centres usually undertake *training* for health professionals and educators, and health education and health promotion groups for women from the community. The comparatively new Victorian service, Healthsharing Women, is an example. The Brisbane Women's Health Centre and Melbourne's Women's Health Information Resource Collective (the word 'Information' was added to their name in 1988) are similar, and they also include a vigorous *advocacy and health policy lobbying* dimension in their work. A *referral system* (formal or otherwise) is often part of these services.

In addition to health information and education, most centres have at least some individual clinical services. There remains, however, great variety: which services and for whom? The list that follows is more or less hierarchical in that centres offering the services further down the list tend to have the others as well.

Counselling of some kind is nearly universal among the centres that offer individual services, and the similarity between 'information' and 'counselling' blurs the distinction between centres giving only 'information' and those that also offer 'clinical services.' A woman who tells a centre worker about her history of domestic violence or personal suffering of some other kind may not instigate a formal therapeutic encounter, but the workers who make referrals and give access to information usually find that they must acquire at least basic counselling skills to enable them to deal with clients and to protect their own emotional well-being. Most centres have at least crisis counselling, followed by referral for longer-term support (e.g., Lismore and Gosford). Whether centres also offer ongoing counselling is more variable, and may change within one centre from time to time depending on current funding and staffing. Counselling is generally seen by staff to be resource hungry but also absolutely basic: an indispensable service.

Another basic service furnished almost everywhere is *primary gynaecological care* (pregnancy tests, Pap smears and breast checks, tests for sexually transmitted diseases, treatment of vaginal infections, contraception, abortion referral). In the early days of the movement, these services were delivered by a range of workers, many of whom had no explicit medical qualifications but had learned 'on the job'. Such work being done by supposedly 'unqualified' staff was a source of hostility to centres, and now primary medical care tends to be the responsibility mainly of doctors and nurses, although women's health workers without medical or nursing training often undertake at least some of the work under the nominal supervision of staff with professional qualifications.

More *general primary medical care* (treatment of colds, flu, injuries, etc.) is somewhat less common. Many centres are forced to refer general care to women GPs if possible or to community health centres in order to reserve their clinical staff for gynaecological work. Others insist on taking 'holistic' care very seriously and are concerned not to relegate care for different parts of the body to different agencies. The Multicultural Women's Health Centre in Fremantle is an example of such a generalist service. They have been scrupulous to publicise that they are not seeking to take clients away from local GPs, but the women who come to the Centre have often not had any health care services apart from hospital care for the births of their children or medical emergencies. The Aboriginal Congress Alukura service in Alice Springs includes infant and child health, recognising the relevance to a woman's health of the well being of those for whom the woman cares. If Congress Alukura gets permission to provide birthing services as well, it will become one of the most complete women's health centres in the country in terms of the range of services available.

Some centres offer non-conventional or *alternative therapies* (such as iridology, naturopathy, homeopathy, massage, herbal remedies). These are the original or exclusive focus in some centres, especially those that are not government funded. Examples include the Women's Healing Centre in Glebe (formerly in Annandale), the Clinic of Preventive Medicine for Women in Canberra, and the Acacia Bark Clinic in Adelaide. In government-funded centres, alternative therapies are usually a later addition to the array of services, particularly if the centre is located in a conservative community (for example Gosford), although several funded centres have always had a commitment to offering a mixture of orthodox and less conventional services. The centres at Bankstown, Coffs Harbour and the Blue Mountains have included alternative therapies in their clinics from the time they originally opened.

Child care is another resource-hungry service, but it is an ideal everywhere, and a priority in many centres. All four of the government-funded centres in the Adelaide region have some kind of child care, for example. Often, child care is arranged informally, using any worker who happens to be available for the duration of a woman's consultation. Sometimes, it is just a matter of a box of Lego and books on the floor of the reception area, with whoever is on the reception keeping an eye out. The Coffs Harbour Centre has a register of volunteers who come in when they are needed, a creative solution to the problem of the unpredictability of demand. Others stipulate the days on which child care will be available, and advise mothers of young children to book in at those times. At Gosford, a properly equipped child care facility is available to the children of women attending the Centre for clinical services or group sessions.

Centres occasionally organise other *groups* (coffee mornings, general discussion groups, reading groups, English language classes, etc.) to facilitate social contact for isolated women. This is another case of a blurry line: when is a group a 'health education' or therapeutic group, and when not? For isolated women, social contact may be vital to the promotion of their health. To a woman who does not speak English, language classes may be more significant to her future health status than some explicitly 'health' education classes or clinical services. Similarly ambiguous '*non-health*' *services* such as legal advice, debt counselling, or more general community education and community development programs are available in a few centres. The Hunter Region Working Women's Centre in Newcastle, which opened in 1975, defined itself from the beginning as a multipurpose women's centre that included health services rather than a health centre providing ancillary services.

Apart from dealing with women and health in the very broadest sense, the various women's health centres are united by an ideological commitment which both originates within and contributes to contemporary feminism. The next chapter discusses the relationship between women's health and the women's movement, showing how a vision of the possibility of reclaiming control over their own bodies and health has unified women from a variety of personal and political backgrounds, inspiring and enabling them to do the work of women's health centres.

2 Women's health and the women's movement

Australian women's health centres are distinctive in some ways, but they are also part of a movement throughout the English-speaking world, a movement that has been called 'the rebirth of feminism' (Hole and Levine, 1971). Leichhardt was the first women's community health centre in Australia, but it was not the first women's health centre to arise out of the contemporary women's movement. That distinction probably belongs to one of the six or seven feminist self-help clinics opened during 1971 in cities all over America, including Berkeley, Seattle, Baltimore and Los Angeles (Price, 1972; Ruzek, 1978: 61). But long before the advent of contemporary women's health centres, women have been assisting one another to learn about and care for their bodies. Marieskind discusses, for example, health care by women, for women as a centuries-old tradition that was practised in ancient Egypt and Sumer and has continued, despite periods of suppression, throughout recorded history (1976: 63–4).

A question frequently put to advocates of women's health services is, 'Why women's health?' Although not always asked in a spirit of genuine curiosity, the question is a legitimate one, which actually contains two questions: why *women's* health, as opposed to men's or people's health; and why women's *health*, as opposed to equal pay or education or some other right or resource that women might advocate instead of health? Answers to both sub-questions can be gleaned from considering the relationship of the women's health movement to the contemporary women's movement. In the course of the discussion, we will also examine the role of feminist thinking in formulating both the theory and practices of the women's health centre movement.

There are several perspectives from which to consider the importance of women's health to women's lives, and hence to understand why women's health and women's health services are socially and politically significant. Three perspectives will be explored here: that of the women's health movement itself, a sociology-of-health orientation, and a more abstractly theoretical approach which explores the discursive connections between femininity and illness. A section of this Chapter is devoted to each of the three perspectives, which are introduced in brief here before they are developed in detail in the separate sections.

First, because women's health centres are the focus of this book, it is necessary to understand how the women's health movement formulates the issue. The question here is, how the women who organise and work in women's health centres understand the broader significance of their work. My objective is to describe the feminist analysis that forms the basis for women's health centres. These questions take us back to the beginnings of women's health centres and to an examination of the women's movement's formulation of women's health care as a political problem, what factors make it problematic, and how women's health is related to women's social position more generally. I discuss four particular sub-areas on which the feminist movement of the 1970s concentrated attention: reproductive health and birth control, gynaecology, medical training and research in women's health, and mental health.

In the second section, women's health is discussed from the perspective of the sociology of health and illness. This orientation deploys mainstream social science understandings of professionalisation, medicalisation, and social organisation to shed light on the circumstances within which the women's health movement has developed. The material in this section supplements the women's movement's basic analysis by identifying mechanisms in the social construction and management of health and illness in advanced western societies. It begins by introducing the central critical social science perspective on medicine, and goes on to discuss specific social scientific debates about women's health status. The concepts introduced here provide a basis for understanding the social model of health which informs the women's health movement.

Third, I turn to a theoretical analysis not encompassed within either of the two previous perspectives. This analysis examines the relationship between femininity and illness as socially constituted concepts, and it suggests that the work of the women's health movement may be a radically important intervention, but for reasons in addition to those identified by the movement itself, or by sociological insights.

WHY WOMEN'S HEALTH?

In an ideological environment which presumes that equality means sameness, and that liberation for women simply means access to arenas of male privilege, separate women's health services appear to be a step backward, a concession to notions of feminine deficiency that should be overturned. However, such a view does not represent adequately most schools of contemporary feminist thought. In the feminist formulations that inform the women's health movement, separate services are not second best: they are a vital part of feminism's double agenda—to improve the lives of women in contemporary society, and also to change the fundamental values and structures of society. Contrary to the model that defines 'liberation' as requiring women to imitate men's lives, and therefore to conceal any need or quality distinctive to women, the women's health movement has always acknowledged and indeed affirmed women's different bodies and particular health needs. The current revival of theoretical interest in female embodiment (see, for example, the special issue Number 5 of *Australian Feminist Studies*, Summer 1987) represents a theme that is a continuing commitment for the women's health movement. Hence, in the women's health movement, it is no concession to begin by acknowledging that women have a distinctive perspective on medicine as a consequence of distinctive health needs.

Reproductive health

For many people, 'women's health' is synonymous with reproductive health. And certainly, as we saw from the beginnings of Leichhardt, Australian women's health activists focused initially on reproductive health, particularly on birth control. Almost every discussion of feminism acknowledges that birth control is crucial to women's well being, and counts improvements in contraceptive technology as 'advances' for women. So it is no surprise that one of the initial demands of the contemporary women's movement was for free, safe contraception and abortion. In late twentieth-century Australia, the law stipulates that access to many effective forms of contraception and virtually all medically safe terminations of pregnancy will be controlled by medical personnel. Hence, demands for birth control are, effectively, demands on medical institutions, and it is logical that one of the foundations of the movement for women's health centres has been women's need for access to high quality reproductive health care, especially birth control.

From the perspective of the 1990s, when condoms are discussed on television and pictured on the sides of buses, it is difficult to appreciate how restricted access to information and contraceptives was in Australia until quite recently. 'From the 1920s to the 1960s there were only three birth control clinics operating in the whole of Australia, and they provided information and devices only to married women, and only to suitably "eligible" ones at that' (Matthews, 1984:134). Although the situation improved during the 1960s, the most reliable contraceptives prescribed by doctors were still available only to married women, and terminations of pregnancy were expensive or dangerous, or both. Oral contraceptives were welcomed by Australian women, but many doctors would not prescribe them to unmarried women. Consequently, birth control was an urgent, practical issue in the late 1960s and early 1970s. Indeed, before the advent of AIDS, contraception was almost exclusively a women's issue (Luker, 1975), and in many ways, it remains so.[1]

Many of the feminists who first identified problems of access to birth control were unmarried. Consequently, it may initially have appeared to be an issue only for a radical or extreme 'fringe' rather than a concern for Australian women more generally. The press and the public have always been ambivalent about feminism and feminists, so the fact that health, sexuality and birth control were subjects in early feminist forums and consciousness-raising groups did not necessarily make these issues matters of more general concern. But soon, working- and middle-class married women who did not identify as feminists began to reveal their difficulties: the embarrassment, the humiliation of having to obtain their husband's permission to get contraception, the judgmental behaviour of doctors who disapproved of 'artificial' birth control and thus refused to prescribe it. When women's marriages ended, they found that their sexual lives were also expected to end. Married or single, women complained of the unwanted effects and health hazards of medical contraception, the messiness, inconvenience and ineffectiveness of non-medical contraceptives (such as foams, pessaries and creams), and the expense of all kinds. Until 1972, contraceptives were subject to sales tax and import tariffs of 'between $7^{1}/_{2}$ and 45 percent' (Matthews, 1984:135). Thus, a diverse range of women became united by their common dissatisfaction with restrictions on the provision of birth control, with the limited and inappropriate choices available, and with their physical and social consequences.

If contraception initially placed women's health on the feminist agenda, struggles over the management of pregnancy and the process of birthing itself consolidated health as a feminist issue. The power struggle surrounding the medical takeover of childbirth was prolonged. Although many Australian mothers in the late nineteenth and early twentieth centuries were attended by untrained midwives, the obstetric training of doctors was so poor and their tendency toward unwarranted intervention so great that the outcomes of midwife-attended childbirth were often better than doctor-attended ones until after the Depression (Willis, 1983:120–1). American research shows that in the late nineteenth century in New England, lying-in hospitals run and staffed by men had higher rates of infant and maternal mortality than a hospital run by women (Howell, 1975: 53; Lorber, 1985). Perhaps not incidentally, the women-run hospital also maintained better records. During the years following World War I, the supervision of childbirth in Australia gradually shifted from home to hospital, and from midwives to general practitioners to specialist obstetricians. This 'medical takeover', as Willis describes it, involved a transfer of responsibility for attending childbirth from working-class women to middle-class men, a transfer which was substantially complete by 1930 (Willis, 1983: 93). Increasingly, pregnancy became medically and socially defined as a disease, childbirth as a potential medical or surgical emergency, and both as processes that women and their babies could not be expected to survive without medical (eventually specialist) intervention. While infant and maternal mortality were high, the promise (whether founded or not) of greater safety led women to welcome these changes (Bates and Lapsley, 1985: 66).

By the 1960s and 1970s, however, some women began to resist these changes, objecting to their personal impact, and questioning the claim that medical intervention was responsible for the long-term secular decline in infant and maternal mortality (Haire, 1978; Tew, 1985). Reports of apparently needless pain and injury began to appear; the humiliation and brutality of some hospital routines were exposed, and some after-effects on both mother and baby were found to be negative (Oakley, 1980). Women observed that the transformation of care for pregnant and parturient women involved a shift of power and control. This was a shift of power away from the birthing woman and her female attendants, into the hands of male doctors and large, bureaucratic medical institutions. Obstetrics ceased to be the 'Cinderella' of medicine (poorly paid and low status), and became the 'happy specialty', rewarding emotionally as well as financially,[2] and the availability of hospital beds made it possible for obstetricians to confine in medical facilities many healthy women who were undergoing uncomplicated childbirth (Oakley, 1984). Women who believed that the change was beneficial to their own health or that it insured the welfare of their babies welcomed or at least accepted it. But as doubts began to circulate more widely about the efficacy and safety of medicalised childbirth, and concerns were expressed about the possible negative impacts on both mother and infant, challenges began to be posed to this superficially progressive (and implicitly irreversible) alteration in the location, conduct and control of birthing.

There is nothing necessarily feminist about efforts to change childbirth. Several non-feminist organisations such as the Childbirth Education Association became involved in attempts to reform birthing practices and infant care, but on certain issues, particularly decision making and control, these groups usually deferred to medical authority (Reiger, 1988). By contrast, the feminist analysis sought to diminish medical control over pregnancy and birth by imparting as much information as possible to women and encouraging women to ask questions, seek the support of a friend or advocate, inform doctors of their preferences, and refuse unnecessary intervention (for example, see publications by the Boston Women's Health Book Collective, 1971, 1976, and 1984). Feminist health groups typically advocated the return of control over childbirth to birthing mothers and the birth attendants (many of whom were women) chosen by the mothers (Rothman, 1982; Broom, 1984c).[3] Doctors who support such initiatives have been subjected to the censure of their professional colleagues, as in the case of British obstetrician Wendy Savage, who was suspended from clinical duties for over a year (Savage, 1986).

Gynaecology

Another concern that put health on the feminist agenda was gynaecological problems (Frankfort, 1972). Often regarded by doctors as trivial, menstrual problems, the 'minor' infections, discharges, and other symptoms associated with pelvic and vaginal malfunctions were afflictions traditionally suffered in silence. Lennane and Lennane (1973) studied the tendency of doctors to attribute gynaecological disorders to psychosomatic origins, an attribution for which there was little foundation and which did nothing to alleviate real distress. These medical beliefs and attitudes made women reluctant to go to doctors for the treatment of gynaecological problems, sometimes until the symptoms had become intolerable. When women did seek help, some doctors were evidently uncomfortable about conducting pelvic examinations and other investigations, or simply thought them unnecessary (Bacon and Moore, 1978). Consequently, women were prescribed inappropriate or ineffective remedies, and then were blamed for the fact that they did not get better (Barry, 1972). Many doctors were clumsy, insensitive and unskilled in performing pelvic examinations, thus causing the woman distress and discomfort or even pain and injury. Some women who had been injured by precipitous, prolonged or inexpertly managed childbirth found it difficult to persuade doctors that their symptoms were significant enough to warrant attention. The women's movement gave women both the permission and the opportunity to express the distress occasioned by these situations, some of which involved years of suffering. Such women spoke courageously from the floor at abortion debates during 1971 and 1972, and at the 1973 Women's Forum in the (standing-room-only) Sydney Town Hall. Several who had never addressed a group larger than their household or perhaps a classroom found themselves telling their stories of illness and distress caused by too many pregnancies, of condescending doctors who refused to listen to them, and of friends and sisters who were injured or killed by illegal abortions. The women's movement validated such histories and sought to understand and respond to them. Feminists argued that the medical neglect and mistreatment of 'women's complaints' is not incidental, but arises from the fact that the problems are unique to women, and hence of little interest to medical men.

Medical training and research

Studies of medical training identified some of the mechanisms whereby doctors consolidated and legitimised their professional ignorance (in both senses of the word: not knowing, and not giving attention) of women's health needs (Scully, 1980). Education for general practice contained only limited coverage of obstetrics and gynaecology, and it was a standard joke that the gynaecology lecture would include the display of a *Playboy* centrefold as one of the 'clinical plates'. Medical textbooks instructed the new doctor to expect women to be mentally unstable, masochistic, infantile and dependent (Weiss, 1977). Gynaecology texts typically omitted research on female sexuality and women's health (Scully and Bart, 1973). Whether trainee doctors believed them or not, texts encouraged a view of women as neurotic, dependent, and hypochondriacal. Alarmingly, two decades of feminism have not transformed Australian obstetrics and gynaecology textbooks. A study of texts used in contemporary medical training shows that women are still being represented as sexual objects for male pleasure. For example, the caption of a plate in a textbook used at three major Australian medical schools commented gratuitously that 'One might wonder where she hid the tumour when she sunbathed in her bikini' (Beischer and Mackay quoted in Koutroulis 1990: 79). Overall, the texts dichotomised women as virgins or whores, and prone to neurotic complaints. As a consequence, psychiatry and gynaecology have become oddly blurred, in gynaecology texts at least (Koutroulis, 1990).

Despite this undistinguished record, in the United States there have been suggestions that gynaecologists should be the primary medical professionals for women. Ruzek labels this move 'gynaecological imperialism' (1978: 11). There could be no clearer signal that women have been symbolically and functionally reduced to a collection of reproductive organs than having gynaecologists replace generalists in women's health care. In response to such thinking, American women's health activist Barbara Seaman proposed, perhaps not entirely in jest, a complete ban on the entry of men into obstetrics and gynaecology (1975: 45). Marieskind, however, argued that the very existence of the specialty is a medical reflection of 'the wider social ideology which views women as sex objects and reproductive organs' (1975: 48).

Women's health research has been comparatively poorly funded, and much health research has failed to include trials on females, animal or human. A recent review of US biomedical research found that 'men have been the primary research subjects for studies of diseases, studies of diagnostics and studies of treatment and cure' (Sibbison, 1990: 166). In Australia, investigation of women's health receives only a tiny fraction of total funding, and the research that is done continues to concentrate on reproductive matters to the neglect of other priorities identified by Australian women (O'Connor et al., 1990). Research into new methods of contraception has concentrated more on the economic and industrial potential of new products than on the safety and other concerns of users (Cowan, 1980; Korenbrot, 1980).

Although breast cancer is 'the most common cancer. . .and the most common cause of cancer death in Australian women' (Commonwealth of Australia, 1990: 15), debates about appropriate treatment have continued for over 100 years without resolution. Some observers claim that 'survival rates are little affected by any of the current methods used' (Skrabanek, 1985: 316–17). American surgeons were slow to adopt less radical approaches to the surgical treatment of breast cancer (Seaman, 1972: 191). In view of the drastic and mutilating nature of much breast cancer surgery, it is remarkable that clinicians and researchers should still disagree about whether breast cancer is one disease or several, and over the curability of the disease or diseases. Age-standardised mortality from breast cancer has, if anything, increased in the last twenty-five years (Australian Institute of Health, 1989; Devesa, 1986). Although breast self-examination (BSE) is routinely recommended, 'no mortality data are available from prospective randomised trials of BSE' (Commonwealth of Australia, 1990: 17). All in all, the individual and epidemiological picture of women's reproductive and gynaecological health care falls short of what could be expected in rich developed societies.

Mental health

Another concern that placed women's health high among feminist priorities arose out of women's mental and emotional health. The higher incidence of psychoneurotic disorders among women had long been considered evidence of constitutional deficiency, of an innate tendency toward mental instability and emotionality. The new feminist analysis introduced arguments that, in some instances, ran parallel to the anti-psychiatry movement of R.D. Laing and Thomas Szasz. According to this view, most women with mental or emotional problems were not insane at all; they were being labelled 'mad' in order to marginalise and discredit the difficulties they had in conforming to acceptable feminine behaviour. Another, related argument held that women were being driven mad by male oppression and conflicting social demands, caught in a chronic double bind; or they were depressed by the isolation and monotony of conventional femininity (Brown and Harris, 1978). According to a third view, there was no overall sex difference in the incidence of mental and emotional disturbance, but men expressed the disturbance in ways such as alcoholism, illegal drug use, and personality disorders, while women were more likely to suffer from emotional problems and neuroses.

Whatever the explanation, women consistently report higher rates of psychoneurotic disorder such as anxiety and depression. For example, on the basis of data in the 1977–78 Australian Health Survey, more women than men in every age group were judged to be suffering from a psychiatric problem (as measured by the General Health Questionnaire, GHQ), and women suffered on average from a larger number of problems than men (Australian Institute of Health, 1988: 59). Furthermore, there was evidence that women suffering from anxiety or depression were liable to be drugged and incarcerated (Chesler, 1972). More prescriptions overall are written for women than men, but the over-representation is higher still in the case of psychotropic (mood altering) drugs. Data from the 1983 Australian Health Survey show that more than one and a half times as many women as men reported taking tranquillisers and hypnotics in the previous two weeks (Commonwealth Department of Health, 1985: 11). The heavy burden of mental and emotional distress carried by women called for a response.

General health care

These facts alone would have been enough to make health a feminist concern. Gradually, however, evidence began to accumulate suggesting that women's general health care was also often inferior to men's (Corea, 1977). For example, my observations in the surgeries of general practitioners in the ACT found that doctors were less likely to answer a woman patient's questions than a man's, they were less likely to give technical information about the condition or therapy, and less likely to offer the woman patient alternative approaches to treatment: all this despite the fact that women typically played a more active and inquiring part in their consultations than did men with similar health problems (Broom Darroch, 1978). An American study confirmed that women patients asked many more questions than men, but that doctors tended not to 'match' the level of technicality of the question as well for women (Wallen, Waitzkin and Stoeckle, 1979). British research also confirmed doctors' tendency to define women purely in terms of domestic responsibilities, and to respond to women patients in condescending ways that promoted their dependency on doctors and drugs (Barrett and Roberts, 1978). Such studies were confirmed by the personal stories of women seeking treatment for general illnesses and injuries, not only problems unique to women. That is, health care in general—not only gynaecological and reproductive health care—has been shown to be problematic for women.

These difficulties are compounded by women's disproportionately high levels of need and utilisation. By nearly all measures, women suffer higher rates of illness, and they use most medical goods and services at higher rates than men. For example in the 1983 Australian Health Survey,

67 percent of females (compared with 57 percent of males) experienced one or more illness conditions in the previous fortnight, and 78 percent of females (compared with 64 percent of males) took some sort of health-related action such as reducing normal activities or going to the doctor. These differentials are typical of morbidity measures (although there are exceptions, for example, see Waddell and Floate, 1986). Women, then, come in more frequent contact with doctors and other health workers, so any deficiencies in health services are more relevant to women as a group than to men, and they are relevant more frequently during an individual woman's life. The demography of the Australian population also makes health care a 'women's issue'. Men's higher age-specific mortality means the population contains more elderly women than men, and the elderly have high rates of utilisation of medical goods and services. Women's use of medical facilities in health as well as in illness further elevates rates of exposure to medicine when consulting doctors for contraception, care during pregnancy and birth, and as domestic health workers when caring for other members of the house-hold. Therefore if medical care is problematic for anybody, it is worse for women who are more likely to be exposed to it, and who are exposed to more of it.

Reclaiming control of our bodies

The women's movement responds to this analysis in a variety of ways. In the early 1970s, one activity was the formation of consciousness-raising (CR) and women's health groups. Not all CR groups formed around health issues, but many took up health problems as part of their agenda. While CR groups concentrated on a kind of 'talking cure', women's health groups also prompted action. Women obtained inexpensive plastic vaginal specula and used them at group meetings to view their own cervixes. The experience was profoundly consciousness raising. It gave women knowledge of and visual access to a part of their bodies from which many had traditionally been estranged. The group gave its members permission to touch and see their own genitals. They thus reclaimed a part of their own bodies that in some ways had belonged more to doctors than to themselves. The self-examination served as a metaphor and a practical example of one battle cry of renascent feminism: 'taking control of our own bodies'. A popular poster from the period proclaims the power that is restored to women who have a speculum and the knowledge of their own bodies (see Figure 2.1).

Women's health groups also undertook 'action research' by listening to and recording women's own experiences of health problems and ways of managing them. They read about health care in China. They studied non-traditional therapies such as herbalism and naturopathy, and taught one another to use home remedies to deal with conditions that doctors

Figure 2.1 Wonder Woman with her speculum
(This poster appeared in many women's centres in the 1970s)

had been unable or unwilling to treat. Trained professionals were often willing accomplices in the process, gladly teaching lay women to do various procedures themselves. Often, women were surprised at how easy some of the techniques were. In a presentation to the American Psychological Association in 1972, feminist health activist Carol Downer claimed, 'Abortions are so simple they are downright dull; vaginal infections are diagnosed with a microscope; pap smears are easier to do than setting our hair; fitting a diaphragm is less complicated than stuffing a turkey. We can do these things' (quoted in Ruzek, 1978: 54).

Self-help was carried into women's health centres (Hornstein, 1974). Not all women who started women's health centres had originally formed self-help groups, but some began that way. And in any event, the recognition that traditional medicine was often ignorant of women's health needs and occasionally hostile to women clients encouraged women's health centres to help women take responsibility for their own health. This emphasis was reinforced by a particular reading of the history of healing in which lay women were thought to have been the original therapists whose knowledge and authority were gradually usurped by medical men. 'Modern medicine, in de-skilling women has deprived them, it is claimed, of quite precise powers over reproduction in particular and the body in general' (Brown and Adams, 1979: 45). Thus the emphasis on self-help was a significant strategic response to the understanding that female healing powers had been stolen by male medicine. Furthermore, 'Self-help . . . is not simply "do-it-yourself-doctoring" '. It involves conceptualizing health and illness in a fundamentally different manner' (Ruzek, 1975: 80).

The Australian women's health movement encompasses a range of views about how improvements in women's status, including health status, are best achieved. They are united by dissatisfaction with existing medical services, a critical view of modern medical professionals, a determination to bring about improvements in women's circumstances, and a vision of a radically different society. It is a vision of a society in which women are not oppressed or systematically disadvantaged, and which is consequently not sickening to women, either directly or indirectly. It is also a society in which girls learn to enjoy and be proud of their female bodies, and women are enabled to be responsible for the promotion and development of their own health and well being, with access to the goods and services necessary to health development. In such a society, women's reproductive organs and processes would not exclude them from normal social life or disadvantage them in any form of social participation. And in such a society, women as well as men would be involved in providing appropriate and high-quality health care.

If a society so described sounds utopian, it has, nevertheless, oriented the work of the women's health movement and guided the work of women's health centres. This vision has been an essential resource in moving a diverse group of women from analysis into action. Results of that action are the substance of this book.

THE SOCIAL CONSTRUCTION OF MEDICINE

The pattern of poor care, medical ignorance, trivialisation of women's problems, and excessive and inappropriate treatment became the object of feminist research and theorising. What emerged was a detailed (if unsystematic) feminist critique of modern medicine. In order to understand the feminist critique, it is helpful to review the general critique that was being developed at the same time by writers such as Ivan Illich (1975), Vincente Navarro (1976) and Paul Starr (1982). Feminists both drew on and contributed to this general critique, which has foundations in the sociology of medicine and in more or less left-wing commentaries on powerful social institutions, of which medicine is an exemplar. Traditionally, medical institutions and their staff have been presented as if they were governed entirely by twin commitments to science and healing. That is, medicine has claimed for itself a special status, separate from everyday life which is—by contrast—acknowledged to be governed by ordinary human motives and weaknesses, and shaped by social and economic pressures. Based on the observations of the sociology of medicine, both feminist and other discussions of contemporary health care have disputed medicine's claim to special status, stressing that medicine is a social institution like any other, and as such, it is subject to the social processes that structure institutions and pattern behaviour. Medicine has been analysed as a profession seeking occupational dominance and privilege (Friedson, 1970; Johnson, 1972), as a form of magic (Roth, 1957), as an agent of capitalist and imperialist interests (Navarro, 1976), and—most important for our present purposes—as an institution for the social control of deviant behaviour (Zola, 1972 and 1973).

At the simplest level, if health is the norm, then illness is a deviation from that norm and medicine serves to control such deviations. However, the concept of medicine as an institution of social control can be deployed considerably beyond this almost incidental analysis. The concept has been used to identify the processes underlying patterns such as the application of non-medical criteria to decisions about access to care (Glaser and Strauss, 1964; Roth, 1972), the compulsory medical treatment of unwilling patients in order to contain socially disruptive behaviour, and the imposition of medical diagnosis on social deviance such as homosexuality (Ehrenreich and Ehrenreich, 1974; Schneider and Conrad, 1980). There are many examples of medical personnel enforcing norms of middle-class respectability on poor and working-class clients;

similarly, clients from non-Anglo ethnic groups may find that culture (as much as language) is a barrier to adequate and suitable medical care when medical personnel seek to impose 'appropriate' forms of illness behaviour. In a subtle reversal, instead of defining illness as deviance (from health) requiring control through alleviation or cure, deviance of many kinds becomes illness, and illnesses are conditions over which doctors are the main legitimate authorities. But because the ideology of medicine connects it with help and healing rather than with punishment or the imposition of social norms, the operation of medicine as an institution of social control remains covert and usually informal, but nonetheless powerful. While the 'sick' person is not usually blamed for their illness, they may lose rights through medicalisation of their deviance. For example, compare criminal with medical incarceration. A criminal is usually given a specified sentence of imprisonment, may appeal against the sentence through the courts, and may serve a shorter sentence if their behaviour is good. A person committed involuntarily to a mental hospital, by contrast, serves an indefinite sentence and has fewer formal mechanisms of appeal. Even after voluntary admission, discharge may be delayed although the patient does not suffer from or report any symptoms (Rosenhan, 1973).

Radical critics of contemporary medicine have often cast doctors as agents of 'the establishment', serving the interests of a hegemonic social order by labelling, drugging, and medically incarcerating people who engage in disorderly or subversive behaviour. The extreme example of such medical control was the Stalinist practices in the Soviet Union, which labelled political dissidents as insane and confined them to mental hospitals. Less dramatically, in the west doctors have been accused of acting (however unintentionally) to mute dissent and contain rebellion, thus serving the interests of capitalism and patriarchy. For example, British community workers have suggested that the response of the National Health Service to the health problems caused by poor housing, poverty, isolation, and women's double burden is to 'act as an agent of social control: to keep women functioning so that they can continue to bring up their families, whilst suppressing any tendency to question, or rebel' (Dixon, Johnson, Leigh and Turnbull, 1982: 65).

Medical institutions and personnel do not simply control deviance. They also produce it. This is partly a matter of interpreting, labelling and sanctioning behaviour that is socially disruptive or disapproved, such as abortion. Additionally, deviance is produced by norms for what kinds of deviance are gender-appropriate. Social expectations encourage women who do not conform to norms of acceptable femininity to conform instead to norms of deviant femininity. Illness (including mental illness) is, as Schur says, 'a "favored" female deviance' (1984: 191).

Simply because of their greater exposure to doctors and medical institutions, women are more likely to be subject to medical social control. However, some forms of feminine behaviour are particularly prone to medicalisation according to the logic that deviance by a female is more liable to be understood as 'sickness,' while in a male it may be defined as 'badness' (Edwards, 1988: 169, 179–85). For example, petty theft by males is generally dealt with by the criminal justice system, but shoplifting, where women are the majority of offenders, is increasingly defined as an illness which is referred for psychiatric management. Thus, it can be argued on several grounds that while the process of medicalisation has enlarged the realms of daily life that are open to medical surveillance, a larger segment of women's lives than men's is vulnerable to medical control.

This interpretation applies general observations about the social functions of medicine to consider the particular relevance to women of the contemporary critique of medicine. It does not, however, engage a distinctively feminist perspective which would go on to observe that when doctors and patients interact, the typical encounter occurs between a male doctor and a female patient, and that the sexes of the participants shape the character of the doctor/patient relationship. It may be thought that this only matters if sex is explicitly at issue during the consultation, for example, if the patient has a sexually-transmitted disease. However, sex is relevant to the medical encounter regardless of the patient's reason for presenting. It is, perhaps, not obvious how the processes, organs or tissues that are common to both sexes could be the basis for different treatment of women. After all, a gall bladder is a gall bladder; its malfunction and removal should be based on the same diagnostic and prognostic criteria. But a woman's body has been constituted throughout her life through distinct psychic and cultural processes that do not cease to apply simply because the organ in question is also present in male bodies, and the social meaning of 'a woman's body' is discursively produced by (among others) medical texts and practices.

In some instances, the processes whereby the apparently asexual processes and parts of the body become 'sexualised' in women occurs through the supposed interference by women's reproductive organs or hormones in the functioning of other organs. The case of hysteria is the most obvious example of the process. At times, hysteria was believed to be unique to women, arising as the word implies from the uterus itself. A common contemporary example is the medical notion that the so-called 'female hormones' disturb the body's natural balance.

Thus, the sexes of the participants may be less *overtly* salient if the consultation does not involve the patient's genitals, but both doctor and patient remain embodied beings and sexed subjects, whether that is explicitly acknowledged or not. In the typical medical encounter, the doctor is a man, psychically inscribed as separate and powerful, imbued with the presumption of agency, sexual dominance and strength. The patient is a woman, psychically inscribed as connected and relationally oriented, and imbued with the presumption of dependency, sexual subordination and passivity. (If, as is often the case, the patient's class location is inferior to the doctor's, a differential opens between them along another dimension.) These embodied sexualities are not once-for-all accomplishments, but lifetime projects in which subjects are constantly engaged; and each requires the Other for its own constitution. Doctor and patient need not discuss these matters for the dynamics to inform their interaction. If the doctor is a woman, the dynamics will change, but sexuality will not thereby become irrelevant. . .only differently relevant. Furthermore, when a woman consults a doctor, there is no escaping that the patient's female body is the object of their interaction. Even in the case of mental illness, the possibility of organic disorder must be considered, and most consultations concern what is mutually agreed is a malfunction of the body. As Moira Gatens has observed, bodies are not sexless, even if—at the conscious level—we are busy trying to behave as if they were (Gatens, 1983).

Women get sick, men die

While feminist activists were preparing critiques of conventional medicine, initiating self-help, and launching women's health centres, medical sociologists were striving to develop explanations for women's higher rates of morbidity. What does the aphorism mean—'women get sick, men die'—and how has it come to inform social science research and theory and health services planning and delivery? Studies based on data in which medical professionals actually examine people are typically regarded as more valid than self-reports, and such studies usually find that women have higher rates than men for hypertension and rheumatoid arthritis. The results are more ambiguous for other conditions, and in some cases—notably diabetes—sex differentials vary from time to time and from place to place (Wingard, 1984: 444). More generally, studies using examinations, medical services utilisation, and self-report data indicate that at most ages women are more likely than men to rate their health as poor. They also use medical goods and services at higher rates, and they have higher rates of most acute conditions (except accidents) and of many chronic and disabling conditions (Verbrugge and Wingard, 1987).

The issue of women's 'excess' morbidity has thrown up two major arguments: first whether women are 'really' ill more often, or whether the apparent difference is a social artifact; and second, if they are 'really' sicker, whether the causes of their illnesses are organic or psychosocial. It is important to remember that discussions of sex differences in illness are plagued by the same conceptual and measurement problems that afflict all studies of health and disease: namely, the impossibility of drawing sharp distinctions between organic states and psychosocial conditions or personal circumstances, and consequently of distinguishing absolutely between illness, illness behaviour, and medical care.

To illustrate, *death* appears to be the one unambiguous measure of (lack of) health, containing no contamination by psychological states or social relationships. It is absolute: there can be no argument about degrees of severity. However, there is considerable disagreement about *what death rates tell us*. That is, writers do not agree about what factors are most significant in producing death rates that differ along socially defined lines. Some commentators insist that death rates are reflections of access to or adequacy of medical care, while others are equally certain that they indicate the effectiveness of public health measures in the population. Except in populations with fairly high rates, death rates (with the possible exception of infant mortality) are not sensitive measures of quality of life. And whatever is measured by death rates, we know that they are strongly correlated with socioeconomic status (McMichael, 1985). So even here, we do not have an unambiguous health measure.

Other ways of assessing health, such as questionnaire-based reports of illness conditions, self-rated health, days spent in bed or in hospitals, consulting doctors and other health professionals, taking medicines, and so on. . .all are clearly influenced in various ways by factors apart from the organic condition that is supposed to be the real disease. Furthermore, the social dislocation, embarrassment, pain, and other disrupting characteristics of a condition may, in some cases, be more important to how people define and act upon illnesses than the 'objective severity' as it would be assessed by a doctor. In my judgment, these issues cannot be satisfactorily resolved. It is enough to observe that the disagreements they provoke thread through all the social scientific literature on women's health, and leave us unable to state categorically in all cases how illness behaviour is related to organic disease. However, the point is not to establish conclusively whether women are 'really' ill more often than men, but rather to note that women's illnesses are sometimes construed as deviations from 'normal' patterns of illness; and that there are widespread social beliefs that women's illness behaviour is itself, in some sense, deviant and a problem to be explained if not eliminated. For example, comparative statistics often make a point of excluding (often labelled 'controlling for') obstetric and gynaecological conditions in calculating rates of consulting or hospitalisation. Although the reason for this exclusion is obvious and plausible, it can imply indirectly that the statistical elimination of these conditions accomplishes a social elimination, as if these were not important experiences in women's lives and significant to the understanding of health, medicine, and women's bodies. A literature that discusses women's 'excess' morbidity establishes in its very language that male patterns are the norm against which female patterns are to be measured.

The belief that women's illness is an 'artifact of reporting' (that is a feminine propensity to complain of symptoms more than men) should have been laid to rest very early in the debate, by an article by Gove (1973). His review of data on differences in death rates from various causes by sex and marital status shows that the 'marriage advantage' (that is, death rates are lower among married people than among the single, divorced or widowed) is larger for men than for women, and that differences by marital status are greatest 'with those types of mortality where social factors would appear to be especially important' (p. 60). To establish these claims, he compares deaths from causes such as accidents, lung cancer, and diabetes (where psychosocial factors should be significant in exposure to risk or effective management) with death's from such causes as leukemia (where 'psychological state has little effect on either etiology. . .or treatment'), and finds that there are minimal differences by marital status for the second group of causes, but marked differences for the first group. He also demonstrates that selection effects (healthy people are more likely to marry) cannot explain the findings. Thus, he shows that people's personal and social situations can—at least for certain causes of death—have a measurable impact on their health. By breaking the homogeneous group 'women' into a few, crude categories, Gove begins to unpack some of the sub-patterns concealed by generalisations about women. These data establish conclusively that at least some of women's health problems are not reporting artifacts, and foreshadows an interest in the social factors that may influence health.

In the case of writing about women's health, however, acknowledging the relevance of the social tends to be deflected by a kind of mind/body dichotomy that splits real bodily illness from psychosocial factors that are only 'illness behaviour', or conditions that are psychosomatic and hence imaginary. However, the dichotomy is a false one, separating elements that are always bound inextricably together. 'Illness' is a fundamentally social category. There may be human diseases that have no impact on the person, but human actors can have no knowledge of them. A person must feel something (pain, fatigue, vertigo), do something (faint, vomit, decline to go to work), or have something done to them (take their temperature and declare them feverish, order them to bed, label them as contagious) in order for us to define the person as sick. On the other hand, there may be conditions where the only accessible indicator is the sick person's self-report but for which there are no detectable organic signs. However, we cannot assume that all or even most of these disturbances exist only in the 'mind'. Pain is often such a symptom; in the absence of vomiting, so is nausea. What are called hysterical conditions are, nevertheless, experienced in the body and can be as disabling as conditions for which organic causes can be found. In sum, (with the possible exception of outright malingering) all illnesses are simultaneously both psychic/social and bodily. Hence, the dichotomy between the categories obscures rather than enlightens understanding.

In sociology, the confusion created by the split is evident in attempts to account for the higher incidence of diseases among women by suggesting that the 'feminine role' is more compatible with sickness than the 'masculine role' (for example, see the frequently cited article by Nathanson, 1975). In this context, 'the feminine role' apparently means doing unpaid domestic work, as opposed to paid work in the public sphere. The idea is that women (because they are less likely than men to be in paid work) have fewer scheduled obligations and more free time to engage in illness behaviour, while men soldier on in the face of symptoms that send women to the doctor or to bed. According to this view, women are probably not 'really' sicker than men: they only act that way.

In a related argument, Nathanson and others have also suggested that it is comparatively easy for women to reveal that they suffer from symptoms (especially, but not exclusively, symptoms of emotional distress) and to engage in other illness-related behaviour without violating the norms of conventional femininity. By contrast, conventional masculinity is less compatible with admitting that one has symptoms and making allowances for them. This hypothesis is frequently given to explain (or explain away) women's patterns of morbidity and illness behaviour. Such reasoning has also led some people to propose that men's higher age-specific mortality results from their propensity to postpone admitting to themselves or others that they have symptoms; hence men supposedly delay seeking medical attention until their conditions are too far advanced to be satisfactorily treated. The limited evidence, however, suggests that there is little sex difference in delays in consulting for serious conditions such as cancer (see, for example, Marshall and Funch, 1987; Marshall, Gregorio and Walsh, 1982). Furthermore, research has not substantiated the claim that adherence to feminine stereotypes would predict illness behaviour (Thompson and Brown, 1980).

Among sociologists who agree that women's illness behaviour is significant because it is related to patterns of illness (rather than incidental because it represents differences in taking up the sick role), a second debate has been conducted concerning the underlying causes of elevated morbidity among women. Gove and Hughes (1979) have advanced a 'nurturant role hypothesis' which says that women's illnesses result from the domestic demands, particularly on married women, that 'interfere with their ability to take care of themselves'. They also suggest that the poor mental health of women who are subject to heavy 'nurturant role demands' contributes to poor physical health. Gove and Hughes (1979 and 1981) claim that the sex differences in morbidity are negligible among men and women who live alone, and that this confirms that the sex differences in illness rates among men and women living in families are real rather than artifactual. They also say that the differences result from women's heavy domestic responsibilities. Their evidence is confusing and ambiguous, and has sparked an inconclusive debate in the literature (for example, see Marcus and Seeman, 1981a). In part, the debate was inconclusive because it tended to focus on methodological issues, although there were important measurement problems such as assessing 'fixed role obligations' without considering the care of young children or the elderly as such an obligation (Marcus and Seeman, 1981b). Nevertheless, the debate introduced into mainstream social science the possibility that women might be physically harmed by their devotion to domestic duty, a proposition that feminist critiques of marriage and the family had been at some pains to establish (Bernard, 1972). Gove's earlier (1973) research showed that among women deaths from homicide and motor vehicle accidents are an exception to the rule that married people's death rates are lower than those of the unmarried. For these two causes of death, single women are at less risk than their married sisters (page 51). Although Gove did not make the point, women are in greater danger of being killed by men they know, especially husbands, than by strangers. This is another finding that lay dormant in the literature until feminists concerned about domestic violence became active in raising awareness (e.g., Scutt, 1983).

The debates about the basis of women's patterns of illness and illness behaviour remain unresolved and are probably unresolvable. But they were useful for their extensive examination of the part played by social factors in the experience and management of ill-health. They suggested, at times indirectly, that health could not be adequately understood (and hence that health services could not be appropriately designed) if the models were based entirely on advice from doctors and pre-established medical criteria. Furthermore, although it was probably not the authors' intention to do so, the debates introduced several considerations that have been taken up by women's health activists. By translating the often pejorative language of social science, we can extract several useful ideas:

1 Women and men may differ in the ways they typically experience their bodies, and hence in how they experience, define and respond to symptoms of illness. For example, women may have more awareness of internal bodily changes and states. If this were understood as legitimate, coherent human variation with intelligible (and inseparable) social/psychic and organic foundations, then social and medical ideologies and practices would not need to control women's 'difference'

2 Compared with men, women may engage a different process, or invoke different criteria, in the decision to take illness-related action such as consulting medical professionals, reducing activity, taking

medicines, or going to bed. Once again, this difference need not be construed as a problem, but can instead be understood as a variation with costs and benefits to all concerned, which could usefully be taken into account in planning health services

3   Doctors may respond differently to women than to men with 'similar' organic conditions, perhaps attributing different etiology or prognosis, or prescribing a different course of therapy for similar symptoms. Such variations in professional behaviour may compromise the standard of care patients receive, and hence call for change

A social model of health

The women's health movement, which is interested in the whole woman and her social environment and material circumstances, adopts a more 'holistic' approach to health than the fragmentation fostered by contemporary specialist technical medicine. This perspective has come to be called 'the social model of health' (in contrast to the medical model) and it has been affirmed by the Australian Women's Health Network and in several State and national women's health policies. This social model of health and illness is rooted in the same soil as the new public health. It recognises the relevance of social and economic factors to the cause and prevention of ill health, disability and premature mortality.

The medical model, with which the social model is contrasted, locates disease within the person and conceptualises the sources of disease in terms of germs, physical insult or defects in the individual's physical structure or function. It takes the environment into account only insofar as it exposes individuals to infectious, toxic or injurious agents, and allocates 'health' resources to medical or surgical services for sick individuals. By contrast, the social model locates people in social contexts, conceptualises the physical environment as socially organised, and understands ill health as a process of interaction between people and their environments. It stresses the fundamentally social character of the distribution of illness and injury, and the contribution of improved living conditions to the historical increase in longevity. It argues that for the greater health of all people, prevention should be emphasised at least as much as treatment in the allocation of health resources.

A social model of health fits well with the notion that women's illnesses are frequently either caused or made worse by the material, social and psychic circumstances of women's lives. It opens the possibility of considering the cultural foundations of women's bodily experiences, and hence the possibility of non-medical approaches to the management and prevention of illness and the development of health. Within a social model of health, bodily experiences may be understood as structured and organised not by the blind forces of brute 'nature' (e.g., germs), but by the social and political environments (e.g., housing, working conditions) within which people live. A social model does not claim that there are no infectious or injurious agents or physical defects. However, it draws attention to the fact that such agents and defects are not shared equally or distributed randomly in the population. Instead, illness, injury and disability are distributed according to patterns that largely follow lines of social, economic and political disadvantage. According to most measures of illness, the poor are much more likely than the rich to get sick and die prematurely (Black et al., 1980). And if the social, economic and political orders are connected to the distribution of health, it follows that the gender order can also be considered as one significant element in how health is socially located, managed, and experienced.

The advent of the social model of health enables women's health activists to resist the medicalised model that attributes all women's difficulties to our defective bodies and constitutions, an approach which depoliticises women's protest and trouble by 'naturalising' symptomatic behaviour. According to some views, it is either impossible or inappropriate to interfere with patterns that are products of 'nature'. As Lieven (1981) argues, people often claim that 'if it's natural, we can't change it', although this dictum is applied selectively. But even when it is deemed possible to intervene in a 'natural' event, the basis of the intervention is politically different than when the circumstances are understood as socially based. Defining conditions as natural[4] has been an effective ideological means of excluding those conditions from the arena of human responsibility (Broom, 1984b). Natural disasters are not unjust, and our response to the suffering they cause is a matter of compassion, not justice. Similarly, if problems are defined as illness, it is inappropriate for people to demand redress as of right, although they can hope for (and in some instances buy) effective therapy. The social model of health recognises that health problems and other social and economic inequities are interrelated, and that health cannot be restored, protected, or promoted if it is defined and approached as if it were simply biological. Although they are enjoying some currency, the ideas underlying this model are not new.

IS 'HEALTHY WOMAN' A CONTRADICTION?

The power that doctors and medical institutions exert over women is both symbolic and material. I have already discussed how the women's health movement argued that doctors control women and women's bodies, by denying access to goods and services, and by imposing unnecessary and inappropriate treatments. Concern about the imposition of such control ignited the women's health movement during the

1970s. But the impingement of medicine on women's lives goes beyond these material manifestations. It functions equally powerfully through ideological and symbolic channels (or perhaps more accurately discourses). To understand these processes, we must focus not only on the social and cultural practices of medicine, but also on medical and other discourses that are involved in the production of social meanings, especially the meanings of health, illness and femininity.

In a society where health and the body are socially defined as medical matters, the odd situation prevails in which male doctors have, to a considerable extent, become the experts on women's bodies, empowered to label normal and abnormal femininity, and to prescribe the appropriate means of restoring normality. The links between masculinity and medicine on the one hand, and femininity and illness on the other, complicate and reinforce medicine's power in women's lives. I have proposed elsewhere that illness itself has come to be understood as feminine in some senses, and reciprocally that femininity has connotations of illness or disease (Broom, 1989). For example, the qualities associated with sick people (such as weakness, passivity, dependency) are similar to qualities associated with certain forms of femininity, particularly that of bourgeois white women during the Victorian era when feminine pallor and fainting were romanticised in a 'cult of invalidism' (Ehrenreich and English, 1973: 47; Sontag, 1977).

Health professionals, as well as lay people, form this connection. A landmark study asked clinicians to describe a mentally healthy male, a mentally healthy female, and a mentally healthy adult. The qualities these professionals used to characterise the mentally healthy man and those to describe the mentally healthy adult were very similar, but the mentally healthy woman was described in such different terms that the authors observed that 'this constellation seems a most unusual way of describing any mature healthy individual' (Broverman et al., 1970: 5). The profiles of the healthy man and of the healthy adult both included qualities such as independence, activity, confidence, and directness. However, the profile of the healthy woman contained such characteristics as being conceited, excitable, submissive, and emotional. Qualities such as aggressiveness, which are congruent with healthy masculinity, may be seen as symptoms in an adult woman (Standing, 1980: 136). The study suggests that, in the minds of these clinicians, there is a symbolic link between normal adult femininity and ill health, or at least qualities associated with ill health. While mature masculinity and health are closely related concepts, mature femininity appears to be infused with notions of sickness and defect. The very concept of a 'healthy woman' may, in some senses, be a contradiction in terms (Broverman et al., 1972). A later study of GP's perceptions of their patients found that doctors rated the prognosis of women more poorly than that of male patients with similar conditions (Wallen, Waitzkin and Stoeckle, 1979: 143).

In medical discourses, the female body and its normal functions are often discussed as if they were aberrant, by definition. The treatment of pregnancy as a disease and childbirth as a surgical event illustrate this pattern; these examples were mentioned above as they alerted and motivated contemporary feminists to action in the women's health movement. In the present context, however, we are interested in the discursive practices that constitute women's bodies as 'medical material', in order to develop a feminist analysis of the the relationships between the female body on the one hand, and women's socioeconomic circumstances and their social experiences of being female on the other. Rothman (1982) describes in detail the construction of reproduction as a medical matter which cannot be expected to proceed normally unless subject to meticulous supervision and regulation by qualified professionals. Martin shows how medical texts define labour as a mechanical process which must be subject to close monitoring to ensure that it conforms to strict standards, and appropriate technical intervention to correct errors in progress (1987: 58–61). Doctors who oppose homebirth and other less interventionist approaches to childbirth stress the inherently hazardous nature of pregnancy and birth, the unpredictability of the female body, and its propensity to go awry. They also stress that they alone can be relied upon to protect babies and mothers from the dangers of the uncontrolled female body. In these medical discourses, the notion of the 'unassisted vaginal delivery' is now the exception rather than the rule, and in some hospitals, it seems that any vaginal delivery (rather than Caesarean section) may soon become exceptional as well (Bates and Lapsley, 1985: Chapter 4; Lumley and Astbury, 1980).

Similarly, menopause is now widely defined as an illness, more specifically a 'deficiency disease' like diabetes, and like diabetes, requiring daily chemical treatment for the rest of one's life (McCrea, 1983). Writing about menopause is writing about degeneration and malfunction.

> In both medical texts and popular books, what is being described is the breakdown of a system of authority ... ovaries cease to respond and fail to produce. Everywhere else there is regression, decline, atrophy, shrinkage, and disturbance (Martin, 1987: 42, 43).

Menopausal women may be threatened with becoming 'intersexed', ugly and crippled if they do not take hormone replacement therapy. However, women themselves may not adopt an 'illness' orientation to menopause. In one study, professional women were least likely to view menopause as a disease, blue-collar women were most likely (Frey, 1981). And women who are experiencing or have experienced menopause are less likely than younger women to think of menopause as a distressing experience that requires medical intervention (Martin, 1987: chapter 10; Neugarten, Wood, Kraines, and Loomis, 1968).

From the nineteenth century until the 1960s, medical representations of menstruation were fraught with images of pathology, although menstruation is rarely considered as a clinical disorder today (Martin, 1987; Rothman, 1984). However, this is not the first time in western history that menstruation has been considered 'normal.' On the contrary, writers as early as the ancient Greeks and Galen apparently stressed the similarity between male and female bodies, and suggested that men had analogous processes for dealing with 'plethora'. While menstrual blood might be seen as contaminated, menstruating was not regarded as pathological. Martin (1987: 31–7) discusses the transformation of menstruation into a bodily 'disturbance' during the nineteenth century. For example, consequences of a menstrual period are depicted by a late nineteenth-century writer as

> leaving behind a ragged wreck of tissue, torn glands, ruptured vessels, jagged edges of stroma, and masses of blood corpuscles, which it would seem hardly possible to heal satisfactorily without the aid of surgical treatment (Heape, quoted in Martin, 1987: 35).

Menstruation may no longer be so overtly defined as pathological, but it remains an anomaly: bleeding in the absence of a wound. Gallop suggests that it confounds the impulse to dichotomise women into either madonna or whore, since menstrual blood 'cannot. . .be absorbed into the category of female sexuality as phallic turn-on', but neither does it signify maternal reproductive accomplishment. 'Thus it remains an embarrassment for either classic feminine representation' (Gallop, 1988: 54). The contemporary medical imagery used to represent it refers frequently to failed production, disintegration, and death (Martin, 1987: 46–9). In a medical symbolism that has been internalised by many women, menstruation stands for wasted reproductive capacity.

Analogous processes in the male body, or processes common to both sexes are not represented in such terms, however. Martin illustrates how different are the metaphors used to describe the distinctly male function of spermatogenesis (p.48) or parallel (to menstruation) bodily processes such as the regular shedding and replacement of the lining of the stomach (p. 50). In these cases, the metaphors suggest health, vigour, abundance and renewal. Female functions appear to be subject to peculiarly negative representation in medical discourse. It is no accident that research stressing the debilitating potential of menstruation was most popular in the postwar years when women were being pushed out of the labour force. The focus of medical attention currently is more on the premenstrual phase of the cycle than on menstruation itself. Premenstrual syndrome has been formally recognised as a disease requiring active treatment if women are not to be deranged by these imbalances and their families placed at risk.

Even in the absence of specific symptoms, cycles themselves are considered aberrant. The hormonal fluctuations associated with the menstrual cycle are often discussed as if the normal, healthy human body were not cyclic, and as if changes (apart from menstruation itself) associated with hormonal cycling are pathological and require therapeutic intervention in order to restore health. All of these examples illustrate the deeply held cultural conviction that the normal, healthy body is the male body, and that the female body, even in its 'natural' state, is defective. The existence of the speciality of gynaecology (where there is no cognate speciality for males, unless one counts urology) is testimony to the symbolically problematic and morbid nature of the female body. Pateman has argued that because of the female body, women have been understood as disorderly and 'naturally subversive of men's political order' (1988: 96). The permeability of female bodily boundaries is thought to conflict with the integrity of the body of the free individual which is actually the male body.

Such symbolic associations might be only of intellectual interest were it not for the rise of medicine and the ascendancy of therapeutic institutions and practices during the nineteenth and twentieth centuries. In both popular and medical discourse, disease is considered as 'a misfortune, caused by non-human (or "natural") physical factors' (Edwards, 1988:143). For the purposes of the discussion here, there are two important consequences of defining a condition, event or behaviour as a 'disease'. First, sick people are not responsible for their condition, although they may be expected to participate appropriately in its management. Unlike a crime which is motivated and in which someone is responsible for the deviance, illness implies helplessness and dependency, the action of impersonal natural causes rather than personal or social agency. Second, society's authorities on illness are doctors. When these two apparently obvious aspects are related to the previous discussion linking illness and femininity, we have circumstances that simultaneously conceal and legitimise medical definitions of acceptable femininity and medical domination of women's lives.

ON NOT TAKING IT LYING DOWN

The ways in which medicine is implicated in the subordination of women can read like a catalogue of unrelieved horrors. There is no need for me to balance that impression by cataloguing medicine's contribution to women's welfare: that task has been undertaken with zealous dedication by others (see Shorter, 1983, or Graham, 1950 for examples). But it does need to be said that women are not the passive victims of medical control. Medicine does not simply shape and control women as it pleases. There are several reasons why the 'effects' of medicine on women are more complicated than that.

For one thing, medicine is not perfectly consistent in what it says and does. The messages of medical discourses are often contradictory. The notion of a healthy woman is deeply ambiguous, carrying simultaneously the implication of the abnormal female body and the implication of freedom from disease and disorder. Neither one is the 'true' meaning of 'healthy woman'; both elements coexist in uncomfortable proximity. Such disjunctures create opportunities for qualifying, questioning and undermining oppressive meanings.

For another thing, medicine is not the only game in town. Most childbirth may be appropriated to medical settings and attributed to the efforts of doctors rather than women, but the discourse of natural childbirth imputes to women the power and corporeal knowledge to give birth (Odent, 1984). When medicine offers oppressive or unpleasant options, some women may look to other sources of health care in alternative therapies or home remedies. When science defines women's complaints as imaginary or trivial, some women may seek out other sources of validation in self-help or support groups.

Even within medical interactions and institutions, it is sometimes possible for women to turn adversity to advantage and use medical authority to legitimise and organise the distress that they experience, and to mobilise medical resources in the effort to obtain relief. More than one new mother has expressed appreciation at post-natal hospitalisation because it allows her a brief 'vacation' from domestic work and child care.

Women are not only the objects of medicine: they are also active agents in the constitution of their bodies and themselves, participating in other (sometimes conflicting) discourses, at times accepting and at other times resisting medicine's impositions.

Finally, women may convert their individual concerns and criticisms into organised resistance. The women's health movement is exactly such organised resistance. The analysis presented in this chapter, particularly in the last section, suggests that superficial changes within medical practice—making medicine more 'woman friendly'—will, by themselves, not be adequate. However important it is to reform prevailing medical institutions, these changes do not address the participation of medicine in the discursive production of femininity and the female body. To intervene in this critical site, it is necessary to develop oppositional discourses. That is exactly what women's health centres can do.

3 The women's health movement and the state

The state plays a key role in the drama of women's health centres, but the question of the relationship between women and 'the state' is a vexed one in contemporary feminist thought.[1] Especially during the heyday of socialist feminism, feminists spent much energy seeking to understand the nature of the modern state, its role in women's oppression or liberation, and its relationship to other powerful social institutions. In the post-socialist, post-feminist 1980s, the emphasis shifted slightly to a call to develop a 'feminist theory of the state'. Although we are little closer to such a coherent statement, it has become increasingly apparent that existing theories of the state (such as liberal humanist and socialist) are limited in their capacity to shed light on the differential impact of the state on the two sexes. Feminist scholars are striving to understand this institution and its relevance to women's lives and feminist struggle, as is evident in the recent upsurge of Australian feminist publishing (Sawer, 1990; Yeatman, 1990; Watson, 1990; Franzway, Court and Connell, 1989).

Henrietta Moore identifies six distinct issues that have occupied feminist analysis of the state: welfare provision by the state; 'ideological state apparatuses' such as the media or political parties; state responses to women's organisations and initiatives; the differential impact of state action on men and women; the differential access of women and men to state resources; and the role of kinship and gender in the emergence of modern states (1988: 129 and 132). To that list, an Australian observer makes two important additions: the role of the state as an employer of women, and the part played by some of those women—femocrats—in the effort to shape state policy and action in terms of feminist objectives. Except for Moore's final category (dealing with the emergence of modern states), elements of each of the feminist concerns about the state are relevant to the activities of women's health centres.

Questions about the relationship between women and the state remain confused and unresolved in part because writers often fail to acknowledge the multiplicity of meanings embedded in the term *women*, or the variety of structures, ideologies and practices encompassed by the concept *the state*. Even within one society, 'women' means (at least) females of various ages, classes, ethnicities and races, life stages, and household circumstances. Likewise, 'the state' means (at least) government in some general sense; the institution with the monopoly on the legitimate use of force; the various branches of government such as the legislature and the judiciary, the law, the police and the army; government policies; public agencies including welfare and regulatory bodies; and various levels of government (national, state and local). Obviously, the relationship between women and the state is one thing when the woman is a senior officer of the Commonwealth public service (in which case she is in a sense part of the state). But it is quite another when the woman is a Spanish-speaking migrant who seeks emergency funds and housing from the state, which is represented by a young male Anglophone clerk on the counter at a local office of the Department of Family and Community Services. The fact that there are two women in relationship to the state is much less significant analytically or personally, than the class and ethnicity of the women, the particular circumstances that bring them into contact with the state, and the components of the state with which they are interacting.

Thus, we must specify in any particular instance which aspect of the state (and which women) are at issue if analyses of their interactions are to be fruitful. Otherwise, I am inclined to agree with Judith Allen that ' "the state" is too blunt an instrument to be of much assistance (beyond generalizations) in explanations, analyses or the design of workable strategies' (1990: 22). Still, one might say much the same about any institutional analysis; the concepts of the 'family', the 'economy', 'medicine', 'education', 'law', and 'religion' are also used as if their contents were simple, self-evident and consistent. Insofar as they have been used in that fashion, they yield less analytic fruit than if we seek to be more historically, culturally, and structurally specific.

However, our understanding of the state is also confused because of the complex and deeply contradictory character of the relations between women and the state. Feminists have thought of the state as both a source of women's oppression and as a resource for women's resistance. Even though they may have used the concept rather vaguely, the arguments warrant consideration. Let us consider each of those understandings briefly.

Most feminists note that the state serves patriarchal interests (Barrett, 1980; McIntosh, 1978). Historically, the most basic legal rights of citizenship such as the franchise were denied to women. Married women were legally subsumed by their husbands, and lost even the limited rights to own property or establish a residence that were accorded to single women. The famous 1907 'Harvester' judgment in the Federal Arbitration Court institutionalised Australian wage discrimination. Although several legal measures (womanhood suffrage and married women's property acts) during the nineteenth and twentieth centuries have redressed many of these formal disadvantages, inequities remain, such as rape laws that exclude the possibility that a married woman can be raped by her husband. In the health field, the state regulates medical practice and stipulates the qualifications and licenses required before anyone can undertake such therapeutic procedures as prescribing drugs or performing surgery. The consequence of such regulation has been to limit severely the kinds of activities that can be performed by health workers who are not medical practitioners; and while most doctors are men, most other health workers are women. Thus, the state enforces medical dominance of other health workers which, in effect, is male dominance of females.

State policy and administrative practice also contribute to the reproduction of a patriarchal gender order (Williams, 1989). For example, many social welfare schemes presume that a woman who lives with a man will (or should) be supported financially by him and therefore do not grant benefits to a woman who cohabits. As Shaver puts it, 'Australia's welfare state is without question patriarchal: its income security system, probably the most gender-neutral of its apparatuses, presupposes, symbolises and maintains economic incentives for a particular sexual division of labour' (1987: 109; see also Shaver, 1983). Similarly, health and welfare services often rely on the unpaid caring work provided (largely by women) to sick or disabled family members, sometimes at the expense of their own health (Dale and Foster, 1986: 100). For example, the shift out of institutions toward 'community care' places a greater burden on families and specifically women (Bryson, 1987; see also Bryson and Mowbray, 1986). The traditional reluctance of the police to enforce assault laws in cases of domestic violence has left women and children vulnerable to violence in their own households. On a number of counts, the welfare state has reinforced women's financial and emotional dependency on men and consolidated women's investment, sometimes to their disadvantage, in rendering health and welfare services to their families. This pattern of state activity also has examples in the health field, such as restrictions on the advertisement and distribution of contraceptives, and limitations on access to terminations of pregnancy. In some cases, these restrictions have force of law, as when abortion is legally prohibited; but in other cases the restrictions may be a matter of more or less voluntary standards or codes of conduct with which the state requests that the relevant professionals or industry comply, as when advertisers refrain from promoting contraceptives on television.

On the other hand, feminists have advocated—sometimes successfully

—for the state to intercede on women's behalf. Recent affirmative action and equal opportunity legislation are examples of efforts to use the coercive power of the state to require employers to stop discriminatory hiring and promotion practices. Judicial decisions in 1969 and 1972 mandated equal pay. Income support once grudgingly granted only to worthy widows is now available to single parents of both sexes whether or not they were previously married. Several States have reformed rape laws, and police responses to domestic violence are changing in some jurisdictions. None of these changes has come about easily or spontaneously, nor are they immutable. All have been achieved as a result of long-term and concerted pressure on the part of women who objected to injustice and men who supported their cause.

In sum, the feminist verdict on the state appears to be chronically ambivalent. The state acts simultaneously as part of the problem and part of the solution for women. As Sara Dowse put it:

> despite my scepticism about the so-called democratic process of government and my philosophical abhorrence of the modern capitalist state, when I want something done I look to just that arena. My expectations are low, but my directions are clear ... To put it simply, while women are unlikely to achieve equality through the operations of the state, they are even less likely to buy it through the market. (Dowse, 1984: 139 and 143)

To the list of more or less successful claims made by feminists on the state in Australia one must add the funding of an array of feminist-run community based women's services such as rape crisis services, refuges, information hot-lines, and women's health centres.

The pre-existing relationship between medicine and the state is likely to influence the options that are available, or at least that are perceived to be available, for alternative services. For example, it appears that Britain has little to approximate Australia's feminist women's health centres. Because the National Health Service (NHS) delivers free medical care, 'alternative services always run the risk of appearing to promote private medicine, while at the same time being likely to attract an entirely middle class clientele' (Doyal, 1983: 23). Thus, British feminists have been reluctant to advocate separate women's health services (Elston, 1981: 203). Some Well Women Clinics have been set up along feminist lines, but many are simply renamed Family Planning Clinics, do not operate full time, and do not enjoy the same rights (for example, specialist referral) as ordinary GP practices. In Britain, 'feminist health care is being provided, albeit on a very small scale and often in a watered down form' (Foster, 1989: 346). For women to become involved in feminist health care, most must be prepared to volunteer their time because few avenues of funding have been identified within the NHS.

The self-funded Women's Therapy Centre in London is a notable exception whose success Doyal attributes to the large unmet need for psychotherapy, and the fact that psychotherapy is difficult to obtain on the NHS. Conservative attacks on the NHS have drawn feminists into the struggle to defend the Service, while at the same time striving to bring about changes to make the NHS more appropriate to women's needs.

In this Chapter, the discussion of the state concentrates on several different public-sector actors, mainly Commonwealth and State politicians (and their policies), officers of Commonwealth and State health departments, and some local officials. It has relatively little to do with other elements of the state, such as the judiciary, the legislature, the police, or formal law. But even limiting attention to the components of the state that have been directly relevant to women's health centres, there is some diversity. Far from acting with one conspiratorial accord, these various elements have disagreed with one another, frustrated one another's objectives (both intentionally and accidentally), and at times presented women's health workers with a bewilderingly contradictory set of instructions and requirements. Reactions of officials and politicians have ranged from active hostility through more or less benign neglect to vigorous support and encouragement. Nevertheless, a general concept of the 'patriarchal state' and somewhat more specific notion of 'male bureaucracy' have been significant in shaping the way women in the women's health centre movement have defined their ways of operating and how they have conducted relations with potential or actual funding sources. In this Chapter, the focus is on the impact of the state on the women's health centre movement, and how the movement has understood and interacted with the state.

I explore the issues of 'the relationship between women and the state' in the context of women's health centres seeking funding from government sources. The Chapter describes in some detail the origins and aims of the Commonwealth's Community Health Program (CHP), initiated under the Whitlam government, because this Program supplied the initial funding for most of the first dozen centres. During this period, the general atmosphere in the Commonwealth public service was also being shaped by new agencies and procedures designed to give advice on women's issues and to monitor the impact of policies on women. Nevertheless, during the 1970s, the prospects for funding women's health centres were linked with the fate of the Community Health Program, and the Program effectively went into hibernation between 1976 and 1982. By the time it was revived, women's health centres had gained wider sources of funding, and the Commonwealth was no longer a significant actor in sponsoring the foundation or continuation of women's health centres. Consequently, in the latter part of the Chapter, attention turns to the more diverse methods to which centres resorted for State funding because they were dealing with more diverse policies and programs.

Before turning to those specifics, however, we must examine briefly the underlying perspective on the state in the women's movement of the 1970s as it informed the foundation of the first women's health centres. It is important to consider the women's own definitions and understandings of the state, because those understandings have shaped how they approached what has been a difficult and, at times, antagonistic relationship.

THE PATRIARCHAL STATE

During the 1970s, feminists writing about and discussing the state stressed its complicity in protecting the interests of men and in reproducing patriarchy. Attention was drawn to the way the law treated women and children as objects, as the virtual property of males. Some of these concerns were reviewed briefly above. Furthermore, feminists pointed out the obvious yet previously unremarked fact that most of the powerful agents of the state are men: politicians, senior bureaucrats, judges, police and the military. Although a few women have joined those ranks in the last two decades, most state power remains in male hands. At the time Leichhardt opened, feminists approaching the state dealt almost entirely with men. Thus for the women who founded the first wave of women's health centres, the state was a 'male' institution serving men's interests.

The state was understood to be patriarchal in another, less obvious sense, arising from its bureaucratic character. Feminist analysis of bureaucracy points out that such hierarchical power structures simultaneously legitimise and conceal domination, domination of both the junior employee and of the client. Far from being a neutral system that mechanically achieves explicitly stated objectives, bureaucracy depoliticises resistance to existing power relations, silences resistance and functions to reproduce prevailing power relations. In a bureaucracy, employees and clients alike are 'embedded in a system that so automatizes, disindividualizes, and objectifies their activities and relationships that the power relations therein are synonymous with the activities themselves' (Ferguson, 1984: 88). As an arm of the state, the bureaucratic public service was one of the main examples of a form of social organisation hostile to women and to feminism.

In sum, the women's movement regarded the state with a healthy degree of scepticism. As we have seen, for some women's health centres the scepticism was so strong that it led them to eschew any formal relationship with the state, and they declined to accept state funding. Others reluctantly sought funding, but their militancy and unwillingness to compromise with the patriarchal state eventually contributed to a breakdown in relations with their sponsors. A British group summarised the dilemma succinctly, saying, 'Resources we need involve us in relations we don't ' (London Edinburgh Weekend Return Group, 1979: 42). Most compromised, more or less gracefully, took the money (sometimes with deep reservations), and have had reason both to celebrate and regret the decision.

The health centres in this study can be divided into two major periods of initiating activity: 1974 to 1977, which corresponds to the active life of the Community Health Program, and 1983 to 1988, ending with the release of the National Women's Health Policy and Program. These two periods are separated by five years during which no women's health centre was established on newly allocated funding from either Commonwealth or State governments. These changes illustrate that the 'patriarchal state' presents various faces to its ambivalent feminist clients. As Franzway, Court and Connell put it, 'we must reckon with a balance of forces rather than a unitary patriarchy' (1989: 29).

PARTY POLITICS AND THE COMMUNITY HEALTH PROGRAM (CHP)

For both women and the state, there was a happy conjunction in the early 1970s between the growing women's health movement and the Whitlam government's Community Health Program (CHP). The reborn women's movement was advocating vigorously for social change. Soon after the rebirth of feminist activism, Labor was elected to government for the first time in more than twenty years. Whitlam became Prime Minister with no history to defend, and he approached government with a mandate for reform. Although they were both drawing on common streams of influence, the women's health movement and Labor's CHP arose from substantially independent origins: the women's health movement from renascent feminism, and the CHP from a broad social medicine movement now called (or closely related to) the new public health or health development. Leichhardt was certainly not a 'response' to the CHP, nor were the subsequent centres. If women's health centres responded to any government initiative, it was International Women's Year (IWY) and the announcement of funding for *women's* projects. Women in Perth, for example, had already been talking about a women's health centre, but they were inspired by IWY to seek government funding. They thought IWY might fund their centre, although like the other women's health centres, they too were funded by the CHP. IWY had comparatively limited funds, mostly for short-term projects. The Leichhardt women did not know about the Program when they made their decision to establish a community-based women's health centre, and as far as I am aware, they did not tailor their plan to fit the Program's objectives. They did not have to. What they intended to do already conformed in most significant respects with the sorts of initiatives the policy-makers in the CHP were keen to support. The good match between feminist women's health centres and the CHP is shown in a press release from the Prime Minister's office in June 1975. In it, the Prime Minister announced the establishment of the Hunter Region Working Women's Centre, and expressed the hope that centres similar to the one at Newcastle would be 'established throughout Australia'.

The proposal for a Community Health Program was the first priority of the Interim Committee of the National Hospitals and Health Services Commission, a creation of the newly-elected Whitlam government, although steps to improve access to medical services had been taken as early as the 1940s. (The political history of the CHP is described in detail in Milio, 1984.) The Commission's Chairman was Dr Sidney Sax, who had been recruited from the New South Wales Health Department, one of the more innovative States in the health field at that time. Sax and the Commission elaborated the idea for the Program remarkably rapidly, perhaps in part because it had been foreshadowed in general terms in Whitlam's 1972 policy speech (Milio, 1984) and in part because elements of the Program had been anticipated in a book by Sax (1972: chapter 4). In a matter of weeks from the formation of the Hospitals and Health Services Commission, a three-year Community Health Program had been planned, approved by Cabinet and funding appropriated by Parliament, a sequence of developments that could never occur with such speed today. Significantly, no legislation was involved in the establishment of the Program, enabling the Program's architects to take a highly flexible and innovative approach. The only complete statement of its basic concepts and principles appears in a 29-page document published in 1973, A Community Health Program for Australia (National Hospitals and Health Services Commission, 1973). Over 600 projects were funded in the first eighteen months alone. Between 1973 and 1976, over 700 projects were funded, including the first eight women's community health centres and 21 women's refuges whose history has many close links to that of the health centres.

According to Sax, the CHP was conceived as a mechanism of funding primary health care and illness prevention activities of State health authorities and non-government organisations. Initially all of the funds were to be from the Commonwealth, with a gradual weaning process during which the State would assume increasing financial and administrative responsibility. The Commission sought proposals that would emphasise certain principles such as the provision of services by health care teams, an orientation toward illness prevention, community consultation, accessibility, comprehensiveness and efficiency; but the requirements were not rigid. The Commission expected variation in the kinds of projects, and encouraged experimentation in the hope that the Program would throw up creative initiatives, trusting that there would eventually be some consistency. This open approach certainly promoted creativity, but it made the Program vulnerable to critics who wanted quantitative evaluations of its activities, and to treasuries that required strict accounting for public funds.

This flexible, innovative, comparatively relaxed framework was ideal for women's health centres, which were self-consciously different, community-oriented, and organised around a team of staff operating as equals and sharing the work. Leichhardt was one of the first initiatives of the CHP. The Commission welcomed its application, which conformed well with its general objectives: 'high quality, readily accessible, reasonably comprehensive, co-ordinated and efficient health and related welfare services' (National Hospitals and Health Services Commission, 1973: 5). The Health Department's journal published an article proudly describing the Centre about a year after it opened (Commonwealth Department of Health, 1975). John McCauley, head of the Health Department Branch responsible for the CHP overall, was an enthusiastic advocate for the Program, for women's health centres, and especially for the refuges. Colin Bailey, executive director of the Program, was also sympathetic, and Hospitals and Health Services Commission Chairman Sidney Sax welcomed the women's health centres. When the AMA and NSW State politicians attacked Leichhardt, accusing the women of being unqualified, Sax visited the Centre and saw nothing that concerned him. When I interviewed him, he explained mildly, 'They all seemed to be perfectly reasonable, rational people who knew what they were doing, so I came back and told Doug Everingham not to worry about it. All I had to do was satisfy myself that what they were doing was reasonable; it seemed to me it was perfectly reasonable and I was prepared to defend it if I had to'.

McCauley was similarly supportive of the work of the centres, working to facilitate funding, remove barriers and defuse opposition. Several women involved in founding the first centres remembered him and praised his effectiveness; Lyndall Ryan refers to him as 'an unsung hero'. Both McCauley and Sax were on the receiving end of complaints about the projects, and some of the more controversial activities obviously made difficulties for them. For example, they both recalled the uproar that followed Leichhardt's distribution of the booklet 'What Every Woman Should Know' to adolescent girls outside high schools.

The booklet contained basic information on sexuality, contraception, and gynaecological health. Its diagrams were entirely clinical line drawings—none of the supposedly 'pornographic' cartoons from Leichhardt's pamphlets appeared in it, and most of the text was simple descriptive information on the anatomy and physiology of reproduction, with details of various methods of birth control. But the pamphlet took a strong position on every woman's right to know about her body and to decide for herself about sex and pregnancy, asserting

All women, married or single, need to be able to control pregnancy . . .

67

the worry and responsibility of preventing pregnancy must rest with the woman. The man cannot be trusted to be careful enough about contraception, *and his mistakes are your problems* (italics original).

Some parents and politicians who saw copies of the booklet were outraged that teenage girls would be given such information and the encouragement to be responsible for their own decisions regarding their sexual behaviour. The statement that men could not be trusted gave ammunition to those who sought to paint women's health centres as man hating. Such incidents made life difficult for the public servants (mainly men) who supported the centres, and who occasionally found feminist militancy difficult to understand.

The CHP received comparatively little public attention compared to the publicity surrounding the introduction of the national health insurance scheme, Medibank. The CHP was represented in the media as if it were nothing but health centres, more specifically health centres employing salaried doctors. The press presented the Program as a battle between two giants: the Commonwealth government, which was taking a policy initiative, *versus* the medical establishment, which was fighting any incursions into fee-for-service private practice (Milio, 1988: 197–226). But there were many projects in addition to health centres, and even among the centres (women's and mixed sex), only nineteen employed salaried doctors (Milio, 1984). The programs ranged from a single community health nurse stationed at a remote, isolated outpost which lacked any other health services, to a polyclinic at Mt Druitt which employed a range of health practitioners in a densely settled but under-serviced area of Sydney. The variety of projects was made possible by the CHP's exceptionally wide terms of reference, which blurred the traditional distinction between health and welfare. Thus, for example, women's health centres could include in the budget child care workers and assertiveness training classes. Although refuges were not part of the original planning, there was no barrier to their inclusion when Elizabeth Reid, the Prime Minister's special adviser on women's affairs, was looking for an administrative home for the refuge program. The mandate of the CHP constituted an environment where services were developed that would later be defined as representing the social model of health. As we have seen in Chapter 2, this model has become a key concept for women's health centres.

Despite the speed with which it appeared, the Program was designed in consultation with the State health authorities, and funding flowed through these authorities. This coordination with State health authorities was intended to insure that projects were appropriate to local needs. The collaboration with the States was also designed to promote a constituency for community health in the States, so that the concepts behind the Program would have advocates outside the Commonwealth bureaucracy. Some State officials were reluctant participants, happy to take the money but preferring a 'no strings' approach that would allow them to spend the money as they chose; others supported the objectives of the Program, and were willing to be involved. They cooperated even though they could not act entirely independently. In some cases, such as the centre at Collingwood, 'State rights' took priority over the development of a national Community Health Program, and women's health centres were incidental (or perhaps not so incidental) casualties. In a few cases, the Commonwealth bypassed a State that refused to fund a promising project. Indeed, special legislation was passed for the CHP funding arrangements to stipulate that States must be consulted, but absolving the Commonwealth of the duty to channel funds through them.

The Program stressed improving services to areas of high need, which were defined in terms of specific groups (such as women and migrants) as well as geographically (proximity of existing medical facilities). Between a quarter and a third of the projects were initiated by non-government organisations such as those that founded women's health centres; the rest were projects of the States themselves. The Commission anticipated a variety of arrangements for funding: some to specific projects, others through block grants, with the former designed for 'subsequent incorporation in the integrated systems to be supported by block grants' (National Hospitals and Health Services Commission, 1973: 22). It realised that the first year required special funding arrangements because of the speed of the start-up process.

It is difficult to estimate how much the existence of this radical CHP influenced the subsequent history of women's health centres. Although the women did not necessarily experience the establishment process or negotiations with government as simple or straightforward, relations with the state were less constrained than ever before or since, and women's health centres enjoyed explicit policy protection in Canberra. (The advent in 1989 of the National Women's Health Policy [Commonwealth Department of Community Services and Health, 1989] and Women's Health Program may signal a return to such commitments in Canberra. This book concludes its systematic coverage with 1988 and does not, therefore, discuss these recent Commonwealth initiatives in any detail.) Leichhardt's first-year grant had been paid without a requirement that the Centre or the State contribute any funds. But in December 1974 they learned that the funds for Liverpool would not be made available unless the Women's Health Resources Foundation or the NSW Health Commission showed that it could meet 25 percent of the capital costs and 10 percent of the operating costs. They were also informed that in future Leichhardt would be expected to find supplements to Commonwealth funding. Although these arrangements are spelled out in the original document (National Hospitals and Health Services Commission, 1973), the women were clearly unprepared for the change, and apparently the Commission had not told them when the initial grant was made that 100 percent Commonwealth funding would not continue. The NSW Health Department was not forthcoming with money to bridge the gap. Unless the centres charged fees (which they refused to do), they could see no way to meet the requirement, and in a press release, they described the $16 900 required for Liverpool as an 'astronomical sum', which—on their budget—it was.

From the Commonwealth's side, solutions to the problem were politically complex. Some people (particularly members of the conservative coalition parties) believed there was a Constitutional prohibition on the Commonwealth funding health services directly. Normally the Commonwealth gives financial support to the States who are in charge of service delivery. However, the Attorney-General's Department advised the Commission that there was no Constitutional impediment to direct Commonwealth funding, and the 1973 legislation establishing the Commission incorporated the relevant wording from the 1946 amendment to the Constitution which allowed payment for medical and dental services. Still, Department officers were aware of the danger in drawing unfavourable attention to the Program, and they were anxious to avoid provoking controversy. In May 1975, a meeting was held in Canberra between officers of the Commonwealth Department of Health and representatives of all the women's health centres. At the Department's suggestion, a key agenda item was the formation of a national women's health centre body to permit full Commonwealth funding of those centres whose States were unwilling to contribute (Queensland and Victoria, for example). If the funds were paid to a national organisation, the issue of direct funding to the centres could be circumvented. The centres would thus be saved from having to charge clients or look elsewhere to supplement their funding.

For their part, women from several of the centres were sceptical of some of the provisions of the proposed national body. They were also unhappy about the confusion surrounding the negotiations, and the speed with which they were expected to agree to the arrangement. No time was allowed for them to consult with other members of their collectives to reach consensus on such an important matter. In the end, the national women's health centres body was never incorporated and various other methods were found to address some of the centres' funding difficulties. Some of the reluctant States eventually agreed to fund the gap, and in a few instances, the Commonwealth bypassed a State and allocated direct funding. The Commonwealth's willingness to search for solutions to such problems illustrates the way the ideological commitments of the Whitlam government, exemplified in the CHP, meshed with the approach to health care of the women's health centre movement. Each suited the other's purposes remarkably well.

With the CHP as the funding source, other developments in Canberra under the Whitlam government helped create a political environment supportive of the women's health centres. Elizabeth Reid was appointed in 1974 to serve as the Prime Minister's special adviser on women's affairs, and a Women's Affairs Section was established first in the Office of the Prime Minister, later in the Department of Prime Minister and Cabinet, to serve as the 'nucleus of a network of women's policy units to be established in the various functional departments' (Sawer, 1990: 33). The Section became a Branch in 1975, and by 1976, there were twelve women's policy units in functional departments including one in the Department of Health. Stefania Siedlecky, Leichhardt's first doctor, served as a family planning consultant and later also women's health adviser in the Health Department, bringing the perspective of the women's health centres inside the state itself. From this position, she was able to advocate for the centres, although she had no power or resources to deploy on their behalf.

Because the source of their funding was the Commonwealth, the first centres could network nationally to assist one another in seeking funding and conforming to the CHP's minimal requirements. Although circumstances varied from State to State, Canberra had a strong commitment to the Program and was willing to facilitate relations between the States and their centres when difficulties arose. For example, Commonwealth officers tried (unsuccessfully in the end) to resolve the conflict between the Women's Health Centre at Collingwood and the Victorian Hospitals and Charities Commission. The Queensland health department's refusal to participate necessitated direct project funding of the Brisbane Women's House Health Centre. The Commonwealth also suspended some of the usual expectations of the CHP when these would have impeded progress. For example, proposers of projects were normally supposed to consult with local medical professionals. However, because the AMA was hostile to community health centres in general and women's health centres in particular, that loose requirement was waived for some of the centres. It was a heady time for everyone involved. Innovation was suddenly welcome in substantive programs and in the government machinery that dealt with them. In an interview, the CHP's executive director Colin Bailey told me, 'Government administration has never again been so dynamic'.

While some States were obstructive, officers of State health authorities were not always opposed to the centres; some were as enthusiastic about women's community health initiatives as those in charge of the Community Health Program in Canberra. For example, when the Leichhardt women were finalising their original submission, Professor Palmer suggested they talk to an officer of the NSW Health Department, and gave them the name of someone he knew. Lyndall Ryan was surprised to find the man Palmer had suggested most interested in the submission. He read it with care, and then said, 'But you haven't included a car. You'll need a car!' He proceeded to revise the submission appropriately, helped re-check the figures, and explained what to include in the covering letter. In the event, they did not get the car, but this encouragement to revise their submission upward signals what different times those were.

From reading the documents and talking with some of the Commonwealth officers of the period, I gained the impression that they knew it could not go on. The original plan for the CHP was only for three years, stipulating that there could be no funding for new projects after December 1975 (National Hospitals and Health Services Commission, 1973: 21), unless, one assumes, Parliament had by then decided to extend the life of the Program. It also contained expectations that the Commonwealth would gradually become less directly involved and that States would become more responsible. On grounds of sheer practicality, arrangements would have to be changed. As the number of projects increased into the hundreds, it became more and more difficult for the staff in Canberra to maintain close, personal oversight of each individual project, as they had done to begin with. A sense of urgency had been generated by Labor's long period (23 years) out of office, and the belief that Whitlam would have only one term, or at most two, in government. Consequently, some people felt that the priority should be to get buildings built and projects in place that would be difficult to dismantle. But even the pessimists could not have anticipated how short Whitlam's term would be, or how rapidly his government's community heath initiatives would be attenuated.

When Whitlam was removed from office in November 1975 and Malcolm Fraser took over as Prime Minister, the CHP lost its main political sponsors. As a comparatively small initiative established without legislation, it was vulnerable. Although the coalition government was not explicitly hostile to the Program, its 'new federalism' policy and preference for a high level of State responsibility prompted it to revise the funding arrangements. Instead of funding individual projects, in 1976 States were given block grants for community health. The new arrangement permitted States to allocate funds according to their own priorities and political orientations rather than having to conform to the loose guidelines established by the Commonwealth. In the following year, Commonwealth finance for community health was reduced to 75 percent of operating costs and 50 percent of capital costs. The new Medibank health insurance scheme was altered (Gray, 1984), drastically changing the funding possibilities for women's health centres. The 'death of a thousand cuts' continued in 1978–79 when the Commonwealth share of the community health bill was reduced to 50 percent. In 1981, money for the CHP disappeared into general tax sharing grants to the States, thus ending any possibility of Commonwealth direction.

During this same period, hospital costs increased sharply, and the

States were desperate to find funds to cover the increasingly expensive hospitals. In the overall 'health' budget, the allocation to the CHP was trivial: in 1976 the CHP received around $55 million compared to nearly $900 million for hospitals and $1.4 billion for Medibank (Milio, 1984: Figure 2). Without a strong policy commitment to the preservation of community health projects, the Program disappeared in two senses. The money was incorporated into general tax sharing grants, and the projects ceased to be given priority in funding decisions.

HOLDING THE LINE: 1976–1982

In light of these changes, it is little wonder that the atmosphere for women's health centres was chilly after Labor lost government. Only the Centre in Alice Springs opened on new CHP funding after the coalition came to power, and that Centre was more a refuge with some appended health services than a full-fledged women's health centre. All the others started during the 1976–1982 lean years either ran on volunteer staffing, fundraising and donations (for example Gosford, Wagga, and Blue Mountains); or they took over the grants previously allocated to another centre (Adelaide Women's Community Health Centre, and Women's Health Care House in Perth); or they managed to obtain other sources of funding (such as Bankstown, and WICH in Melbourne). As the proportion of Commonwealth financial support shrank and was absorbed into general State coffers, centres had to economise, cut services, and negotiate much more aggressively with State officials. The politics of the particular State had always been relevant to the centres, but during the Whitlam years, the centres all had one major sponsor. Also, it was at least possible—when the State refused—to obtain direct Commonwealth funding. Under Fraser, this all changed, and a new, even more varied and complex environment evolved.

By the time the CHP had disappeared as far as women's health centres were concerned, several other changes had occurred in the political and policy environment. With or without government grants, many health centres depended on the payments they received from bulk-billing Medibank for consultations with medical practitioners. In 1978, the Fraser government limited bulk-billing to pensioners and disadvantaged clients, so centres without grants were no longer able to deliver the same range of free services to all women. Even those centres which still received government funding lost an important source of income that had often been used to 'top up' the grant or cross-subsidise other activities. Thus, even changes in the national health insurance scheme that were not directly aimed at the CHP impinged directly on their activities.

The Fraser government was also less sympathetic to the women's policy units that had been established in Canberra, although Sawer regards the 1976–83 period as a time of 'quiet bureaucratic entrenchment' of women's policy machinery at both Commonwealth and State levels (Sawer, 1990: 33). Sara Dowse had become the head of the Women's Affairs Section (later Branch, later still Office) following Elizabeth Reid's resignation. A Minister Assisting the Prime Minister in Women's Affairs was appointed in June 1976, and a National Women's Advisory Council was established in 1978, chaired by Dame Beryl Beaurepaire. The appointment in 1977 of a new (and hostile) permanent head to the Department of Prime Minister and Cabinet led to the demotion of the Office of Women's Affairs to the new Department of Home Affairs, 'then ranked 26th out of the 27 Ministries' (Sawer, 1990: 46). Dowse resigned in protest, and the Office remained in the bureaucratic wilderness until 1983. In 1981, a cost-cutting 'razor gang' recommended that the women's affairs machinery be eliminated and their functions located in individual departments. Lobbying by Dame Beryl and the Head of the Office, Kath Taperell, managed to save the Office and the Women's Bureau (which had been created during World War II, and had existed continuously since 1963), but it was soon clear that eliminating the women's units in the departments had also eliminated much of their function (Sawer, 1990: 51). It would seem that a low point was reached simultaneously in both the community health area and in the women's policy areas.

The women's refuges were also potential casualties of the devolution of community health funding. However, the refuges were not all feminist in their politics, and shelter for victims of domestic violence was more politically palatable to the conservative government than the activities of overtly radical women's health centres. The femocrats in Canberra were forced to concentrate on what they could do. Organising Commonwealth funding for new refuges was politically feasible; money for new women's health centres was not.

Always resourceful, women's health centres had to become even more adaptable during the lean years. The Bankstown Women's Health Centre in Sydney is an example of how one centre coped with the difficulties of this period. Its committee had lodged seven unsuccessful submissions for funding with the NSW Health Department between 1974 and 1978. (Why they did not apply to the CHP is not clear.) Like others thwarted in their efforts to obtain government support, they eventually opened with volunteer staff, offering clinics one day per week in each of three baby health centres. Several months later, in May 1977, they received $4000, and in June of the following year another grant, of $11 000, from the Commonwealth. In October 1978 they obtained a combined grant of $18 000 from the NSW and Commonwealth governments, and the Bankstown Council provided them with a house rent free, enabling them to open five days a week in their own premises. The Council later moved them to the house in which they are now located (still rent free) in Restwell Street, and sponsored an extension to the house with the assistance of TAFE students in building trades courses. Their accommodation is quite extensive because they can use a Scout hall next door when additional space is needed for such activities as yoga and exercise classes. Although they have never been funded for it, they now offer child care two-and-a-half days per week because they were concerned that mothers of young children should have access to the Centre.

The generosity of the city council did not compensate for minimal grants, and during 1980, staff chose to work one week per month without pay in order to maintain the service. The Centre gets small supplements from diverse sources. For example, a full-time child sexual assault worker is paid by the Department of Family and Community Services, and they have obtained adult education grants to pay health educators. Practitioners offering naturopathy, massage, and some other services are not paid from the Centre's funds but charge clients a fee. Workers paid by the Centre, however, have functioned as a collective, maintaining a commitment to equal rates of pay, avoiding hierarchy, sharing responsibility, and protecting worker autonomy. An internal review conducted in 1988 identified the benefits of collectivity as advantages of their form of organisation. In the absence of adequate funding, the devotion of the workers became the main resource. The personal cost of their commitment is evident in low rates of pay, overwork, lack of personal space for workers (they are so crowded that counselling must sometimes be done in the kitchen), difficulties with such modest needs as taking lunch breaks, and limitations on paid time for professional development.

I have described Bankstown because it shows how dedication and personal sacrifice come to substitute for material resources when government funds are lacking or limited. Bankstown appears to have been sustained by a high level of commitment despite inadequate funding. The strong support of the local council may go some way toward maintaining the sense that the work is valued, even when other tiers of government are less encouraging. Another strength of the Bankstown model is that it resorted to several sources of funding rather than depending entirely on a single sponsor. Although their major source of financial support is the NSW Health Department, by obtaining some funds from other departments they have been able to enlarge their range of services and staff beyond what would be possible under a strict medical model definition of 'health'. Such strategies, however, require the Centre to invest time and energy in seeking out funding sources and preparing submissions which diverts resources from other pressing work.

The lean years were also a time of several dramatic takeovers and closures which are discussed in more detail in Chapter 4. The Brisbane Women's House Health Centre at Roma Street was the first to be closed amid crisis, scandal and recrimination. Funding to the Women's Health and Community Centre in Glendower Street in Perth was 'suspended' at around the same time; Women's Health Care House opened some months later on the money that had previously funded the Glendower Street group. In 1980, the Hindmarsh Women's Community Health Centre in Adelaide was subject to a takeover by the South Australian Health Commission, and after several months of confusion, a newly funded women's health centre was opened in North Adelaide, leaving a new group of women at Hindmarsh to continue that service on a volunteer basis. Soon after funding was withdrawn from Hindmarsh, the South Australian Minister for Health visited the Northern Territory. Both Northern Territory centres (Darwin and Alice Springs) lost their funding in 1980, and until the Aboriginal Congress Alukura opened in Alice Springs in 1987, there was no women's health centre in the Territory. It is impossible to establish with certainty, but it seems unlikely that so many centres would have closed if their original funding arrangements and relations with the state had not been vulnerable to such drastic change.

As far as I can tell, none of the changes in medical insurance, health policy, and health administration were aimed specifically at sabotaging women's health centres, but they certainly had that result. To some extent, the difficulties were unintended consequences of struggles that had little to do with women's health: struggles between political parties, between the government in Canberra and the individual States, and between the medical establishment and comparatively left-wing governments. Nevertheless, the women's health centres were probably pawns in these struggles. And there is no doubt that when Labor lost power in Canberra, the health centres became much more vulnerable to those who had opposed them from the beginning. The Fraser government may not have had a policy of constraining women's health centres, but neither did it have a policy of promoting or protecting them. Consequently, when local opposition gained momentum, centres had no 'top cover'. As we shall see, that meant that any internal conflict could be used as an excuse to close down a centre. It is perhaps the nature of the state that it can often contain and constrain radical social movements not through outright opposition, but through the more subtle procedures of regulation, insecure funding, and surveillance.

THE REVIVAL OF COMMUNITY HEALTH?

When Labor returned to power nationally in 1983, it announced a commitment to revive the Community Health Program which had been virtually suspended for several years. Prime Minister Bob Hawke allocated $20 million in new funds to the CHP, which was supposed to restore, in real terms, the level of funding in 1975–76. However, he did not establish any new machinery for the Commonwealth to monitor expenditure, nor were explicit guidelines worked out. Consequently, a 'de facto' policy emerged, shaped by 'various other economic and political priorities and events. . .[which] essentially supported the immediate needs for hospital cost control in the States through the CHP's emphasis on secondary and tertiary prevention for the aged and disabled' (Milio, 1988: 105–40; quote at 132). Although the Commonwealth once again contributed funding to community health, effectively, the policies of the individual States and their financial status had become the key to community health initiatives.

Consequently, establishing women's health centres has come to reflect conditions in specific States. South Australia was the first to move. The Bannon government appointed Liz Furler as Women's Health Adviser and devised a policy on women's health in 1984 (Sawer, 1990: 149–50). With a new Labor State government and an enthusiastic minister, Dr John Cornwall, three regional women's health centres opened in 1983 and 1984. At least one of these (at Elizabeth) had been approved in 1979, but was stopped when the South Australian Labor government was defeated in an election. Adelaide was host to the 1985 End-of-Decade National Women's Health Conference, sponsored in part with federal funds, at which the women's advisers from the States established a Commonwealth/State Coordinating Committee on Women's Health.

At about the same time that Bannon appointed Furler, a committee was convened in New South Wales to review women's health policy, but it had been a long time coming. New South Wales women's services mounted a vigorous 'defend and extend women's services' campaign, beginning in 1981 in response to the change in the Commonwealth–State funding arrangements. The Women's Health, Information, Resources and Crisis Centres Association (WHIRCCA) was formed to lobby on behalf of women's services, and succeeded in arranging regular three-monthly, co-ordinated consultations with the Health Department. The NSW Women's Health Policy Review Committee (which included a representative from a women's health centre) submitted an interim report in 1984 which recommended funding for new women's health centres. It then undertook a rolling program of statewide consultations with individuals and organisations. A Women's Health Unit was established in 1985, headed by Carla Cranny. The substantial final report, published in September 1985, recommended (among other things) the development of a women's health policy and program, regional women's health advisers, and funding for women's health centres (Women's Health Policy Review Committee, 1985). Ten women's health centres were established in NSW country towns and metropolitan Sydney suburbs between 1984 and 1987.

Victoria acted slightly later. A Women's Health Policy Working Party distributed a short discussion paper entitled 'Why Women's Health?' in November 1985, seeking the views of women throughout the state and inviting them to respond to the discussion paper. They too conducted extensive consultations and submitted an interim report which recommend that Victoria fund a women's health information service and women's health centres. Vigorous lobbying by community health and welfare groups, including a Women's Health Action Group formed especially to spearhead the campaign, should have left the government in no doubt of public support for the initiatives. The final report announced the establishment of the Women's Health Policy and Program Unit in the Health Department, a new women's health centre, and the Healthsharing Women information centre (Victorian Ministerial Women's Health Working Party, 1987). It also recommended eight regional women's health centres. The Women's Health Service in Footscray and Healthsharing Women both opened in 1988, followed in 1989 by centres at Geelong and Bendigo, with two more in the planning stages during 1990.

The Victorian Women's Health Unit, initially under Manager Christine Giles (who had been executive assistant to South Australian Health Minister Cornwall from 1982–85), was not entirely welcome within the Department, and the Unit is much smaller than the staff of five announced by the working party report. Women's health initiatives were accused of being separatist and wasteful because they duplicated services that were supposedly already available. Nevertheless, the Unit was able to mobilise support from other sources. For example, members of the ALP women's caucus in Parliament (which included members such as Joan Kirner, Caroline Hogg, Maureen Lyster, and Kay Setches) were willing to advocate for women's health even when it was not obviously to their political advantage to do so. Kay Setches chaired an ALP women's health sub-committee (consisting of women members from the Party's women's policy committee and the health policy committee), which was instrumental in getting women's health on the agenda and developing support from Health Minister David White. Support also came from some of the regional directors, and from the 'bottom up', including some traditionally conservative Country Party areas, indicating the possibility of broad coalitions forming around women's health issues.

The policy of Western Australia has been more ambiguous. In 1986 a women's health working party recommended a women's health unit be established. Such a unit was created in the Health Department in 1987, headed by Thea Mendelsohn. She built on what had been done by the working party, and conducted four consultations with women around the state. Following these inputs from Western Australian women, the Unit was to develop a policy on women's health centres, but after a draft policy was developed (1988), they were instructed that there would not be a separate policy on women's health. Nevertheless, by the end of the 1980s, Western Australia had four women's health centres: Women's Health Care House in Perth, the Multicultural Women's Health Centre in Fremantle, and small centres in Kalgoorlie and Whitfords (an outer northern suburb of Perth) both opened in 1989.

The history of the Multicultural Women's Health Centre at Fremantle is similar in some respects to that of Bankstown, although it has relied more on the commitment of a single individual, Co-ordinator Ronelle Brossard. Brossard grew up in suburban Perth, and later settled in Fremantle, to which she is devoted for its landscape, way of life, ethnically diverse population and culture. During a few years in Canada, she was involved in a community centre in Vancouver which served more than 60 nationalities, and she was eager to start something similar when she came home to live in Western Australia. In 1984, a small committee developed the initial vision of a very ambitious comprehensive women's resource centre offering such services as general information and advocacy, health services, legal advice, meeting facilities and child care. The group contacted the major community services in the area, all of whom endorsed the concept. However, their attempts to obtain premises and establishment funding were unsuccessful and the group gradually disbanded. Brossard felt that something more modest might still succeed, and she was willing to live on the dole until it could be established.

It is remarkable that a centre starting after the revival of the Community Health Program had as much difficulty as those that sought funding during Fraser's period in Canberra. The Multicultural Women's Health Centre opened in 1985, and ran entirely on donations and volunteer labour for about three years. The Fremantle Migrant Resource Centre supplied an office and equipment, a consulting room and paid the phone bill plus limited travel and secretarial expenses. Brossard obtained a grant of $1000 from the Multicultural and Ethnic Affairs Commission, another grant of $1500 for 'out of pocket expenses' from the WA Health Department, and assistance and moral support from the Fremantle Hospital, Family Planning Association, and Women's Health Care House. Eventually, the Centre succeeded in obtaining a grant from the WA Lotteries Commission to pay rent on a house for the Centre (the first time the Commission had ever granted funds for rent), and they opened in their own premises.

Doctors at the Centre donate part of their Medicare rebate to running the Centre, and the WA Health Department finally made a grant that paid salaries for one full-time worker (Brossard) plus a half-time receptionist. Despite the fact that numerous other applications for funding have been unsuccessful, they still offer all services free, including five multi-lingual women doctors and a woman gynaecologist who are fully booked. The Centre has health promotional material in fifteen languages, health promotion lectures for women's groups, clinics in specific languages with qualified interpreters, night clinics (also fully booked), and mobile clinics which have been successful in attracting Aboriginal women. They also offer a referral service, advice and assistance to other health workers and agencies, counselling, discussion groups, alternative and preventive health services (physiotherapy, reflexology, massage), relaxation, nutrition and exercise groups conducted by a health educator, a meeting space for community groups (at minimal charge), and free child care for women attending the Centre. The house had a swimming pool, and the Centre had planned to offer water exercises and swimming classes to help develop fitness and confidence, and prevent osteoporosis. However, they could not afford to maintain the pool or hire qualified instructors, so the idea had to be abandoned and the pool was filled in.

This Centre is testament to what can be accomplished by the dedication and persistence of a remarkable woman with little or no backing from the State. It furnishes a valued, respected, and well utilised service to a disadvantaged population. On the other hand, it also shows the costs of running a women's service with inadequate funding. At times, the limited resources of the Centre have been exploited by financially well-off institutions. For example, the Centre has been asked to give lectures to medical students on culturally appropriate health care for migrant women. On one occasion, Brossard was paid 'in kind' by a box of rusty vaginal specula that were ready to be discarded. Some of the equipment could never be used, while the rest required hours of scrubbing to make them functional. Because she knows how important better trained doctors are to the health of migrant women, she has tolerated such insults. Like many other committed women's health workers all over the country, at times Brossard has paid a personal price in terms of her own health and well-being while trying to maintain and develop high quality services. The tendency for women's health workers to overwork and burn out has been exacerbated by the very elements that inspire them: the vision of a transformed society, a determination to contribute to positive social change, and the belief in women's rights to knowledge and choice regarding their own health. These contradictions are discussed in Chapter 5.

The ACT began the process of developing a women's health policy in 1989, and it was completed early in 1991. The advent of self-government complicated the process, as did repeated changes to the structure of the ACT's health bureaucracy. The saga of a women's health centre for the ACT must have been as long as anywhere in the country. Women were exploring possibilities and applying (unsuccessfully) for grants to establish a centre as early as 1974. However, generalist community health centres were established in the ACT as part of the 1970s Community Health Program, and the Department of Health felt that these centres would meet women's needs. Subsequently, a women's health centre was opposed because it might perform abortions. In 1990, funding was finally obtained from the National Women's Health Program and the ACT Health Department. A government funded and managed Women's Health Service has been operated (since 1987) by the ACT Health Department.

In April 1990, the new Labor government in Tasmania appointed a senior policy officer to develop a women's health policy and program for that state. The Labor election platform included promises of women's health centres in Burnie, Hobart and Launceston. The Hobart Women's Health Centre has survived since 1987 on small one-time grants, volunteers, and fund raising.

The prospects for women's health centres in Queensland were also transformed by the election (in 1989) of a Labor government after a long period of conservative rule. The new government established a Women's Health Unit, headed by Jude Abbs, the former co-ordinator of the Brisbane Women's Health Centre. The Brisbane Women's Health Centre itself was finally funded by the Queensland Health Department and the National Women's Health Program in 1990, and moved to improved premises with expanded services. These changes were dramatic for a centre which had subsisted for years on low levels of insecure funding, all from sources other than the Queensland Health Department. Late in 1990 the Women's Health Unit was planning a women's health education officer and a women's health information network. The Northern Territory appears to be the only hold-out, with no policy and only one women's health centre, Congress Alukura, which still does not conform to its original proposal. An Aboriginal women's health centre is planned for Darwin.

A COINCIDENCE OF INTERESTS

A superficial analysis would attribute these periods of new activity to the presence of a Labor government in Canberra and the lean years to the government of the conservative coalition. It is certainly clear that the first women's health centres were greatly facilitated by access to funding from Canberra through a program that was friendly to many of the aims of the women's health movement, and in an atmosphere that generally opened government to feminist participation. It is also clear that the gradual dismantling of the Community Health Program between 1976 and 1982 deprived prospective new centres of what had been their major source of establishment funding. However, there are reasons to believe that things would have changed even if Labor had retained government in 1975. Whitlam did not control the Senate, the government was under attack, and the media used women's issues—especially IWY—to attack the supposed triviality and wastefulness of the Labor government. At the same time, the economy had begun to deteriorate, and it was unlikely that the level of expenditure would have been sustained. The Federal government was under pressure to reduce the size of the public sector.

The women involved in the centres were not necessarily politically naive, but most of them were not interested in the workings of government administration or in playing politics. They wanted to be at the 'coal face'—working for and with women. Indeed, this describes most of the women I have talked to who currently work in women's health. Consequently, women at the first dozen centres learned what they needed to know to get the funding to do their work (or at least most of them got some funding to do part of the work), but they relied substantially on one basic formula which revolved around the CHP. When the CHP disappeared, the women had to learn how to deal with State politicians and health bureaucracies much more directly and extensively than they had previously. They no longer had a powerful advocate in the health bureaucracy in Canberra, nor could they benefit from the incentive of Commonwealth funding being offered to the States. The CHP had not been formally eliminated, but as far as women's health centres were concerned, it had ceased to function. During the five-year drought, many groups made submissions for funding, but none were successful.

The return to a Labor government in Canberra, and its announcement of a revival of the CHP, coincides with resumption of funding to women's health centres. However, the coincidence may be just a coincidence, and women's health centres might have begun to recover (probably in a somewhat different form) even if Fraser had remained in government. By 1983, the women's health centre movement was working out ways to deal with their State health authorities, and finding other ways (less reliant on the community health concept) of supporting their work. For example, Commonwealth Employment Program funding was used in several centres (such as the Shoalhaven Women's Health Centre in Nowra and the Lodden-Campaspe Women's Health Service in Bendigo) to hire project officers or women's health workers. Women in South Australia had been seeking funding for a centre at Elizabeth since 1979. The progress was halted by the crisis at Hindmarsh and the split, but they resumed their efforts and had very nearly obtained funding (from the conservative government) in 1982 when yet another general election in South Australia brought about yet another change of State government. With a sympathetic new minister, they made rapid progress and both the Elizabeth and Southern Women's centres were funded in 1983. This illustrates the impact of State policy in the period from 1982: two of the three centres funded in 1983 were in South Australia, as was one of the two funded in 1984. As Dowse puts it, 'the limits to reform are set by the political economy—not by the particular government in office' (Dowse, 1982: 206).

I am reluctant, from a feminist perspective, to credit the patriarchal or fraternal state with the role of the key player in these changes. It is clear that without the feminist movement, and the women with the vision, commitment and energy, the state by itself would not have done the work of women's health centres. But the state made resources available, exerted pressure, constrained activity, and in other ways contributed to and changed the conditions of possibility within which women's health centres were established and developed. Equally, it must be acknowledged that women's health centres have had a reciprocal impact on individual public servants and politicians, and on the procedures and policies for which they are responsible. Although these impacts have yet not been investigated systematically,[2] a summary impression can be gained from Palmer and Short (1989: 219–26).

In the next Chapter, I consider the characteristic 'life cycle' of women's health centres. Activities of the state figure at several points in that life cycle. Relations with the state are also a central concern in Chapter 5, which examines in detail the fundamental contradictions of running a state-funded feminist women's health centre.

4 The natural history of a women's health centre

When a woman recognises how medicine figures in her oppression, it can be a radicalising experience. For those who decide to do something about it, the process can be even more radicalising—and sobering. Although many workers and collective members have come to women's health centres as feminists of long standing, others have discovered the women's movement through their work for women's health. Several women told me that the work was the best job they ever had, full of learning, proud accomplishments and personal development. Nearly all of them have found it challenging and exhausting. For a few, it has been a shattering turning point in their lives, cutting them off perhaps permanently from women who have become enemies. A few have left the women's movement entirely as a consequence of conflicts at a centre.

What processes can produce such varied and dramatic results? When they are happening, they may seem to the participants to be unique personal experiences, like falling in love, and so in some ways they are. However, like falling in love, the processes that occur in a health centre have identifiable qualities that may be better understood in terms of the life cycle, the ebb-and-flow, that characterises many of the centres and affects the women who are connected with them.

A publicly-funded women's health centre undergoes a 'natural history,' a sequence of predictable phases. Probably no one centre passes through all of these phases, exactly as described here. Rather the sequence outlines a typical history. Sheryl Ruzek's study of the American women's health movement identifies three stages in the development of social movements: constructing awareness, determining policy, and institutionalising reform (1978: chapter 8). Her categories are a useful point of departure for describing the natural history of a women's health centre. However, they were devised to describe the development of an entire social movement of which a health centre might be one part, rather than to make sense of what happens within specific organisations.

The four phases described in this chapter overlap to some extent with Ruzek's, and they also follow the general pattern identified by Newman's (1980) study of worker collectives. Sharing the vision, setting up shop, the crisis, and settling in for the long haul are phases I have identified in the life cycle of these health centres. The first phase is quite similar to Ruzek's 'constructing awareness of women's health issues', and the similarity makes sense because the phase refers to the period mostly before the actual establishment of centres during which the general women's health movement had not yet given rise to a critical mass of women's health centres. The subsequent phases, however, differ from Ruzek's, as would be expected from the service-oriented agenda of the centres, in contrast to the more general objectives of an entire social movement. Women's health centres share the broader transformational objectives of the feminist movement, but their commitment to delivering services introduces a distinctive dynamic. After describing the four stages in the development of women's health centres, I illustrate their expression through a detailed description of the rise and fall of the Hindmarsh Women's Health Centre in Adelaide. Finally, I discuss the problem of institutionalisation which underlies many of the difficulties experienced by the centres.

SHARING THE VISION

The formal opening of a centre may be its first manifestation to the community at large, but the opening is typically preceded by a period of months, or even years, of informal discussion in which women develop their ideas about women's health and formulate a commitment to having a centre. This stage is often initiated by a focus on the health of the members of the collective itself, rather than on women in the community more generally. The discussion of the process of placing women's health on the feminist agenda (Chapter 2) is, in effect, a review of the phase of developing a shared vision.

Usually, the first step is to collect and distribute their own information. Women compile lists of sympathetic doctors and gather information about common complaints and medications. For example, the early collectives researched the side effects of oral contraceptives, devised home remedies for vaginal infections, told each other where to get a safe abortion. Such exchanges quickly uncovered the need for more information and better access to it. Roneoed leaflets began to appear, books and articles circulated, some women used a speculum to see their own cervix—and perhaps that of another woman—for the first time in their lives. Women determined to reclaim control over their own bodies must take responsibility for their own health. For them, leaving it in the hands of medical men was no longer an alternative. When women became concerned to make such information and health resources available to other women who had neither the opportunity nor the inclination to involve themselves in feminist gatherings, they hit upon the idea of establishing women's health centres.

The centres that opened during the 1970s all went through this phase. Those opening in the 1980s and 1990s do not, as far as I know, retrace these trail-blazing steps, or at least not to such an extent. The 'first dozen' had cleared that part of the path, and later centres could proceed with at least a partial set of shared understandings. The view that medicine serves the interests of patriarchy was an established principle in the women's movement. Women's right to information and choice, and the need for access to appropriate services have all become standard feminist claims, part of the package of shared values. This does not mean that they are necessarily accepted in society at large or in medical circles. But within the women's movement, the second and subsequent waves of women's health centres did not need to rediscover these values. The centres of the 1980s have typically been preoccupied at the start with more mundane, practical issues of incorporation, finding a building, community consultations and submissions for funding which did not figure so prominently in the development of the earlier centres. I deal with those tasks in the next phase.

SETTING UP SHOP

Once a group becomes committed to the idea of a centre, it must explore what the centre might do and how it should be run. Most women's health centres in Australia rely on state funding. A group of women seeking to start a centre will have explored the sources, terms and conditions of funding, and they will have invested a lot of womanpower in meetings and correspondence with officials from State and perhaps Commonwealth departments, and occasionally in lobbying politicians. Women in country towns often find it more difficult than those in cities to arrange meetings with administrators and politicians, and this may delay or even prevent successful funding. The Wagga Women's Health and Support Centre had the misfortune to open just as the Community Health Program was being dismantled (see Chapter 3), but it was also impeded by its geographic isolation, which resulted in a long period without government funding (1978–1984).

Even when sources of funding are identified, and the chances of funding look bright, a great deal of organisational and developmental work is required. Sometimes small grants are made available to hire a project officer who carries some of the burden of such work and provides secretariat services to the women from the community who are putting forward the idea. The South Australian centre at Elizabeth had the benefit of a project officer working out of the YWCA to spearhead and support the development of its proposal. The centres established in the late 1980s and early 1990s such as Footscray and Bendigo in Victoria have had the benefit of this resource. Nevertheless, women from the community must be prepared to invest many hours of unpaid labour if a centre is to be established. Until the centre hires staff to provide health services, all of the establishment work must be done by volunteers. Such a pattern is not, of course, unique to women's health centres or even to women's services. Most non-government community organisations go through the same process.

The translation of feminist theory into practical women's services has been contested from the 1970s on, so the process of establishing a centre is often fraught with conflict. An example can be gleaned from events surrounding the opening of Leichhardt, which coincided with the opening of Elsie Women's Refuge in Glebe. In some circles, Elsie was seen as politically correct because it was entirely volunteer and had no dealings with the patriarchal state. To the women who held that view, Leichhardt was a sell-out, and the staff at Leichhardt were accused of 'living off the fat of the land'. Some of the Leichhardt women felt caught: the need for the Centre was recognised, but their way of obtaining funding branded them as having sold out. One member of staff resigned before the Centre even opened because she felt they were not radical enough. The Collective discussed the issues raised in such criticism, and were keenly aware of the danger of being swallowed up by the general health system. Their reaction was to strive to be markedly different, always revolutionary. Their subsequent emphasis on non-conventional and alternative therapies may, in part, have been stimulated by the early criticism.

Some apparently simple tasks such as locating appropriate premises can be surprisingly time consuming. The criteria that Leichhardt, Hindmarsh, Liverpool, and many others applied—working class area, with a high proportion of 'disadvantaged' women such as lone mothers and women from non-English-speaking backgrounds, convenient to public transport—remain priorities for most centres. Usually, organisers insist that the facility must be accessible for women using prams or wheel chairs, and of course the building itself must accommodate various uses. Most centres need at least one large room for group work, several smaller rooms for individual counselling and clinical work, space for reception, facilities for sterilising and storing equipment, and office space. If the centre is providing child care, the garden must be securely fenced and accessible from an indoor area for children. Any group work that involves vigorous movement such as exercise classes requires quite a large space. All those facilities must be financed on a strictly limited budget. Leichhardt was lucky to find appropriate accommodation relatively quickly. Their landlord was enthusiastic about the project, and went out of his way to be sure that they (rather than other tenants) got the lease, and at a favourable rent. Some collectives spend months searching for a place to set up a centre, and if a lease runs out or the building is sold, they have to start all over again, as has happened several times at Lismore.

The process of legal incorporation, which is required if the group is to receive government grants, is superficially straightforward, but it is not easy to translate the values of a feminist collective into the language of a formal constitution and articles of incorporation. From the vantage point of the 1980s and 1990s, women proposing to establish centres often have the benefit of hindsight to warn them of the hazards of a carelessly worded constitution which might leave them vulnerable to manipulation or takeover by hostile forces. At the same time, they must fulfil the legal and administrative requirements of the funding body. All this takes time, a new vocabulary, and painstaking care.

The preparation of the submission for funding (or the tender document as it is now in Victoria, for example) has become a daunting task. Increasingly elaborate administrative requirements, terms and conditions hedge the process. The structure of the centre must usually be spelled out in detail, along with job descriptions and the formal qualifications required for each position—not an easy matter for a feminist collective intent on job sharing. Needs surveys are often called for, but without resources a volunteer group will be hard pressed to undertake the appropriate research. It is no longer enough to stake the claim on the basis of women's personal experience: a full statistical description of the catchment area from which clients would be drawn is usually required, as well as details of other services which might meet the needs identified. For example, the Women's Centre of Albury-Wodonga's 1988–89 submission to the NSW Department of Health contained more than 25 pages of text, supplemented by tabular presentation and supporting documents. The submission itself, for a centre that had already been funded for two years, is notable for its heavy emphasis on statistics. This is one example of many where needs identified by women's direct experience must be depersonalised, translated into what amounts to a foreign language, in order to be seen as a legitimate basis for funding.

Quite often, the bureaucratic procedures are so cumbersome, the need for a centre is felt to be so urgent, and the commitment of the women so strong, that they decide not to wait for funding. The centre is established with donations and perhaps with a nominal fee from clients. Such centres inevitably rely on large amounts of voluntary labour from staff. Volunteer centres may limit their services to supplying information and referrals, but only a few find ways of offering clinical services without funding. For example, the Melbourne Women's Health Collective, which was active in Collingwood during the mid-1970s, did primary gynaecological care and counselling for about two years despite the fact that it was never funded. In another example, the Multicultural Women's Health Centre in Fremantle started on a limited basis, giving information and referrals to women from non-English-speaking backgrounds. It operated from a donated office in the Fremantle Migrant Resource Centre. Small grants from the Western Australian Health Department and the State Lotteries Commission enabled the coordinator, Ronelle Brossard, to rent a house and organise clinical services and small groups. The main resource for the Centre has, however, always been the quiet, poised determination of Ronelle Brossard and the commitment she inspires in other women.

Getting a women's health centre established often involves long hours of physical labour, renovating buildings, moving furniture, painting and decorating. The women at Leichhardt designed and built all their own furniture, although this is one activity that did not become a precedent for other centres. The first doctors at Leichhardt sewed the sheets and drapes for medical examinations, and most groups find a member or two to make the curtains and paint the house. Many centres are furnished with old desks, chairs and lounges scavenged from spare rooms and garage sales. Similar sources supply the basics for the kitchen and the child care area. Second-hand medical equipment is often obtained from doctors who are about to retire. The whole process is like setting up a new home, except that these homes have special requirements in addition to the ordinary needs of domestic life.

Because the demands of establishing a centre are so heavy, the process of 'setting up shop' may be divided into two sub-phases: one including the tasks of establishment, and the second beginning with or shortly after the centre actually opens. Writing about a women's refuge in Texas, Ahrens observed that many of the original members 'had worked to establish the shelter, but were not interested in committing time to its daily operation' (1980: 10). Australian women's health centres pass through the same transition which is often marked by turnover in membership of the collective. The transition seems to be a product of several factors. The simple passage of time eventually draws some participants to other places and projects. This is compounded by the fatigue of a prolonged start-up phase. Women weary of the constant demands, and where much volunteer time is required they may not be able to afford to continue working on that basis. Finally, attrition results from the different kinds of commitments required for the daily operation of a centre. Women with the imagination and determination to get a centre started may feel themselves less equipped, or they may be less interested in the ongoing requirements of running a centre. All three factors combine to prompt the departure of many of the 'originals', and the need to recruit new members.

Whether the participants are originals, replacements, or a combination, running a centre introduces its own problems and rewards, some of which are different from those at the establishment stage. The satisfactions of seeing the centre become a reality are dampened by the necessity to ensure that routine tasks are performed regularly and effectively. A drop-in centre can be dirty, but a women's health centre must be spotlessly clean. A voluntary collective can skip keeping minutes and is accountable to no one apart from its own members, but an incorporated body receiving funding must maintain proper records of its activities and expenditures. In consciousness-raising groups, everyone takes turns being facilitator and member, helper and helped. But in a women's health centre, there are distinct roles for workers and clients. Women who are attracted to feminism in part because they reject the ideologies of feminine duty and service find themselves cleaning, writing reports, and providing services.

THE CRISIS

Nearly all the centres I have studied encountered a major crisis—sometimes several. The first usually occurs within the first or second year after the centre's opening, and may be experienced as a personal and political catastrophe by the women involved. Whatever the details, conflict tends to focus around the perception by some women that the centre is failing to perform the functions for which it was originally established. The situation may be complicated by an initial failure to set out clearly articulated goals. For instance, some women in Alice Springs say that an element in their Centre's crisis was that they did not explicitly state its aims and objectives. However, the crisis usually arises out of the sheer magnitude of the original vision and the scope of its objectives (whether stated or not), and from the contradictions between the centre's various aims. The volume of potential work becomes so great that women soon realise that they cannot do everything they would wish, and often they disagree about which work should get priority. But apart from that, centres usually include women who view some work (for example, a lesbian health workshop or an emphasis on unconventional therapies) as dangerous to the group's survival because it is feared such activities will alienate conservative clientele, sponsors or professionals on whom the centre may depend. Other members of the centre may feel that concentrating on delivering a nicer version of conventional medicine to conventional women is contrary to their basic charter. Such disagreements have disruptive potential. The amount of work makes the disagreements harder to resolve, as staff become exhausted and hence feel less patient and resourceful.

The specific issues that typically underlie the conflict and the resulting crisis are discussed in Chapter 5. The manifestations of the crisis are, however, fairly predictable. Interpersonal animosities among members of staff, or between staff and management collectives do not necessarily signal a crisis, although they always accompany one. The issues may originate in philosophical or political disagreements, but because the women are strongly committed, they tend to take disagreements personally. For those who are most heavily involved, the centre is more than just a job—it is their life, so conflict at the centre has powerful personal repercussions. In addition, women who had not previously been involved with the centre and who may know little about current disputes are often recruited at the time of the crisis. Their presence complicates matters, particularly because they are not likely to be informed about the off-stage politics. On the other hand, having been recruited for the battle, they may stay on for longer-term peace-time work, and they may also expose the warring factions to an order of priorities that is different from those on which the combatants have fixated.

The crisis is usually marked by a drastic turnover of membership of the management collective or staff, both of which may include some of the same women. The turnover can occur because of resignations or by coup. In either case, it represents the choice of 'exit' over 'voice'. That is, some women from the group conclude that they are no longer heard, that they cannot influence the direction or priorities of the centre, and that in the circumstances they prefer to leave the group rather than remain in a situation where their values are given little weight. In a description that could equally have applied to many other women's collectives, Annie Zon said of the crisis at the Darwin Women's Centre, 'Consensus was impossible. . .Morale was rock bottom, cohesion evaporated, trust transformed to suspicion, rumours started spreading, paranoia was rife' (1982: 2). Sometimes one or both factions go to the press or the minister responsible for funding, thus drawing other players with other priorities into the crisis.

Serious conflict within a feminist collective makes it vulnerable to outside forces, which indeed may promote conflict in order to weaken group cohesion and gain leverage. In several instances, crisis in a centre was closely associated with intervention by government funding bodies. The South Australian Health Commission's imposition of a manager and subsequent withdrawal of funding from Hindmarsh is one example; the withdrawal of funding from the centres in Darwin and Alice Springs is another; the suspension of funding in Perth is yet another. The state is not the only actor that can take advantage of dissent within a centre, however. Threats of takeovers by anti-feminist groups loomed large in the dynamics of the drama surrounding Hindmarsh, and in the closing of the Alice Springs Women's Centre.

Some women are almost always lost from a centre during a crisis, but new participants may be recruited. Whether the change in personnel is orchestrated by identifiable factions or results from less organised forces, the centre is likely to have a changed profile after a crisis. Occasionally, the conflict is lethal to the organisation, and the centre is abruptly or perhaps more gradually disbanded. Most centres do come through the showdown, but the aftermath can be traumatic. Both to the individuals involved and to the organisation of a women's health centre, these events constitute a major turning point.

SETTLING IN FOR THE LONG HAUL

If the centre survives the crisis or crises, the subsequent months are a time of establishing new directions. In some instances, the re-establishment is a case of a rebirth with renewed vision. Leichhardt underwent several cycles of collective takeover and reorganisation in the early years, each time ushering in women who had a strong commitment to different priorities than those previously motivating the Centre. In other cases, it is a matter of consolidating what is left after a series of costly losses and trying to rebuild credibility and public support that may have been badly damaged by the period of conflict. One woman described the experience as 'inheriting the wreckage'. In the wake of the funding scandal over the Women's Health and Community Centre in Perth, members of the new organisation—Women's Health Care House—were keenly aware that the cause of women's health had been damaged and that the funding had nearly been lost altogether. They also lost some of the founder members who were in the original Women's Centre Action Group and who had participated in forming the Centre's original vision.

Whatever the consequences of the crisis, in order to continue, a centre must find ways of organising the work, setting priorities, allocating resources, and mobilising resources. These are the tasks—and the dilemmas—of institutionalisation, discussed below.

The description of this more or less typical sequence of events may appear to imply that centres go through the sequence and arrive at a kind of balance where they remain. That has certainly happened at some centres, especially in the last decade. However, the sequence can also become a loop when a high level of volatility and confrontation throws a group back into the necessity to reformulate its vision, redevelop the infrastructure of a centre, and perhaps pass through still more crises before it can arrive at structures and processes that enable it to work effectively in the long term. Sometimes, the period after the crisis can signal a drastic change of direction; in others, it may constitute a kind of revitalisation and recovery of commitment to the original directions. In either case, the typical pattern is that unless a centre is completely co-opted or permanently closed, the cycle of establishment, crisis, and re-establishment is repeated at intervals indefinitely as collectives and environments evolve and change.

Leichhardt Women's Community Health Centre, 1974.

A client arrives with
her children at
Leichhardt.

Leichhardt's first doctor, Stefania Siedlecky, with a patient, 1974.

Counsellor Wendy Martin listens to a client, Leichhardt, 1974.

A client consults materials in the library at Leichhardt, 1974.

Clients' children playing at Leichhardt, 1974.

Leichhardt's first administrator, Judy McLean, 1974. Later, McLean worked for Family Planning.

WICH factory visits.

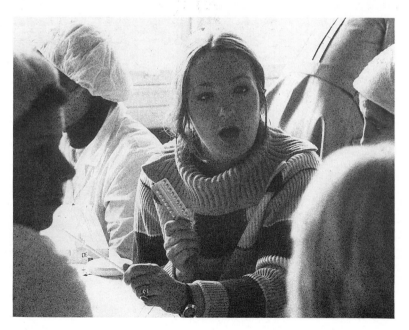

WICH worker on a factory visit explaining the use of oral contraceptives.

Women examining an educational leaflet during a WICH factory visit.

WICH worker shows women anatomical models.

Starting a women's health centre can mean hard physical labour, repairing or renovating old buildings. Robyn Green demolishes the high stable walls behind the Mary Street premises of the Hindmarsh Centre, Adelaide, 1975.

The Adelaide Women's Community Health Centre presented 'Women's Health Matters', a weekly half-hour radio program throughout 1990.

In a two day 'sit-in' in March 1980, several women occupied the Alice Springs Women's Centre to protest against the directions the Centre was taking. *Source: Alice Springs Star*, 28 May 1980.

Public meeting outside the Alice Springs Women's Centre, 25 March 1980. The meeting voted to sack the collective and ask Health Minister Tuxworth to appoint a new committee of management. By courtesy of the *Centralian Advocate* (27 March 1980).

A CASE IN POINT: THE HINDMARSH WOMEN'S HEALTH CENTRE

In order to show how the phases described above are played out, this section reviews in more detail the history of the Women's Community Health Centre at Hindmarsh, which was introduced briefly in Chapter 1. (A short account of these events, stressing somewhat different elements, appears in Auer, 1990.) I have chosen Hindmarsh for several reasons. First, it illustrates clearly the phases and the way they interrelate. Second, the Centre closed in 1984, although the property was not auctioned until 1986, and the final disposition of the remaining funds only occurred in 1989. Consequently, a detailed account of its process is less likely to intrude upon the current lives of the women who were involved or upon a working centre. Third, I have been able to compile a large range of sources bearing on the history of Hindmarsh. In addition to archival information, I have conducted nearly twenty interviews with participants. Finally, although the period of crisis was drastic and in some ways destructive, the longer-term outcomes have included undoubted successes as well as undeniable costs. In some ways, most of the feminists in Adelaide appear to have emerged strengthened and optimistic from what was, at the time, an individual and collective catastrophe.

Optimistic beginnings

The development of the vision at Hindmarsh was similar to the other first dozen centres. They had the inspiration of Leichhardt, but because they began offering services only a year or so after Leichhardt opened, they did not have the benefit of Leichhardt's later experience. The Women's Community Health Centres Group (the Adelaide collective) approached some of the tasks of establishment in a scholarly fashion, researching census data to select the location for the centre, and studying the government guidelines. The original applications went to the South Australian and Commonwealth governments in May 1974, and joint Commonwealth and State funding was formally approved in November of that year. The approval of funding, however, was not the conclusive victory it appeared.

Because Leichhardt had been able to start up so quickly after its funding was approved, the Adelaide women might have expected to receive funding promptly, and if it had been up to the Commonwealth, they would have. However, negotiations with officers of the South Australian Health Department were frustratingly slow, and the group finally decided to open (unfunded) and work out financing later. Initial staff appointments (administrator, counsellor, community educator and researcher) were made in February–April 1975, but apparently ministerial approval was required for the appointment of the doctor, and this was not forthcoming until July, by which time the counsellor and community educator had resigned. When these positions were re-filled, and a nurse hired, they were ready to begin offering services from temporary premises in the Adelaide suburb of Thorngate, in the house of Margaret Taylor, a doctor and one of the collective's founding members. In this small temporary location, they offered limited medical service, with the doctor serving in a volunteer capacity until her formal appointment in July. They had been working under these conditions for about a year before the elegant invitations announced the official opening in March 1976 by the Premier, Don Dunstan, at Mary Street in Hindmarsh.

The Mary Street building was not of an adequate standard for a health centre. The building had originally been an inn (later a doss house), with stables for the horses of guests. Major work (including the replacement of floors, for example, and demolition of the high stable walls) was done by the women, with donated materials, and with help from some husbands and men friends. Between the informal beginnings and the formal launch, women had put hundreds of hours into renovating the building, painting, furnishing and equipping it. Administrative delays also dragged out the process of securing a lease between the SA Hospitals Department and the building's owner for nearly a year.

According to the original submission, the Association, the Management Collective, and the staff were all expected to function collectively, reaching decisions by consensus. Staff were to share duties that involved a wide range of functions: counselling, health education, community liaison, administration, research and child care. Although they planned to share the work, seven distinct full-time positions were identified as comprising the initial staffing. They were concerned to avoid the development of hierarchies, and to encourage the exchange of information and skills. The community of clients was defined in two ways: geographically (centred around Hindmarsh), but also—ambitiously—on the basis of gender, implicitly including all women in Adelaide.

A report describing the first three months of official operation indicated that in that short time, over 2000 people visited the Centre, approximately a quarter of whom were seeking basic health care. Representatives of the Centre went to 25 locations throughout Adelaide where they spoke to over 1000 people. They also held discussions with representatives of more than 70 other community organisations and institutions, made radio broadcasts, and attended conferences. Medical appointments were booked out two weeks in advance.

They ran a vigorous program of groups from Mary Street. The Resource Women's Group met weekly to help prepare women who were interested in working at Hindmarsh or for other community groups. Other groups met to discuss the prospects for improving childbirth services, and to explore the establishment of a rape crisis service. A Greek women's group met, and a tutor from the Department of Further Education ran English as a second language classes. The report on the first three months tersely states that 'The number of individual medical and counselling sessions was reduced in April to allow time for other services' (Report on Activities of the Centre for the months March to May 1976). They had a Greek worker, and they sought the services of interpreters to enlarge the access for migrant women. Evidence began to accumulate that women from non-English-speaking backgrounds were presenting for a complex of physical health difficulties in combination with social, economic and emotional problems. Few of them came simply for a specific gynaecological problem or examination.

The intensity of the work and other factors contributed to high turnover among the staff and the management collective in the next three years of operation, but the Centre maintained a vigorous program of services, groups, and other activities. Energy was invested in contacting ethnic communities to encourage migrant women to come to the Centre. A very practical (as opposed to doctrinaire feminist) approach was taken to this task. For example, they contacted the President of the Greek Orthodox community to inform him of their work and asked his assistance to make the services of the Centre available to the women of that community. During 1978, an 'outreach' of the Centre was established in Christies Beach, south of the city, a precursor of the Southern Women's Health Centre opened in Noarlunga in 1983. Three 'menopause groups' were established in different locations. They were well received and popular support for the work of the Centre was widespread among women of diverse class and ethnic backgrounds. 'The centre attracted women from all over Adelaide. . .By 1978, 22 percent of the total number of clients were migrant women who accounted for 40 percent of medical and counselling work' (Auer, 1990: 210). As a result, English-speaking women were encouraged to try to obtain services elsewhere in order to make more resources available to women who had special need for the support and skills at Hindmarsh.

Increasing pressures

Despite its manifest success, the Centre remained under constant, low-grade bureaucratic and other pressure, which grew rather than diminished over time. For example, they were required to re-apply for funding each year. Although they were given an operating budget and limited control over their finances, they had to go to the State health authorities for every major purchase, as did all health centres. Because they had to justify everything, they kept statistics on everything, constantly conducting what they felt to be trivial research for the bureaucracy instead of getting on with the pressing work for which they had been established. The resulting burden of paperwork was a growing source of frustration to workers and volunteers who were committed to providing needed services. The South Australian health department continued to be a problem for Hindmarsh:

> [It] administered the funding. . .on strict, regulatory notions of accountability which were quite at odds with the health centre's view of what was appropriate. The centre believed that accountability meant spending the money carefully to provide the best possible service to women along the lines drawn in their submission. The department believed that the money should be spent on the items and salaries it traditionally defined as necessary for health services. It was acceptable to spend large amounts of money on medical equipment, medical consulting rooms, and doctors' salaries but not acceptable to spend infinitely smaller amounts on transport for poor, migrant women to get to the centre (Auer, 1990: 212).

The low pay in the health and welfare sector was eroded by inflation. As client demand grew, workloads increased, and some workers sacrificed the original commitment to shared work in an effort to increase the numbers of women served. Staff with special skills (such as foreign language) felt burdened if they were expected to participate equally in all the generalist work in addition to the tasks (such as interpreting) for which they were uniquely qualified. Physical conditions deteriorated as the numbers of staff and clients grew. The old building was structurally unsound and required major reinforcement during a time of heavy service demand. For several months, space was limited and working conditions were dusty and crowded. Rape Crisis, which had occupied the upstairs area, had to move out when the floor became unsafe.

The split

These added pressures made matters worse when, in 1979, the lines of a profound philosophical split began to develop. There had been a major turnover of staff and the management collective during 1978, and the replacements (the third collective) were a mixture of active feminists and more conservative women. All the participants acknowledged that personality clashes created tension and problems, but as I shall observe below and in Chapter 5, these factors exacerbated underlying structural and political conflicts. In the end, personal disagreements may have been as much symptoms of the fundamental contradictions of their situation as causes of their problems. The specific issues that eventually produced the crisis are complex and difficult to disentangle, but they chiefly concerned the relative priorities of the Centre (that is, how their human and other resources ought to be allocated), and the political 'style' of the Centre. The labels 'radical' and 'reformist' hardly do justice to the personal and political philosophies of the women, but I will use the terms for convenience with the understanding that elements of the 'reformist' agenda were quite radical, and similarly that there were moderate issues among the 'radical' group's concerns.

The 'radical' women were found mainly among the Centre's administration and in the later phases of the crisis among the Management Collective and the Association. They were concerned that the original preventive, health education, health promotion and community development objectives had been pushed aside by the pressure to deliver individual orthodox medical services. They placed strong emphasis on advocacy and lobbying, and felt that these activities had been compromised by individual service delivery. They were also concerned that the work, originally shared collectively, had become too specialised and that the Centre no longer operated as a genuine collective. The sessions for staff information sharing were popular when the issue was a clinical matter, but poorly attended when political or theoretical issues, offered by the radicals, were discussed.

The 'reformists' were a combination of more conservative Anglo-feminists and some migrant women on the staff. They feared that the political radicalism of some staff alienated community women, particularly migrants. They felt that they had a somewhat different set of priorities and that they defined the Centre's clientele differently, orienting more toward middle-aged and older women (such as those in the menopause groups), and women from non-English-speaking backgrounds. For example, a Greek worker came to believe that the older, blue-collar women she was seeing would benefit little from an emphasis on sexuality and personal politics. The concerns of her clients were class- and industry-based, such as occupational health and safety, compensation, and access to relevant information in their own languages. She was involved in the early development of interest in what was then called repetition strain injury (the label RSI has now been supplemented by terms such as occupational overuse syndrome, or work-related neck and upper limb disorders).

The radicals vigorously disputed the reformist claim that their politics were detrimental to the Centre or alienating to potential clients. They were also committed to delivering services appropriate and accessible to migrant women, working-class women, and others whose needs were not adequately met by existing services, and they argued against those who represented them as putting politics before people. From their perspective, the dispute concerned the relative emphasis on individual services or allocating more resources to community development work, and the developing tendency toward specialism, which was contrary to the original commitment to skill-sharing and collectivism. Superficially trivial matters took on symbolic significance. Some of the reformists objected to things that had been part of the Centre from the beginning, but had never before been defined as objectionable. For example, one of the doctors took exception to a poster that had been on display long before any of the current staff were hired. Memories are vague but the poster probably concerned lesbianism. Although the radicals had not installed it, they saw no reason to remove the poster since it had been up for years without problems, and although confronting, it was not offensive.

In the face of opposition from some members of staff, pay had never been collectivised, and the issue remained unresolved. Pressure of work increased, and there were rumours of a right-to-life takeover of the Association, which had become inactive, leaving the management of the Centre largely to the staff. The Association was revived, and the lines of conflict more sharply defined. Women from both factions began to recruit others to join.

As early as 1974, Adelaide women had been sensitised to the importance of a sound constitution and the hazard of takeovers. A takeover of the Adelaide Women's Shelter could not be prevented because of the lack of a constitution and specific job contracts for the volunteer workers (Otto and Haley, 1975: 15). In 1979, existing health centres were required to reincorporate under a new South Australian Health Commission act. Consequently, a new constitution for the Hindmarsh Women's Health Centre was drawn up in July 1979 which included provisions that were intended to prevent the feared right-wing coup, but—inadvertently—the new constitution was never formally lodged. The draft constitution required prospective members to 'work toward the basic objectives and principles of feminism and socialism' and to support actively sixteen demands, including 'opposition to the inequitable distribution of wealth and resources', 'the right of women to determine their own sexuality', and 'free, safe abortion on demand'. The draft also required members to oppose the mining and use of uranium. Ironically, one of the most radical clauses was proposed by women who identified with the comparatively reformist faction, against reservations from some of the comparatively radical group. Nevertheless, the entire collective had agreed to the revised constitution. The new document was discussed with the Minister, who expressed no objections at the time.

As tensions increased during 1979, the failure to lodge the draft constitution was discovered. The reformist faction believed the oversight was intentional and sought to have the meeting at which it had been approved declared invalid. Animosities boiled over. Two counsellors were hired as consultants to work with the collective to try to resolve matters, but it was too little, too late. A conservative State government elected in September put further pressure on the Centre to resolve its differences, but things had gone too far.

There were numerous and prolonged collective meetings during the final months of 1979. Sometimes, there were two meetings in a week, and meetings could last as long as five hours. The Association also met frequently during December 1979 and January 1980. At one Association meeting, eight workers resigned from the Association; their resignations were not accepted because, as staff, they were automatically required to be members.

The numerous and lengthy meetings were all the more draining because of the level of emotional intensity that had developed, a characteristic of such organisations in which 'interpersonal tension is probably endemic' (Rothschild-Whitt, 1979a: 521). It is no wonder that the Adelaide women's movement was exhausted by the time it was all over. In the end, even if they could have done so, the women did not have the opportunity to resolve the crisis. That was done for them by the South Australian Health Commission (SAHC), which sent an officer, Dr Barbara Orchard, to administer the Centre. Even the reformists, who felt the radicals were going too far, were alarmed by this development but no one could see any way to prevent Dr Orchard's occupation. Discussions were held about whether the takeover was legal, whether they were obliged to admit Dr Orchard to the premises. The Association sought advice from a QC, and explored the possibility of legal action since they were an independent incorporated body and had not thought of the staff as mere employees of the South Australian bureaucracy. But they had become too divided to find common cause.

Meanwhile, Association members outside the Centre staff were plotting a takeover of their own. It never occurred, but a group of women had planned and organised to remove all the equipment and furniture from the Centre and start up a volunteer centre, independent of State control. Even women outside Adelaide contributed to the action. For example, the Darwin Women's Centre sent $100, probably a substantial proportion of their own money, as a contribution toward a 'fighting fund' for publicity and a possible legal challenge. The guerrilla group had several sub-collectives, one of which found and rented doctor's rooms, signed a lease and paid a bond. Another group developed a press kit to brief the public about what they were doing. The press release was to be published once the raid was complete. Still another group hired trucks with which they planned to move things out of Hindmarsh.

The administrator was sympathetic to the plan, but she was in an awkward position because she had been attacked by the Association for being 'co-opted by male power'. This charge arose from her discussions with a male QC in the effort to obtain a legal injunction to prevent the Health Commission's takeover of the Centre. The cast of the drama changed somewhat. Several women had retired sick and exhausted, while new women had become involved late in the day, some of whom had little knowledge of the existing situation. Their apparent naivete created doubts about their ability to respond appropriately in the circumstances, and about their longer-term commitment. In the end the administrator felt that she would be legally liable and refused to give them the key. At this point, the guerrilla group debated whether to break in to remove the equipment and files. They did not do it, but several members favoured that course of action. One woman from this group told me that in the end, 'there wasn't even a lot of agreement about what the crisis was, let alone what to do about it'.

The aftermath

Early in 1980, the South Australian Health Commission suspended funding. Vigorous lobbying by the Women's Adviser and other publicly known and respected feminists such as Anne Deveson preserved funding for a women's health centre, but not the one at Hindmarsh. The new Adelaide Women's Community Health Centre was established in the middle-class suburb of North Adelaide, and most members of the Hindmarsh staff moved to it. The members of the radical faction were partially dispersed. Some were relocated by the SAHC to other jobs, others left Adelaide permanently.

The battle had clarified convictions on both sides. After funding was withdrawn, those women who moved to the new Adelaide Women's Community Health Centre developed that service in light of the difficulties at Hindmarsh, and the resulting Centre has operated from a position of strength and public legitimacy that has enabled it to help start up three regional centres under the sheltering wing of the 'mother hen'. New positions were funded (a secretary and receptionist, for example), the classification of the new administrator's position was upgraded, and a board of management was formed. Under the capable guidance of Jocelyn Auer, who became the administrator (and later the administrator at Dale Street), Adelaide Women's Community Health Centre developed vital links with the wider community health movement in South Australia, links that continued the community development work that began at Hindmarsh.

The women who ran the now unfunded Centre in Hindmarsh also gained a sharply defined vision of what they wanted a women's health centre to do, and that vision inspired the continuation of what in time became an increasingly non-traditional service provided entirely by volunteers. Only a few women who had been involved in the struggle remained with Hindmarsh. According to Silver Moon, who was one of the new workers, most of those at Mary Street were 'local women who had used the service and wanted it to continue'. They understood that being unpaid workers in an unfunded organisation freed them from the necessity to conform to anyone else's standards or expectations, and they attracted a series of vigorous collectives that ran a successful service for over four years. In 1982, they had four doctors contributing unpaid clinics. They also grew vegetables, grew and packaged herbs, gave space for self-help groups, and managed themselves in a genuinely collective fashion that enabled members to acquire a wide range of skills and self-confidence. Despite the lack of funding, they maintained the service at a high level, and continued to attract a clientele of diverse ethnic and class origins.

Many women worked to try to bridge the gap that had been opened by the crisis. For example, a medical practitioner who had been at Hindmarsh continued to work in both of the resulting centres after the split, earning a living at Adelaide Women's and indirectly using the newly funded centre to subsidise Hindmarsh by working there without pay. For a while, there were monthly social gatherings at one centre or the other. After a time, Adelaide Women's offered Hindmarsh use of a photo-copier. Women from both sides sought to make peace and eventually, the two centres gradually came to co-operate more officially and exchange information, despite lingering awkwardness. Ten years after the split, the wounds sustained during the crisis are mostly healed, although everyone's life was significantly changed. Most can now talk about the events of 1979–80 with insight into their own blunders as well as those of their opponents. A few women remain enemies, but others have healed the breach, and now regard former enemies with respect and in some cases affection.

The events at Hindmarsh are unusually well documented, and in certain respects they are unique. The coincidence of fragmentation within the Centre and election of a hostile government was bad luck. And the plans of the guerrilla group were more imaginative, well-developed, and elaborately subversive than the effort to rescue any other embattled centre. Because of the smaller size and isolated location of Adelaide, the crisis may, in the medium term, have had a more dramatic impact on the local women's movement than similar conflicts in larger eastern cities such as Sydney. However, the process at Hindmarsh has many parallells, not only in other feminist women's health centres, but in any organisation that sets up with the objective of bringing about social change. The key mechanism at work is what sociologists call 'the prob-lem of institutionalisation'.

THE PROBLEM OF INSTITUTIONALISATION

The phrase calls attention to the fact that most of the forces that *give rise* to a social movement are, by their very nature, different from the forces that *sustain* the work of a social movement organisation and enable a new group or practice to become socially valued and estab-lished. The birth of a new religion is usually used to illustrate that basic difference. Although the analogy may not sit comfortably beside a fem-inist women's health collective, there are structural similarities between them (see Roberts, 1984, chapters 7 and 8). Sociologists of religion argue that new religions typically originate as sects or cults that reject estab-lished religions. The new religions stress a high level of commitment from their membership and an ideology of opposition to mainstream society and its values. A women's health collective would be called a 'cult' only by its detractors, but it is similar to a cult in subscribing to beliefs and values that are at odds with those of mainstream society, and in commanding a high level of commitment from members.

Charisma is thought to play a central part in the origins of many new religions, which are often highly democratic and unstructured. Instead of formal positions and rules, the dynamic personal qualities of a special leader unify the members and motivate commitment and personal investment. Charismatic leadership contrasts vividly with other forms of leadership, particularly bureaucratic leadership, which is typically exercised by professional managers who are selected for their positions through a formal organisational appointment, and who exercise clearly defined authority based mainly in their position, rather than in them as individuals. The authority of charismatic leaders, however, is vested in the person rather than the position. Women's collectives, particularly those of the 1970s, aim to avoid having leaders of any kind, charismatic or bureaucratic. Indeed, the collective is intended as a radical alternative to bureaucracy. Feminist collectives usually seek to overturn traditional forms of authority and to vest power in the group or in 'all women'. Nevertheless, the concept of charisma is relevant to women's health collectives in that they have been oriented toward what might be thought of as a charismatic vision. Their work is informed and motivated by the ideal of women freed from patriarchal oppression, healthy and in control of their bodies and their lives, making informed decisions. A defining characteristic of charisma is the capacity to inspire devotion and enthusiasm: the vision of free women in a transformed society has, for women's health workers, exactly that inspiring and motivating quality. More than anything else, their common commitment to that vision carries the work of women's health centres forward, in the face of what we have seen are often large obstacles and major sacrifices.

The comparison with a new religion can also be drawn in terms of the relationship with the surrounding social order. The oppositional ideology of a cult is likely to provoke hostility from the surrounding society. That hostility limits the group's ability to recruit new members, mobilise resources, and pursue its aims. Consequently, if it wishes to endure, it is forced into a series of compromises that moderate its doctrines and practices. Once the original charismatic leader passes from the scene, a cult must identify new sources of leadership and develop other ways of unifying and motivating the membership to do the group's work. In the case of women's health centres, there may be no charismatic leader, but the charismatic vision is likely to be less powerful for later recruits than it was for founders. New members may have a less detailed vision of the social change toward which the centre is committed, and little sense of the history of the work with which they have become involved. According to O'Dea 'religion both needs most and suffers most from institutionalization' (1961: 32), and the same might be said of the women's health movement.

Any new social group that defines itself in terms of opposition to prevailing norms faces that dilemma. Unless it is quickly successful in its intention to transform mainstream society—and major social change is notoriously slow—it has to find a way to survive while it does its transformational work. Such work usually requires resources. Unless members themselves have all the necessary resources, other sources of support must be found. In the beginning, people may be 'willing to make great sacrifices to further the cause. . .[and] willingly subordinate their own needs and desires for the sake of group goals' (Roberts, 1984: 193). There is no doubt that many women's health workers have made and continue to make significant sacrifices. However, the long-term survival of a secular organisation is unlikely to be ensured by purely moral personal commitments. Indeed, very few religious groups apart from some orders of nuns and monks can grow and develop entirely on charity and self-sacrifice, and even in religious orders, self-sacrifice must be instilled, institutionalised, and continually reinforced. Thus, like the new religion, the feminist women's health collective must devise ways of living with, participating in, and recruiting personnel and resources from the very society which it aims to change, while at the same time maintaining its transformational agenda.

The problem of *accountability* is an aspect of institutionalisation that confronts a group changing from a movement to an institution. Social movements seek to mobilise constituencies. The women's health movement has usually had a broad understanding of those women whom it defines as its constituency, either as recipients of services or more active participants in the work of the movement. The question becomes, how does a centre make itself accountable to its constituency? Many women's health centres spend large amounts of time and energy consulting with local women in an effort to find out what they need and want from the centre. Evaluations are intended as a means of checking to see whether performance matches objectives, another form of accountability. When funding bodies are involved, external standards of accountability are also imposed. All of these aspects of accountability generate pressure toward the development of detailed policies and procedures. At the same time, they may reduce the flexibility to innovate and deal with new situations.

Like religions that are undergoing institutionalisation, feminist women's health centres confront 'the dilemma of mixed motivation' (O'Dea, 1961: 33). This refers to the contrast between original members of a charismatically motivated group, and the ordinary members of an ongoing organisation. As we saw in Chapter 1, the first collectives shared a powerful commitment to realising ideals and implementing a set of values. The 'click' phenomenon, when a woman (perhaps quite suddenly) comes to understand her experience in terms of feminist insights, resembles religious conversion: seeing the world with new eyes, understanding the past anew, dedicating one's future to a profoundly altered way of living and working. Of course, not everyone is recruited either to religion or to feminism through sudden conversion, but the process is similar, and has similar consequences. Even among those whose recruitment is gradual, there is a strong dedication to the new vision.

As the group becomes established and organised, and the work becomes more routine, the possibility arises that people will be drawn in whose dedication is not so great, but who take up positions in order to enjoy the power, prestige or income associated with them. Women's health centres, like others in the social-services sector (but unlike established religions), have almost never paid high salaries, nor do they confer much power or prestige in the wider community. Nevertheless, working at a centre for pay introduces a new motivation, and the labour market to which most women have access contains comparatively few jobs at senior levels, so even the meagre salaries and hard work at a health centre may be relatively attractive. Furthermore, the workers typically enjoy a great deal of autonomy, freedom from close supervision, and the opportunity to work for a cause in which they believe. Some welcome the opportunity to work in an all-women environment, free of sexism and sexual harassment. Although centres try to assess job applicants for a basic commitment to women's health, it is inevitable that some workers are there more for the paid job than out of feminist dedication.

Women's health centres are also confronted by a related dilemma of institutionalisation that O'Dea calls the 'substitution of letter for spirit'. The vision or 'message must be translated into terms that have a relevance to the prosaic course of everyday life' (1961: 36). In the case of the health centres, there is no dearth of 'everyday' problems to which the energy of workers can be applied. Unlike many religious experiences, the feminist perspective is inherently and explicitly political. Hence, it is easy to envisage how the ideal of helping women to be autonomous and healthy may be translated into services and activities in a women's health centre. However, as we saw in the case of Hindmarsh, immersion in the prosaic activities of everyday work may overtake the larger agenda, which becomes reduced to routine service provision, 'delimiting the import of the original message' (O'Dea, 1961: 36).

Both new religions and feminist health centres are often highly democratic. Their democracy, however, can make them vulnerable. A study of collectivist organisations in the United States suggested that such groups are prone to crises like the one at Hindmarsh because their commitment to consensus makes any disagreement among members hazardous both to individuals and to the organisation. Rothschild-Whitt observes that 'a majoritarian system can institutionalize and absorb conflicting opinions' (1979a: 521), whereas a collective must resolve all its conflicts. She also suggests that because the members of such groups take up ideas as a matter of personal dedication (rather than as the impersonal rules of the organisation), disagreements are liable to be experienced as personal rejection rather than minor differences of opinion. These dynamics make groups like feminist women's health centres highly volatile, and vulnerable to dramatic conflict. A handbook for people seeking to organise collectives devotes a chapter to 'dealing with feelings' and another to 'special problems of collectives', an indicator of how ubiquitous these concerns must be (Brandow, McDonnell and Vocations for Social Change, 1976/1981).

The analogy between women's health centres and new religions is limited, and in drawing it, the emphasis should be on the similarities in the processes each undergoes. In some respects, the major institutionalised religions, and many of the new religions, are bastions of patriarchy. The congruence between new religions and feminist initiatives concerns how they operate rather than the substance of their message. They do not share a common ideology, but they do share the dilemmas that arise from trying simultaneously to challenge the established order while still working within it.

In light of these dilemmas of institutionalisation, the difficult and often tumultuous life cycle of women's health centres is easier to understand. They have adopted a form of organisation that brings unavoidable difficulties with it, and they face a major problem of being pressed to change their organisations and modes of operating in ways that constantly threaten to undermine their fundamental *raison d'être*. The mechanism at work is common to all social movements that undertake complex, long-term projects promoting social change. The next Chapter explores in more detail the particular issues that have been continuing sources of contention in women's health centres. Although none of these issues is unique to feminist health groups, the combination may well be, and it therefore identifies the distinctive challenge engaged by Australia's women's health centres.

5 Necessary evils

We have seen in Chapter 3 how complex and ambivalent the relation-ships are between Australian women and the state. In the case of women's health centres, the ambivalence is focused on the question of money. Both Sara Dowse (1984) and Marian Sawer (1990) say that since the mid-1970s, Australian feminists have, with little reluctance, taken a 'utilitarian' approach of seeking state funding for a range of women's services. Dowse claims that 'the debate that scarcely happened is closed' (1984:146). While no one could dispute that many groups of feminists have turned to the state for resources, I do not agree that the debate 'scarcely happened'. It certainly did not happen in scholarly writing, and perhaps it did not happen much among feminist employees of the state. Women in the health centre movement, however, have debated vigor-ously about taking money from the 'patriarchal state'. The debate about money is symptomatic of the fundamental problem that is the 'contra-diction' at the heart of this book. The contradiction lies between the basic commitments to feminism on the one hand, and the necessity on the other for women's health centres to co-operate with the medical establishment and the bureaucratic state.

This contradiction arises out of the women's movement's premise that patriarchal society and the oppression of women are partly responsible for women's ill-health. The premise identifies the institution of medicine as an element in women's oppression, contributing both directly and indirectly to women's mental and physical suffering. Consequently, staff in the centres are committed to working in ways that will enable women to improve their health and take greater responsibility for themselves. If the function (however unintentional) of traditional medicine has been to foster feminine dependency and to encourage women to adapt to an oppressive gender regime, feminist women's health centres have a radi-cally different agenda: to expose the social forces that shape women's experience of health and illness, and to empower them to take command of their bodies and their lives. Feminist theory affirms the social model of health and actively rejects the limitations of the traditional medical model. However, women's health centres do not operate in a feminist cocoon. They do their work in a social environment where much of the power and many of the resources to which they need access are controlled by the medical profession or by the state, neither of which has, traditionally, been sympathetic to their project. Insofar as centres are obliged to co-operate with medical institutions and medical bureaucracies (state health authorities), they face a contradiction.

The contradiction arises every time a centre must prepare an official report, undergo a review, or apply for funding. In some political climates, the activities of women's health centres might be tolerated or even, with qualification, welcomed. That was largely so during the brief period of the Whitlam government. But support for the genuinely radical work of women's health centres has been the exception rather than the rule, and even apparent acceptance can come dangerously close to what has been called 'repressive tolerance'. More typically, the centres have felt themselves to be grudgingly tolerated, and to be under continuous (and increasing) pressure to alter their work to fit other definitions of women's health needs. Much of what centres do is, according to the medical and economic criteria that inform state health bureaucracies, peripheral at best or irrelevant and wasteful at worst. Consequently, staff in the centres face a chronic dilemma: how much must they 'repackage' their work in order to make it acceptable to powerful sponsors or funding sources? Must they sanitise or conceal their feminism in order to get along? Is it possible to present one face to state officials and another to women clients? Can they conform to the organisational and procedural formats of the bureaucracy without compromising their fundamental purposes? Or do such concessions actually do more harm than good to their overall objectives? Is state funding a necessary evil, or are its costs too high and should women devise other ways of financing the work?

While the basic contradictions are between a health centre and a patriarchal institution (medicine or the state), the contradictions are most often played out within the centre. Disagreements arising out of these contradictions figured in the conflicts described in Chapter 4. Such disagreements and their resulting crises are not unique to women's health centres; they have also occurred with disheartening regularity in other women's services that were developed during the 1970s and 1980s, services such as rape crisis, refuges and women's advice bureaux. Nor is the contradiction limited to feminist initiatives. Similar difficulties arise in many community-based groups (such as community mental health centres) that place significant social change on their agenda (see Schwartzman, 1980; Freudenberger, 1974; Molica and Winn, 1974, for examples). Employees of the state or of other large organisations who bring a critical and change-oriented perspective to their work also face these problems. Granting that the problems are not unique to women's health centres, the combination of explicitly *feminist* initiatives, and initiatives in the *health* field gives the problems a particular character, infused with a special poignance and urgency. It is the task of this Chapter to explore the factors that form that particular character and to see how it is expressed.

In women's health centres, the contradiction is particularly vivid when the centre writes funding submissions and annual reports, but it does not stop there. It reappears in many other specific and daily conflicts. As we have seen, there have been occasions when the conflicts have been so severe that the centre has been unable to continue functioning. In most cases, the inconsistencies generate tensions that lead to dramatic internal changes in personnel and priorities. Even after such changes, however, the pressure of discrepancies persists, day in and day out. Generally the conflicts are not managed by resolving for one side or the other once and for all. They are mostly dilemmas that must be kept in a delicate balance over the long term because they cannot be banished. The successful centres learn to live with contradiction.

This Chapter explores several typical dilemmas faced on a regular basis by feminist women's health centres. These include questions of internal structure, how to manage power, the place of professionalism, balancing priorities (an ever more urgent concern in difficult economic times), the problem of burnout, developing a constituency, using volunteers, and the ever-present hazard of co-optation.

THE PROBLEMS OF BUREAUCRACY

Even before they have premises and begin to organise services, women starting a feminist health centre confront questions about how to organise themselves to do their work. Politically unselfconscious groups have several models from which they can choose on comparatively practical grounds; but left-wing feminists of the mid-1970s (and beyond) have been keenly sensitive to the politics of organisational structure and function. In order to understand their organisational dilemmas, it is necessary to review briefly some contemporary thinking about modern organisations.

During the twentieth century, bureaucracy has become the characteristic form of state and private-sector organisation, a form which has become so familiar that, to the modern ear, the terms 'organisation' and 'bureaucracy' seem almost to be synonymous. Critiques of bureaucracy have identified two major deficiencies of bureaucratic organisations: the tendency toward displacement of original goals, and the personal costs of working in or with highly bureaucratised organisations. Cutting across these critiques, several commentators have taken up questions about the ways contemporary organisations are particularly problematic for women. Each of these critiques is relevant to the way Australian women's health centres have attempted to deal with the problems of organisation, so they will be discussed briefly before showing how the health centres have defined and sought to solve the problems.

Observers of organisations have commented that bureaucracies are prone to lose track of their formal goals, and to become preoccupied with procedures at the expense of objectives. Means come to be ends of their own, rather than ways of accomplishing the official purposes of the organisation. Over time, the *raison d'être* of an organisation may come to be simply performing functions (regardless of consequences), preserving the organisation itself, or protecting the jobs of its members (or some sub-set of its members, such as management) rather than pursuing the ends for which it was originally created. Situating his own study in the traditions of Marx, Mosca, Michels and Mannheim, Philip Selznick observes that 'ideals go quickly by the board when the compelling realities of organizational life are permitted to run their natural course' (Selznick, 1949/1966: ix). Such displacement of goals is not an aberration of a malfunctioning organisation. It is a predictable consequence of bureaucratic procedure.

Another theme of commentaries on organisations concerns the costs, to both employees and clients, of interaction which is funnelled through bureaucratic channels, so that people are compelled to conform to formal procedures rather than shaping interaction to meet their personal needs. Empirically, this problem is often linked to the displacement of objectives. But the dehumanisation of life within the 'company' can occur even when a bureaucracy is fulfilling its formal aims, because the ideal type of bureaucracy stresses instrumentality and impersonality, the 'value neutrality' of procedures and standards, and the interchangeability of position holders rather than the uniqueness of each person. Such instrumental formality is supposed to protect organisations from abuses such as nepotism and favouritism. But participants pay the costs of these objectives, costs such as difficulties getting needs met, being treated as objects of procedures rather than as intelligent people, and on occasion, personal humiliation.

Feminist critiques of bureaucracy

Feminists have developed a distinctive analysis of complex organisations, stressing the (often covert) gendered character of bureaucratic ideology and structure, and the special problems experienced by women (Kanter, 1975 and 1977; Ferguson, 1984). For example, Kanter suggests that management is a 'male category', not only in the sense that historically most managers have been men, but also because the 'culture and behavior of management' has been shaped by the traditional sex ratio (Kanter, 1975: 34–42). She goes on to observe that 'sexual status [has been]...reflected in managerial ideologies and models of organization, thus helping to solidify the already apparent sex stratification of organizations' (p.43) in which men manage and women provide support services. For example, because the concept of reason has excluded the feminine (Lloyd, 1984), the commitment to rational management has operated to exclude women from senior positions, and to exclude emotionality and 'women's concerns' (such as family responsibilities and personal feelings) from a legitimate part in organisational decision making.

Kanter has also studied how women working in organisations are often not accorded the traditional bureaucratic 'safeguards' of rationality and impersonality. This is most notable among those employed as secretaries, who may be required to perform tasks that are more nearly domestic than office work, and who are expected to display personal loyalty to their bosses, rather than a professional commitment to the organisation or their own careers (1977). Far from conforming to the model of rational impersonality, the secretary–boss relationship is one of *fealty*. The subjects of Kanter's research often used the analogy of marriage to describe the relationship between secretaries and their male employers.

The masculinity of bureaucracy is also significant because large organisations produce gendered and gendering cultural practices and identities (Acker, 1990:140). Organisational hierarchies work both literally and symbolically to reproduce relations of masculine dominance and feminine subordination. For example, access to careers and promotions typically requires the employee to be 'domestically irresponsible' (Moir, 1984), an option which is not explicitly masculine, but one to which men typically have more ready access. Bureaucracies also encode these relations of dominance and subordination in a set of supposedly gender neutral procedures that conceal their gendered character. The implementation of bureaucratic procedures, in itself, disadvantages less powerful groups and individuals even when no officer expresses prejudice or intentional discrimination. These processes are the basis of the concept of 'structural discrimination', and have led Game and Pringle (1983) to refer to bureaucracy as 'patriarchy without fathers'.

Ferguson sees the disadvantaged situation of women in complex institutions as exemplary of the way organisations relate to all vulnerable groups. She calls bureaucracy 'the scientific organization of inequality', and argues that bureaucracy 'serves as a filter for other forms of domination, projecting them into an institutional arena that both rationalizes them and maintains them' (1984: 7–8). As we shall see, the feminist groups that initiated Australia's first women's health centres were keenly aware of these issues when they sought to structure the centres so as to avoid the problems of bureaucracy. 'The radical feminist hostility to bureaucracy is based on a well-founded...opposition to the consequences of hierarchical domination for both individuals and the collective' (Ferguson, 1984: 73).

Activist feminists are not united in their view, but many, particularly those to the left of the political spectrum, have tended to see 'bureaucracies as patriarchal systems of domination and hierarchy that are contradictory to their egalitarian and participatory goals' (Rodriguez, 1988: 215). The forms of feminist organisations reflect this view.

ALTERNATIVES TO BUREAUCRACY: FEMINIST COLLECTIVES

As a consequence of these problems, resistance and alternatives to bureaucracy have emerged within and alongside dominant bureaucratic discourses and organisations. Although the counter-cultural organisations of the 1970s are most familiar, older anarchist and collectivist groups have also sought to go beyond bureaucracy (Ferguson, 1984: 26). Rothschild and Russell identify three major alternatives to bureaucracy which seek to involve workers in decision making or ownership of the firms within which they work: worker co-operatives and collectives, worker-participation programs, and employee-stock ownership plans (1986: 308–9). The organisations discussed in this research are most similar to the worker collectives described by Rothschild and Russell, and conform to their description of such organisations as arising

> from a fundamental ideological commitment to autonomy and self-determination coupled with a sense of opposition to hierarchical authority systems and the inequality that accompanies them. Many participants... were also motivated by a desire to earn a livelihood in a manner consistent with these expressed values (Rothschild and Russell, 1986: 310).

The women who founded the first women's health centres were aware of most of the lines of critique of bureaucracy. Indeed the experiences of feminist activists generated some of the more vivid examples that underpin the critiques. Consequently when they were planning the centres, women often set out to invert many of the classic elements of organisational structure. The founders of Leichhardt, Liverpool, Hindmarsh, Collingwood, Perth (Glendower Street) and Brisbane (Roma Street) women's health centres wanted to create a different sort of organisation: one where the formal structure would be flat rather than hierarchical, where work and rewards would be shared out among all participants, and where power and decision making would be vested in the collective rather than in designated individuals. In these ways they hoped to subvert the tendencies of bureaucracy to displace goals, to concentrate power in a few hands, to marginalise junior members, and to discredit clients. Collective organisation was conceived specifically as a method of resisting bureaucracy and hierarchy and their patriarchal consequences. Some groups also felt that because women's illnesses had social origins, that 'collective problems...should be dealt with in a collective manner by full participation of every person' (Barfoot, 1973: 92).

The exact meaning of 'collectivity' has varied from centre to centre and from time to time, but it has signalled at least a commitment to decision making by consensus and to sharing power and authority among all the members of a group. If these objectives are to be fulfilled, the whole group must be willing to invest time in regular meetings which are likely to be long when complex questions arise. Some centres signified the equality among members by paying all staff the same salaries; a few (such as Bankstown) still do, although doctors are typically the first to be exempted from this rule (as they have been at Bankstown).

Problems with collectivity

The commitment to collectivity has been tested from the very beginning. Funding bodies required groups to be legally incorporated, and to designate officers who would be responsible for receiving the funds and accounting for their expenditure. When politicians and bureaucrats visited or corresponded, they wanted to know who was 'in charge', and they were irritated and confused to be told that anyone and everyone was equally responsible and could answer their questions. State health bureaucracies often insisted that jobs be given familiar labels, and that the occupants of different positions be qualified and paid accordingly. To an extent, it was possible to get around these requirements by agreeing to use such labels for bureaucratic purposes only rather than taking them as accurate descriptions of different positions. As long as the centre maintained control over its budget, it could equalise pay, no matter what the budget stipulated formally. But these informal evasions of formal structure could only be maintained while the entire group remained committed. If anyone was paid on a different basis or was less involved in the collective processes, that differential undermined the sense of in-group cohesion.

Furthermore, collectivity brought problems of its own quite apart from maintaining the political commitment to its implementation. Decisions through consensus usually take longer than those allocated through a chain of command. Thus if most decisions were to be group products, decision making itself became a significant part of the work. This was acceptable in the early stages of the organisation. It made sense to define the nature of the work as a group project. During a crisis, numerous long collective meetings were probably unavoidable. But as a routine method of operation, consensus decision making could become burdensome, taking valuable time away from what were felt to be more important tasks. Galper and Washburne tell a cynical joke about collectives having to reach a group decision before anyone can go to the toilet. They also describe the disillusion with the idea of collectives that is often left in the wake of working in a feminist service (1976), a pattern I have observed among a number of former women's health workers.

Soon the women's movement itself began to document the difficulties with collectives. Freeman (1972) discussed 'the tyranny of structurelessness', including its tendency to allocate power to unelected, unofficial leaders whose actions are more difficult to challenge or limit because their positions are not formally defined. In women's health centres, informal structures emerged even in the most determinedly non-hierarchical, power-sharing, holistic, person-oriented organisations. Indeed, the traditional features of formal organisations—hierarchy, unequal distribution of power, division of labour and specialised positions—all crept into collectivist organisations through the 'back door' of informal structure. In some cases, this process involved what Selznick, in a very different context, called 'the organizational weapon', that is, the illegitimate use of 'a source of power that is latent in every group' (1960: 2). Women with insight, skills and ambitions took advantage of the lack of formal structure to promote their own personal advantage. Usually, however, the ascendancy of individual women to positions of informal power happened more by accident than design. And it was not so much a betrayal of the ideology of feminist collectivism, but rather an instance of institutionalisation in a context where the associated problems take on special significance. The explicit political commitment to avoid bureaucratic structures, and labelling bureaucracy as 'patriarchal' made it all the more difficult to recognise and respond to the unwarranted appearance of informal hierarchical structures in their midst. Because these problems were not anticipated by the first centres, they tended to be defined as conflicts over personalities or political correctness. No mechanisms had been devised for dealing with them, a situation that complicated and delayed their recognition and solution.

THE PROBLEM OF POWER

In the early 1970s, feminist analysis of power focused on the abuses of power that women had experienced from men and male-dominated institutions. Some 'liberal' feminists felt that the problem of power was simply that few women had any, and hence they sought to redistribute power in traditional institutions. More 'radical' discussion and writing, however, centred on an effort to critique power itself, recognising the corrupting propensity of power, typically equating power with domination and linking it with hegemonic masculinity. 'We have considered it evil, corrupting, and male' (Browne, 1976: 34). In these terms, the 'problem of power' is not simply that women are denied access to powerful positions, but that power itself is somehow perverted and contaminating. Some early collectives responded by devising leaderless and structureless organisations.

Through experience and an increasingly sophisticated theoretical analysis, feminists began to recognise that power cannot be banished nor attacked as a discrete entity. Women's health collectives discovered that women with personal, verbal and political skills tended to become informal leaders, and that cliques consolidated informal power despite efforts to avoid hierarchy. Furthermore, feminists recognised that powerlessness is not a virtue, particularly for people who are working for social change and who are interested in advocating on behalf of traditionally marginal groups. Indeed, many of the problems of the women attending women's health centres can be thought of as 'diseases of powerlessness' (Dwyer, 1989: 63). 'Powerlessness corrupts' became a counter slogan, and 'empowerment' became an explicit objective.

Nancy Hartsock suggested that the initial feminist rejection of power was a rational response to formulations of power that were contaminated by particular forms of masculinity. She argues that, due to differing social experience, men and women develop distinct conceptions of power. Traditional theories of power (almost all devised by men) have linked power to virility, dominance and violence ('power over', particularly power over women). Some women (and a few men) have theorised power in terms of agency, capacity and empowerment ('power to') and have sought to re-conceptualise the term (Hartsock, 1983: chapter 9). Other writers with more applied than theoretical orientations designed exercises and courses to facilitate women's empowerment. Empowerment has become a theme for many women's health centres, and the empowerment of both clients and workers has been given high priority.

The discourse of empowerment sometimes appears to be an effort to sanitise unsavoury male power and package it in an acceptable, feminised form that would not offend women's delicate sensibilities or constitute a threat to masculine prerogatives. However, it also contains significant insights, including the recognition that power is not a monolithic, threat-of-force, monopolised by people (men) with formal status or physical strength. It shifts understandings of power away from a focus on force and aggression toward power as energy and creativity (Theberge, 1987). The concept of 'empowerment' allows for an acknowledgement that women's powerlessness is more than a matter of social structure and exclusion from top positions. Women's powerlessness is compounded by women having learned to defer and be patient rather than making claims and expecting justice. That is, women lacked specific skills relevant to the exercise of power, and in order to attain and function in key positions, they would have to acquire those skills, as well as access to the positions. In the case of their health, knowledge is an element of power, and women's lack of access to knowledge about their bodies has contributed to their powerlessness.

Consequently, the basic work of health education and teaching women about their own bodies is valued not only for its health-promoting aspects, but also for its capacity to empower women. Similarly, skills-oriented work such as self-esteem workshops, assertiveness training courses, and job re-entry support may affect health indirectly, but their most explicit value may be to enhance women's sense of autonomy and command over their own lives. These arguments can be difficult for health bureaucrats to understand when such work has few if any measurable, immediate health benefits. Why, they wonder, should they fund 'health educators' to run workshops on these themes when there are inadequate resources to fund 'real' health services like mammography, occupational health campaigns, or immunisation clinics?

Because control over information has been an important mechanism through which professionals maintain power over lay people, one of the methods for power sharing in women's health centres is to give clients access to the information held in their medical records, and the opportunity to enter information and respond to comments made by centre staff. Many women's health centres hand the client's file to her on arrival, giving her an opportunity to read it and add comments before consulting with a health worker. . .a far cry from the situation in conventional medical facilities where records are treated as if they are the property of the staff, and are typically written in language (and handwriting) that clients could not decode even if they were given access. After the 1980 'takeover' of the Hindmarsh Women's Health Centre by the South Australian Health Commission, a major struggle ensued over the disposition of the clients' files which the Health Commission sought to remove. In the event, the files were retained at Hindmarsh for its four years as a volunteer collective, unless the woman herself claimed it or asked that it be sent elsewhere.

Of course not all women go to a women's health centre for personal change, empowerment or information. Some just want to be 'fixed up' so that they can get on with their everyday lives. These women are not interested in health education workshops, the politics of the centre, or a novel and democratised relationship with a women's health worker. They want their immediate health problem solved, their distress relieved. They may have come to see a doctor to unburden themselves of a catalogue of miseries because they feel a doctor is the only legitimate listener, and that a doctor's listening legitimises their distress. They are less interested in the contents of their medical record than in a quick and effective solution to an immediate problem. Such women may even be disturbed to be asked to take responsibility for their own care at a time when they feel dependent and in need of direction. When the

Collingwood Women's Health Centre closed down, an article was published in Melbourne's major metropolitan newspaper *The Age* asking women who had been there to collect their records. Almost none of the more than 3000 women who had used the Centre responded to the invitation. Bon Hull retained the files for two years, and then destroyed them to preserve confidentiality.

Another means of power sharing has been to involve women from the community in the management of the organisation. This approach is valued because it simultaneously draws on the views of local women as a basis for planning the centre's program and builds legitimacy for the centre among the local community, while it also engenders skills and experience in these women. Most of the associations and boards of management of women's health centres are open to women from the community served by the centre, but it usually requires special efforts to attract women with diverse class, ethnic and educational backgrounds to participate. Women with no previous experience may feel that they have nothing to offer, seeing themselves as 'just housewives' who have 'never done anything,' worlds apart from the competent, experienced professionals they see in the staff. Language and ethnicity are also barriers to broad participation. Mothers of young children are likely to have difficulties with child care. Many women lack transport or the time to spend at meetings. A centre seeking broad-based community representation on its management body must make an extensive and serious commitment to mobilising and maintaining the base. Resources (which are always scarce) must be invested in recruiting members and developing the skills of a management group. The Centre in Footscray (opened in 1988 in the western suburbs of Melbourne) is an example of a group which took this element of its operation very seriously, devoting twelve pages of its tender document to the composition, formation and development of a committee of management.

The Women's Health Centre at Dale Street, Port Adelaide is committed to running periodic training sessions for women on their management committee. The Centre supplies child care for policy and planning workshops, reimburses members of the committee for their expenses, and encourages members to treat this reimbursement as a 'right'. The message from their experience and that of Footscray is that by itself, the political commitment to this form of power sharing is unlikely to bring it about. Some of the centre's resources have to be invested in facilitating the participation of women from a variety of backgrounds to enable them to make inputs into the centre's policy and direction.

Ideally, this particular version of power sharing is highly democratic and keeps the organisation open to the views and values of the women of the local community. Ultimately and perhaps ironically, however, it leaves a centre open to a new group with a different philosophy taking control. Depending on which side one is on, this can be interpreted as a return to the original mission or a takeover by hostile forces. In practically every dramatic crisis, there have been efforts (some of which have been successful) to 'stack' meetings with new members whose vote can be counted on. In the early days at Liverpool, a faction successfully ousted women who were seen as not adhering to feminist principles. In Alice Springs, a takeover was promoted by right-wing groups that attacked the radicalism of the Centre. No particular political complexion has a monopoly on such strategies, nor is any group immune from them. The point is that power sharing can open the door to the ultimate overthrow of a co-operative group. Nevertheless, women's health centres have maintained a strong commitment to working in ways that transform power relations rather than capturing and monopolising power (London Edinburgh Weekend Return Group, 1979:145). And even if individual groups go under, the movement itself is strengthened by its refusal to compromise on these fundamental values.

The issue of power is as explosive as any with which the centres have to deal. Mansbridge believes that 'the vision of complete equality has helped destroy a large proportion of the collectives that espoused it' because of a tendency to attribute 'the inequalities that persisted to their members' misshapen personalities' (1979: 194). Activists in the 1990s are in a position to be informed by different ideas of power than those prevailing in the 1970s. These may, in turn, give rise to new ideas of power sharing. Instead of seeing power as a commodity for which individuals and groups must struggle, and the possession of power as a zero-sum game, power can, for example, be understood as 'a generative process: you don't possess it, it is generated in the actual process of being involved in the grid of social interaction' (Fatin, 1990:14). It remains to be seen how the organisation and work of women's health centres might shift in response to shifts in such central concepts. There is no doubt that they have contributed to those conceptual shifts.

PROFESSIONALISM: THE PROBLEM OF CREDENTIALS

Very early, the women's health movement made a commitment to questioning medical monopolies on knowledge and practices. As well as empowering clients by sharing information with them, women's health centres are committed to the notion that all women on the staff have skills and knowledge of value, that they can learn relevant information, and that they can all make equally valuable contributions to the centre's work. The hostility to credentialism was brought home to me forcefully quite early in this study when I asked naively whether any staff at a centre were trained as health professionals. I was told with evident exasperation that professional training was not the basis for staff selection, but that a range of skills and life experiences, plus an interest in women's health were the relevant qualifications. Professionalism is understood to be a problem because it discredits the experiences of women who come to centres as 'clients', casting them in the role of helpless victims who require educated professionals to explain and solve their problems (Dale and Foster, 1986). Such relationships are understood to be disempowering. Feminists, by contrast, seek to acknowledge each woman as an authority on her own life, and to support women who take responsibility for resolving personal difficulties.

Resistance to professionalism has also been an issue in the refuge movement (Rodriguez, 1988; Pahl, 1985) where it has provoked sharp division between feminists and professional social service agencies (Johnson, 1981; Ahrens, 1980). This commitment to every woman's expertise is, however, undermined by professional dominance, credentialism, specialisation and division of labour. If a centre is to run according to its feminist values instead of professionally prescribed formats, it must hire workers and organise itself along consciously and specifically different lines. Some centres give most or all of the staff the same label ('women's health worker'), regardless of their specific qualifications. In addition, many centres seek to democratise knowledge and skills, and rotate functions so that everyone takes turns doing all the jobs. But whatever they think of professionalism in its formal sense, they all strive to be professional in the richest sense of that word, performing their work in an ethical, honest, and competent fashion.

The elements of skill sharing and job rotation are related, but they can be distinguished, and it is possible to make a point of using the group itself as a source of in-service staff development without necessarily sharing out the work. Several of the 'first dozen' centres placed a high priority on the mutual educative processes, and scheduled regular 'learn-in' workshops at which the various members of staff would teach one another. For example, the Hindmarsh Centre set time aside each week for such sessions, and this work remained important after their funding was withdrawn. Sometimes these activities were a fairly direct carry-over from earlier consciousness-raising feminist health groups, as was the case for the Women's Health and Community Centre in Glendower Street, Perth. In any event, they helped to blur the distinctions between staff and clients, because they confirmed the conviction that everyone had both much to teach and much to learn. The members of the collective at Collingwood were always keen to avoid becoming separate 'service providers', and they wanted the Centre to function as a kind of clearinghouse for the exchange of women's knowledge. Doctors and nurses who would participate in this kind of democratisation of knowledge were much in demand for their technical expertise, and because they could teach specific skills such as how to use a speculum, how to take swabs and smears, how to measure blood pressure, etc. Once women without professional qualifications had the appropriate basic training, it became possible to share more and more of the actual work because the doctors were no longer the sole repositories of valuable skills and information.

In the United States, feminists without medical qualifications have challenged the medical monopoly on abortion. For example, the Chicago feminist collective 'Jane' began by providing abortion counselling, support and referrals. Their work enabled them to drive down the price of an abortion and to divert work away from incompetent practitioners. As a result of accompanying women having abortions, some of the members realised that they could learn to do the procedure themselves and dispense entirely with the need to negotiate with commercial abortionists. Several members of 'Jane' were trained and, over a period of four years (until the Supreme Court decision legalising abortion) they performed over 11 000 illegal first-trimester abortions with no deaths (Ruzek, 1978: 25), and an overall morbidity record equal to that of the state of New York when it legalised abortion (Schlesinger and Bart, 1982: 140).

When Australian women without formal medical or nursing training undertook tasks that traditionally had been reserved for doctors and nurses, it provoked a vigorous and hostile reaction. The Australian Medical Association was (and remains) strongly opposed to the use of 'unqualified' practitioners, and warned against the decline in standards of care that would result. The AMA is a powerful political lobby and it has at times made life difficult for women's health centres that are suspected of allowing such challenges to professional authority, let alone centres—like Leichhardt—that publicly announce their challenge. The pressure of professional lobbying has not, however, stopped some centres from defining collectivity in its fullest sense, and sharing much of the centre's work.

If there is resistance to allowing 'unqualified' workers to perform 'medical' tasks, there is also resistance to having doctors do non-medical activities. Some of this reluctance comes from doctors themselves who do not want to 'waste' their time on menial duties. On the other hand, women's health centres have involved many doctors whose political commitment is such that they seek rather than avoid involvement with all the work of the centre. For example, during the rapid start-up phase of Leichhardt, the Centre's first doctors helped make curtains, designed the examination table, and shopped for second-hand instruments. However, other forces work against this kind of commitment; perhaps the most powerful is the constantly increasing workload and consequent need for 'efficiency'. Having everybody do everything requires the allocation of resources to support continuous in-service training. Specialisation may be politically distasteful, but sooner or later most centres move toward it, however reluctantly. Despite a determination not to give special privilege to the doctors, it is difficult to insist that those people with scarce skills or special legal status take their turn at the switch-board or cleaning the toilet. By law, prescriptions must be signed by a qualified medical practitioner. Even doctors who are strongly committed to democratising knowledge will be under pressure to do individual consultations when reimbursement from that work is an important source of income for the centre. Still, compromises are possible. Centres that involve their medical staff in health education and group work are often able to strike a balance between professional dominance and reciprocal skill-sharing. However, everyone in the centre must be vigilant and committed, because the default option is medical privilege, which tends to prevail unless specific procedures are developed to resist it.

RESOURCES: THE PROBLEM OF PRIORITIES

Most women's health centres offer individual clinical services. All provide various kinds of health information and education, and they share an active commitment to disease prevention and health promotion rather than simply illness treatment. For the majority who either deliver clinical services or would like to, a painful dilemma is whether to invest most of the centre's resources in dealing with individual women's problems, or whether to reserve time, money and energy for health education, health promotion, advocacy and fostering social change. Centres with very similar statements of aims and objectives have, in reality, come to very different ways of dealing with these competing demands. For example, while Women's Health Care House in Perth has concentrated on individual services to women seeking reproductive and gynaecological care, the Dale Street Women's Health Centre in Port Adelaide has become involved, among other things, in action by local residents to combat industrial contamination of the neighbourhood environment.

Individual clinical services and community development overlap in the realm of workshops and health education groups which can include both individually-oriented, clinical type work and group-formation, issues-oriented social action. Community health workers Jackson, Mitchell and Wright have sought to bridge the gap between clinical and community development work by discussing community development as a continuum, ranging from what they call 'developmental casework' at one end to involvement in social movements at the other. They suggest that individual clinical services can be approached in ways that foster 'the development of the individual receiving such support, and the creation of links between individual service users' (Jackson, Mitchell and Wright, 1989: 68). Nevertheless, workers in women's health centres have found that the different kinds of work make competing claims. Many women present seeking medical care, counselling, or other personal crisis-intervention; and typically the demand for clinical services exceeds a centre's resources. As one worker put it, 'The woman who walks through the door with a bruise doesn't want a lecture on feminism'. Although it might seem unproblematic to concentrate on such individual services, it presents a social change-oriented health centre with a conflict among its several aims and objectives. Most centres have been established not only to deliver clinical services, but also for the larger purpose of changing the system.

The needs of 'the woman at the door' are immediate and compelling. But basic social change cannot occur if all the centre's resources are devoted to individual clinical work. One of Leichhardt's first crises arose when they discovered in their first year of operation that they had 'developed into a glorified, free, traditional general practice. . .inundated with women seeking medical advice. . .[with] the doctors and the surgeries the focal point of the Centre's activities' ('What Women Have Done at Leichhardt' handout prepared by the Leichhardt Collective, 11 June 1975). This realisation provoked a crisis at the Centre which led to a number of resignations (Petterson, 1975). While some workers were convinced that they had been shanghaied by the demand for clinical services, others felt their first commitment was to meeting the needs of women presenting for care. A decision was made to scale down the emphasis on the doctor–patient couple and to concentrate much more on 'community health education', research and 'circulation of information' (among women's services). As a result of this change of direction, Leichhardt reduced the amount of time reserved for individual services.

In view of the great demand for clinical services experienced by nearly all centres, the decision to scale back cannot have been easy, as the resignations at the time confirm. Women's immediate needs for help are difficult to reject. Purposely deciding to refuse some of these women requires a superficial hardheartedness. Such apparent hardheartedness can only come from a conviction that it is better in the long run to treat the societal disease rather than the individual symptoms, and a commitment to long-term social change that is determined not to be deflected by women's individual crises. Community workers in other settings often face this dilemma, which has been described as choosing between sending an ambulance to the bottom of a cliff to help the injured, or building a fence at the top of the cliff to keep people from falling off. The experience of millions of woman-hours in women's health centres confirms that individual demand will always outstrip the supply of good, basic sympathetic services. Thus only centres that commit themselves explicitly and concretely to something beyond individual services are likely to provide anything else. The Dale Street Women's Health Centre in Adelaide established a balance of activities for its first year of operation, allocating a maximum of 25 percent of time for one-to-one services. Because the needs of 'the woman at the door' are so urgent, at some point, the door has to be closed if centre staff are to avoid burn-out and if the longer-term objectives of the centre are to get attention. This conflict remains relevant because ideology foregrounds fundamental social change, but the daily 'default option' is the provision of personal care. Some centres simply close to individual clients for certain periods during the week. One compromise, taken by Blacktown and Lismore for example, is to nominate a skeleton staff who will be available for crisis counselling during regular periods when the centre is closed to appointments. This enables the centre to continue to offer emergency support while still protecting its capacity to pursue other kinds of work. Overall, centres that do not develop a specific procedure to reserve time and womanpower for health promotion, training, lobbying, advocacy and community development can do little if any such work.

THE PROBLEM OF BURN-OUT

Sooner or later, centres must face a dilemma of balancing the welfare of clients against that of staff. It may seem obvious that the centres are established to serve the needs of clients, but because the demand is so much greater than the resources to meet it, and because—particularly in the early days—there was no formula defining or limiting the work, staff burn-out has been endemic. Centres that always give first priority to client needs without protecting the well-being of staff tend to have very high turnover, and the collective is liable to collapse. Practically all centres were vulnerable to this problem during the early years, and most of them still are. Even in the late 1980s, I was aware that a woman who spent an hour or two in discussion with me would be working back that hour or two, perhaps making a very late end to the work day. There is something perverse about a women's health centre that exhausts the health and well-being of its own women staff in an effort to improve women's health.

Some centres have recognised this irony, and they have devised rosters that reflect the heavy toll taken by constant exposure to what one worker described as 'too many women with too many problems'. For example, while it is not a generalist women's health centre, Canberra's Medea collective offers services to women in emotional distress. It has developed a set of support procedures to ensure that staff members do not leave the centre disturbed by the day's work. Their regular roster includes stress leave. Perhaps the insight leading to such protective systems was facilitated by their explicit awareness that the only real difference between clients and staff is current circumstances. Staff could become emotionally troubled, and clients may deal with their problems successfully and become helpers instead of helped. From my observations, however, Medea's attention to the mental health of staff is the exception rather than the rule. Most centres acknowledge that the work is stressful, but few have such well elaborated systems to prevent burn-out.

On the other hand, centres that always put staff welfare first are correctly accused of failing to be accountable. Although my research suggests that abuse is extremely rare, there have been episodes where staff have used centre resources for private purposes. Such abuses are censured severely by other members of staff. I suspect that public accusations of 'lack of accountability' are usually a legitimate way to express disapproval of the basic philosophy and work of a women's health centre. During a crisis, it is a common charge levelled by one faction against another. The press and state health officials respond to it with keen interest. At least one centre is accused by local feminists of having become so 'inward looking' that its main function is to provide a sinecure for staff who have become conservative and failed to develop professionally.

THE PROBLEM OF CONSTITUENCY

Because they cannot be all things to all women, centres may seek to focus their work on a particular clientele. Which clients will they try to attract? The community as a whole, or some group of disadvantaged women? If the latter, which ones? The first six centres were explicitly located in neighbourhoods with high proportions of ethnic and working-class women, signalling the left-wing origins of contemporary feminism and the criteria of the Community Health Program. Collectives reasoned—and experience has confirmed their impression—that unless a special appeal is made to women from non-English-speaking backgrounds, such women will rarely attend, no matter how great their need. However, catering for a particular group of clients may make the centre less appropriate for 'mainstream' women. Thus the community power base may be narrowed, limiting its lobbying capacity and making the centre vulnerable to takeover or being shut down when some kind of crisis occurs. This narrowing of the power base can occur when the service focuses on an ethnically or economically vulnerable population such as Melbourne's WICH, Fremantle's Multicultural Women's Health Centre, or the Aboriginal women and their families who eventually came to constitute the bulk of the clients at the Alice Springs Women's Centre. The long delays in obtaining permission for births at Congress Alukura in Alice Springs must be partly a product of the political weakness of the clients (Aboriginal women) whom Alukura serves.

The social base of a women's health centre can also become narrow because of feminist elitism or lesbian separatism. In the case of elitism or separatism, the community may come to believe (whether correctly or not) that the centre has become the property of political extremists and that it is not appropriate for 'ordinary' women. For example, I was told of an episode in Perth some years ago in which an older woman went to Women's Health Care House after decades of abuse by her husband. The story, perhaps apocryphal, claims that the counsellor told the woman simply to 'leave the bastard'. Such events need not actually occur for people to be alienated by hearing the stories. The Centre in Darwin (which was closed in 1980) developed quite specific definitions of clientele. For example, during the Timorese crisis, two waves of refugees came to Darwin, one from each side of the conflict. Apparently refugee women from what was deemed to be the 'wrong' side were not welcome at the Centre. Many centres have, at least at times, been seen as actively hostile to men, and perhaps also to women who live with men. When a centre comes to be perceived as that extreme, it is likely to provoke a crisis of dramatic proportions and sometimes devastating consequences. Women in Perth still discuss the withdrawal of funding from the Women's Health and Community Centre (which was charged with extremism) in terms of its continuing impact on the Perth women's movement. The takeover and closure of the Alice Springs Women's Centre remains, if anything, an even more painful influence on the women there. In both cases, these feelings prevail a decade or more after the events.

VOLUNTEERS: THE PROBLEM OF EXPLOITATION

The question of whether (and if so how) to use volunteers has been a concern in virtually every centre. Feminist theory suggests that centres should not use volunteer labour on the grounds that it is exploitative. Too often, women have been expected to do for love or duty work that men do for money (Baldock, 1990: Chapter 8). Even when women are paid, they are often underpaid compared to men who do similar work in the mistaken belief that women do not need as much income as men do, and because women's devotion is supposed to fill the gap left by the inadequate pay cheque. Volunteers may be committed to 'struggle, not charity' (London Edinburgh Weekend Return Group, 1979:139), but there are good feminist reasons for saying 'no' to volunteerism. Especially after the heavy investment of unpaid time and energy required to found a centre, there may be strong reluctance to use volunteers once funding is obtained. Consequently, a number of centres have a strict policy that excludes the use of volunteer labour. Leichhardt has had such a policy; so has Women's Health Care House (Perth), the Hunter Region Working Women's Centre (Newcastle), Bankstown, and Albury-Wodonga.

Apart from the possibility of exploitation, volunteerism is a potential source of other problems. A centre that relies on volunteers may find that it must accept a lower level of commitment from volunteers than paid staff, with a consequently inconsistent level of performance. Volunteers are thought to be more likely than paid workers to renege on commitments to a timetable, and less willing to stick with unrewarding tasks, to submit their work for evaluation, or to undertake in-service training. A volunteer women's shelter in Adelaide had problems from the beginning because one worker, who could afford to be at the shelter all day, virtually took over its daily management and gave interviews to the press in which she identified herself as the shelter's 'founder'. Other volunteers who had different views of how the shelter should be run were unable to remedy the situation because they had to invest time in their paid jobs, and because of the lack of any formal employment contracts with the shelter (Otto and Haley, 1975).

When both paid staff and volunteers work in the same centre, pecking orders can develop. Sometimes unpaid workers get the boring jobs, but not always. An American feminist health centre found that volunteers were reluctant to do the administration, which was regarded as 'shit work' (Morgen, 1986:202–3). In these circumstances, a different kind of exploitation can arise in which paid workers are expected to do all the undesirable tasks on the grounds that they, after all, are paid to do them.

These kinds of difficulties can create splits between paid and unpaid workers. Money and status may buy authority in some organisations, but most women's health centres are opposed to such patterns. Nevertheless, having both paid and unpaid workers does make a difference, and if the differences are not politically legitimate, they can be very complicated to manage. Paid workers may resent the relative freedom of volunteers, and at the same time may feel guilty that they are paid to do what others do for free. Meanwhile volunteers may resent the power and privilege of paid staff and feel that they are treated as second-class citizens. Inevitably, there will be social differences between those women who can afford to volunteer and those who must, of necessity, use their time to earn a wage. Consequently, some centres feel they cannot risk using volunteers.

On the other hand, without the work of volunteers, there would be no women's health centres. Dozens of women have worked for months or even years without pay to found every centre in the country. Some centres such as Wagga, Blue Mountains, or Coffs Harbour would not have survived long enough to receive funding if women had not been able and willing to work unpaid for several years. In any event, when pay is very low, the meaning of 'volunteer' becomes ambiguous. Many women could earn much more elsewhere than they do in women's health centres. In effect, they donate the income forgone. Sometimes that donation is direct to the centre, as in the case where doctors are paid an assigned salary which is lower than the funds recovered from

Medicare in payment for their consultations. Grants have never been adequate to do everything a centre wants to do, and volunteers allow them to extend their reach. And of course the management groups put in many unpaid hours every year.

There are, then, practical reasons for using volunteers, and some circumstances when it is unavoidable. Accepting volunteer inputs also gives a woman the opportunity to put energy back into a centre that may have been extremely important to her at another time. I interviewed several women whose first contact with a centre was as a client. Her appreciation for the support she received was later expressed by her returning to donate time. Working as a volunteer can also be a means for a woman with little paid work experience to acquire experience and skills that she will be able to use in the paid workforce, either within the centre or elsewhere. Some centres deal with this possibility directly. For example, the centre in Gosford has developed systematic training programs for volunteers which impart recognised skills and involve women in regular work that may lead to paid employment. Dale Street (Port Adelaide) also has an explicit policy that permits volunteers only when all parties (management, staff and volunteer) have discussed it and agreed that a volunteer is preferable to a paid worker, and when they enter into an agreement spelling out the nature and extent of the activity, the means of communication between volunteers and paid staff, and the procedures for resolving any conflict.

If a valuable service loses funding, the question of volunteers acquires a new urgency. After the suspension of funding to the Hindmarsh Centre, and the establishment of the new State-funded Adelaide Women's Health Centre in North Adelaide, the Hindmarsh Centre continued to function on an entirely voluntary basis for about four years. The ambiguities surrounding the issue of volunteers are far from resolved, but there is no doubt that the Australian women's health movement has accomplished at least as much through the unpaid work of an army of dedicated women as it has through the ultimately meagre funding from the state.

USING THE SYSTEM TO CHANGE THE SYSTEM: THE PROBLEM OF CO-OPTATION

Centres must negotiate many other balancing acts if they are to survive and thrive. For example, who may be involved in the management of the centre? Agents of the state? The staff? Women from the community? Perhaps incongruously, centres have also struggled over whether it is permissible to have men on the management body or on staff. Given that the underlying concept of the women's health centre is that care should be provided 'by women, for women' this might seem like a non-question. But some funding bodies might seek to prescribe the composition of boards of management, and could nominate men to serve on these boards. The related question of employing men becomes relevant when the supply of women with particular skills is limited. The centre in Darwin was forced to employ men doctors because of the lack of medically qualified women in Darwin during the 1970s. Some women regard these concessions as, at best, a necessary evil. A few see them as a sign of political maturity or even an indicator that they have 'arrived' as legitimate, mainstream services.

How far a centre can afford to compromise with bureaucratic requirements has been an ongoing dilemma. Filling in forms, writing submissions and reports, and keeping records are time-consuming tasks that may be experienced as diverting energy away from the real work of a centre. The dimensions of this problem are discussed in more detail in Chapter 6. In brief, centres have found that scrupulous attention to the details of accounting is vital to their survival. Like it or not, funding is now tightly linked to a capacity to establish need in terms that are as quantitative as possible. The continuation of funding has become absolutely contingent on meticulous bookkeeping.

At the heart of the women's health centre enterprise lies the fundamental contradiction: the necessary impossibility of using a system to change that system. Few women's health centres would be satisfied if all they did was to deliver higher quality, more sympathetic conventional medical care than women can obtain from traditional sources. The centres have much more radical objectives. While their formal aims may not say so explicitly, their most basic purpose is to contribute to the transformation of a social order which causes much physical and mental suffering among women as a byproduct of women's oppression. In simple terms, the women's health movement is motivated in part by the conviction that patriarchal society makes women sick, and the awareness that all the sympathetic, high-quality medical care in the world cannot solve this fundamental problem. The women's health movement is committed not simply to improve the quality of medical care available, but to change the underlying social conditions that give rise to avoidable illness among women.

To bring about such change, however, women's health centres find themselves more or less involved with and partially implicated in the very social structures they are working to transform. They hire and rely on doctors and nurses; they must conform to various codes and regulations imposed by local councils and State bureaucracies; they deal regularly with landlords and suppliers. To obtain state funding they must represent themselves and (to some extent) conduct themselves in accordance with the requirements of the state. Because they are committed to providing health information and services to women on a continuing basis, they are forced to make a variety of concessions in the interests of institutionalisation. The dilemma involves being 'caught up in an effort to develop a new kind of politics that could not be coopted by the system. This involved numerous struggles over ideological, organizational, and internal issues fundamental to the future of feminism' (Bunch, 1987:106).

At the simplest level, this might be formulated as the familiar conflict between reform and revolution. As Ann Curthoys observed, the election of a Federal Labor government in 1972 was a stimulus to the establishment of many new women's services, which meant

> the old revolution/reform dichotomy now had to be confronted, and a
> more precise strategy had to be worked out. The problem was
> incorporation and government control; the promise was effective action
> here and now to combat or at least relieve some aspects of 'women's
> oppression' (Curthoys, 1988:86).

Curthoys goes on to argue that the women's movement has yet to develop the 'more precise strategy' it needs. We have seen that, in one form or another, the revolution–reform dilemma continues to plague women's health centres. As one disenchanted informant expressed it to me in 1989, 'The question is: will we conform and be liked, or will we provide an alternative and be respected?'

While these dilemmas are unlikely to go away, a powerful combination of theory and experience is producing an analysis that may form the basis for different, less polarised ways of thinking about them. Bunch (1987; essay first published in 1977) defines a *reform* as 'any proposed change that alters the conditions of life in a particular area' and which can 'be part of any group's program, whether conservative or revolutionary in ideology'. Reform is distinguished from reform*ism*, defined as the particular ideology that women can gain 'freedom through equality' within the existing system (1987:104–5). Having identified reforms as strategies open to groups of many political persuasions, she goes on to enumerate criteria for evaluating reforms against the objectives of groups with radical (non-reformist) ideologies (pp.111–14).

It seems to me that most women's health centres are striving to be radical groups that rely, to some extent, on reform. This formulation acknowledges the importance of a practical (reform) approach to immediate problems, without compromising the radical political position which orients the approach. With such an understanding, the women's health movement might be able to thread its way more easily through unavoidable contradictions. Running a women's health centre involves moving through a political and personal minefield; insightful analysis might identify the locations of a few of the most dangerous mines. Perhaps the most hazardous ones I have observed are the conviction that there is a simple formula that can resolve the contradictions of a feminist women's health centre, and the belief that the personal and political failings of one's colleagues are the barrier to realising that formula.

6 Antidotes to oppression?

After months travelling the country, conducting consultations on women's health and receiving statements from individuals and groups representing nearly a million Australian women, Liza Newby formed the view that women's health is politically unique in attracting across-the-board support from women. At the time Newby was a special consultant to the Commonwealth Minister for Health, assigned to develop a discussion paper that would form the basis for a national women's health policy (the discussion document was published as Newby, 1988). She concluded that as a social issue, women's health is different from child care or comparable worth, which strike at the heart of conventional arrangements and imply radical social changes. Women who disagree about many other issues are united in their concern about inadequate and inappropriate health services, and they want to see health care improved. More than a decade and half after Leichhardt opened, health remains a powerful issue for women. The worries voiced during Newby's consultations in the late 1980s were remarkably similar to the motivations behind women's health centres in the mid-1970s.

That is not to say, however, that nothing has changed: far from it. If nothing else, women's health centres can never again rely on the 'confidence born of naiveté' (Howell, 1975: 52) which was such an important resource for the first dozen women's health centres. Both the optimism and anger that fuelled feminist action in the 1970s have receded (Fatin, 1990:11), but the work goes on in a continually changing register. This Chapter explores the character and climate of the current environment for women's health centres. It highlights how certain themes have been

The title of this Chapter is adapted from a phrase in Germaine Greer's Foreword to the *Healthsharing Reader* (1990), in which she observes that women are discovering that doctors cannot prescribe 'antidotes to injustice' (ix).

muted while others have been amplified and new themes have been introduced. Overall, it considers how the environment has changed with time, and how the work of the first women's health centres has altered the conditions of opportunity for subsequent generations of the women's health movement. The late 1980s brought several significant developments in women's health and a new crop of women's health centres. What is the relationship between them and their predecessors? How are they continuing the work of earlier centres and how are they being constrained or choosing to alter the original agenda?

In retrospect, it is clear that the initiatives of the women's health movement, including the centres and public forums and 'speakouts' on health, have been politically effective in part because they have threatened the legitimacy of the institutions of medicine and the state. The institutional responses have been complex, and their consequences have not always produced the results feminist activists have intended. Nevertheless, the changes in women's health care during the last fifteen years have altered both the options available and the environment in which interventions occur currently and in the future.

The general discourse on health and health services has been enlarged since women's health centres first appeared, and women's health centres have contributed to the enlargement. A few examples can illustrate this point. At the time Leichhardt opened, its yoga classes were considered quite radical. Several years later, Leichhardt no longer felt the need to offer the classes because they were available from many other sources. Some women's health centres still run yoga classes, but a wide range of health-related services, groups and classes opened during the 1970s and 1980s, sponsored by TAFE's, small clinics, and variously qualified practitioners. Several free-standing (including feminist) abortion clinics opened, which relieved women's health centres of the necessity to perform this procedure, although they have continued to lobby for abortion facilities. There are many more initiatives dealing with occupational health and safety, including initiatives of special significance to women such as programs on repetition strain injury. A vigorous homebirth and birth-centres movement has developed during this time, restoring midwifery to a significant and respected position in the care of women and babies. Mammography and cervical cancer screening programs have been tested. New South Wales piloted a Women's Health Nurse Practitioner program, and other States are considering similar programs. Classes are now routinely available, catering for a wide range of needs and interests: childbirth education, yoga and exercise for women of all ages including expectant and birthing mothers, healthy cooking, self-esteem and assertiveness, menopause and health in the middle and later years, breast self-examination, aerobics and other exercise, meditation and stress management. There are also support groups in most cities for women suffering from many health or health-related problems including eating disorders, RSI, rape, domestic violence, incest, substance abuse, premenstrual problems, HIV infection, and chronic fatigue syndrome, to mention only a few.

Along with this growing array of educational and clinical services, the notion of 'holism' in health has become more respectable, illness prevention and health promotion are increasingly legitimised, and the social model of health is appearing in a variety of government discussion papers and policy documents. The perspectives of 'community development in health' are being elaborated, and resources collated for practitioners who wish to take up such approaches (Community Development in Health Project, 1988). The medical model, with its fragmented, disease orientation may still be dominant, but other voices are now audible.

On the other hand, the achievements have not been won without cost, and their preservation requires continuing action. Several factors can be identified in the current environment that pose a challenge to women's health centres seeking to maintain their commitment to a feminist, critical, and resistant model of their work. Some of those factors have been present since the first day Leichhardt opened its doors, as we saw in Chapters 4 and 5. Others dangers were, perhaps, implicit but have developed over time and have now acquired new salience. Still others are products of changes that have occurred during the last fifteen years.

THE PRICE OF MONEY

Depending on its source and the conditions attached to it, funding tends to shape, more or less directly, the priorities to which a centre must adhere. A study of twelve worker collectives in the United States showed that those that sought funding from other organisations evolved into hierarchical bureaucracies, while those that remained self-funding were able to retain their egalitarian structure and way of working (Newman, 1980). Although such a strict dichotomy oversimplifies the situation for Australian women's health centres, there is no doubt that dependence on outside funding makes centres vulnerable to forces that seek to rewrite the feminist agenda. Morgen observed the operation of this process in her study of an American feminist women's health clinic (1986: 203), a process with many parallells in Australia. Not surprisingly, State health authorities are most inclined to fund programs that deliver individual services at the lowest cost. If they are persuaded that health education and health promotion will reduce the overall cost of service delivery, they may sponsor such initiatives. In the short run, costs may not be affected. Even if health education and health promotion are cost effective in the long run, the fact may be difficult to establish in an ageing population that requires more expensive medical services. Or if the economy deteriorates, the health effects of increased poverty and unemployment may increase the burden on the health and welfare system. That is, external demographic and economic trends may increase the cost of the health sector despite the benefits of disease prevention and health promotion. The health benefits of child care, community development, advocacy, political action, and lobbying are even more difficult to demonstrate and hence less likely to attract funding. For a government whose term in office may be only two or three years, many health initiatives take too long to bear fruit. The results are simply not quick enough or sufficiently spectacular to attract political support.

Consequently, women's health centres are the object of an accidental combination of the tendencies of funding bodies and the immediate needs of individual women, both of which emphasise individual services at the expense of other activities. When a centre is funded, it becomes contractually obligated to perform the designated functions, even if the collective believes that other work should have higher priority. Morgen documents the shift in emphasis through the changing language of her clinic's brochures which began by depicting the work as 'women helping women' and moved to describing ' "paraprofessionals" serving "clients" ' (Morgen, 1986: 204). Given the constant demand to concentrate on individual services, centres are always at risk of being transmuted from social change agencies into social service agencies (Morgen, 1986: 205). 'Agencies are being funded to provide a clearly-defined service in a specifically defined way: they are being forced to become an extra arm of the government' (Flaskas and Hounslow, 1980: 14).

In the First Annual Pamela Denoon lecture in 1989, Senator Pat Giles observed that during the 1970s, 'we gave a whole new meaning to the word "submission" '. There is truth in that, but it is also true that submissiveness remains a sub-text beneath the surface text of the formal request for funding. The first submission for Leichhardt was a short, strongly worded declaration of intent. More recent collectives have typically been much more circumspect in their wording as well as longer. There are many ways in which seeking money from the state requires a group to submit to a set of procedures, priorities and values that may be far removed from the vision motivating the group to ask for money in the first place. Grants create a good deal of attendant administrative and clerical work. In the years since the Community Health Program, the processes of obtaining, administering and reporting on grants has become more complex, requiring the centres to have staff or board members with expert knowledge of the legal and procedural requirements of the funding bodies. A volunteer group can be casual about record-keeping, but once they get a grant they must be accountable for the expenditure of the money, and that includes detailed and systematic records of what they do and for whom. Future funding depends on it. The CHP began with limited requirements for accountability and evaluation, but contemporary funding sources usually build elaborate procedures directly into the granting process. As far as women's health centres are concerned, there are three major drawbacks to such procedures. They are are time- and resource-consuming; they impose rules of formality on previously informal, co-operative centres; and they push centres away from collective organisation toward task specialisation and hierarchy.

Time and womanpower spent preparing submissions and administering grants (maintaining official records, documents, and accounts) cannot be devoted to political action, community development or care of women who come to the centre for help. But on the other hand, without paid staff, there may be no centre available to undertake services and advocacy. Sometimes it is hard to know when the effort ceases to pay off, but the free clinic studied by Rothschild-Whitt surely passed the point of diminishing returns. Its staff were spending three-quarters of their time seeking funding (1979b: 228). Among the first dozen Australian women's health centres, several were run by collectives that fiercely resisted the intrusion of such bureaucratic procedures. A few flatly refused and paid the price: no funding.

But if funding-related administration was a nuisance in the early days, it has increased exponentially since then. Staff at almost every centre I visited complained about the growing burden of paperwork. Few now object to the principle of accountability as such, perhaps because those who object have left the field to those who are willing to compromise. But the *form* of accountability is often burdensome and inappropriate. I gained the impression that centres are particularly resistant to the exclusive emphasis on 'upward' accountability from workers to management, to the State health department and ultimately to the Minister. They are much more receptive to 'lateral and downward' accountability in which other workers and the local community become participants in the process, but which is apparently less popular with health bureaucracies (Community Development in Health Project, 1988: chapter 2). But all objected to the amount of tedious work entailed in 'upward' accountability, and many had reservations about the appropriateness of the criteria and formal procedures to which they are subjected. For example, a women's health worker at the Shoalhaven Women's Health Centre told me they are now required to submit quarterly (rather than simply annual) reports and statistics. They are also called upon to prepare separate submissions, including separate cost allocations for rent and administration, for each of the Centre's distinct activities, rather than for the Centre as a whole. Consequently, at times, they have 'to curtail direct servicing in order to fulfil the statistical reports'. In view of the fact that women's health centres are committed to giving women adequate time and attention to understand and address problems, they can never process individual clients as quickly as more conventional clinical services can. They are already under pressure to see more women and spend less time with them. The intrusion of additional clerical work simply makes this problem worse.

Submissions and reports require centres to represent their activities in terms that fit bureaucratic categories, but bear little resemblance to the centre's work. As one woman put it, 'What we do doesn't fit on their form!' The fact that forms are irrelevant to what the centres regard as their real work compounds the sheer administrative and clerical load. The terms of 'program budgeting' recently introduced in New South Wales, if applied strictly, would require health centres to measure the floor space allocated to each activity for budgeting purposes, and to maintain separate ledgers for each activity. The resulting proliferation of paperwork is mind boggling. These procedures constitute headaches for all community-based service groups, not only women's health centres. But such legalism and fragmentation are especially offensive to groups whose ideological commitments are to integration and holism. The situation prompted one worker from Liverpool to remark sarcastically, 'Woe betide the person who does counselling in the group room!'

Part of the problem with the administration and clerical work is its requirement for formality. For example, from the beginning, most centres have sought to operate so that women do not need to have a health problem to go to the centre—they can just go for social contact and companionship. If loneliness and isolation are understood as 'health' problems, this policy is a sensible health service. As restrictions are imposed, each woman who goes to a centre must be categorised as suffering from a specific health problem and receiving a specific relevant service. Women's health centres have preferred to avoid splitting hairs over whether or not a given problem is 'really' a health issue, so the growing formality is experienced as an intrusion on a successful way of working. In any event, if a woman has language or other difficulties, the gradual process of gaining confidence in a centre may contribute to her ability to seek help for more traditionally defined health problems at a women's health centre or in conventional medical facilities. Under regimes of economic rationalism, continued funding depends (among other things) on the numbers of women served, so every contact must be noted, coded, and recorded in the terms of an official format. The notion that women can just drop in for a 'cuppa and a chat' becomes difficult to sustain when everyone must be a classifiable case. The volunteer-run 'Jenny's Place' in Gosford was committed to serving as a kind of drop-in centre. When they began to need official statistics, they had to establish a reception area to record every visitor and her reason for coming. The change from the informal home-like atmosphere was summed up by a regular visitor to the centre who asked indignantly, 'Who put that desk in the middle of our lounge room?'

The third problem with applying for and administering grants is the pressure they exert toward specialisation. Of necessity, administrative and grant seeking tasks are usually allocated to one or a few women who have the specialist technical knowledge and skills. Although the knowledge and skills could be taught to other staff members and hence the tasks could be shared, in practice the official requirements of funding effectively impose specialisation. Government demands for 'evaluation' exert pressure for one or a few members of staff to specialise in the relevant tasks. Even if the terms of a grant do not require the appointment of an administrator or a bookkeeper, the nature of the work leads to such appointments and hence to increasing specialisation in the divisions of labour. Depending on the definition of collective, divisions of labour may not be inimical to collective organising, but they make it much more difficult.

The contrast between the Hindmarsh centre in its volunteer phase with many of the funded centres illustrates the dilemma of funding. The women who volunteered at Hindmarsh found it empowering, enriching, and self-healing, and they were able to maintain a valued, high quality service for four years with no government grant. Indeed, from the accounts of the women involved, the value and quality of their work was, in some ways, achieved because of, rather than in spite of, being unfunded. Liberated from bureaucratic constraints, they were able to respond to the needs of local women and their own impressions of how best to meet those needs. They formed a vigorous and productive collective that functioned 'like an extended family', free of the rancour and hostility that so often plague feminist collectives. They reached consensus readily and drew in women from working-class as well as middle-class backgrounds. Because no individual was in charge, every woman took responsibility and found ways of contributing to the work. Those who were shy about joining in the clinical activities or groups might initially choose to work in the garden, only venturing inside the building as their confidence increased. Consequently, the goods and services were more varied than those offered at a conventional health centre. As one volunteer told me, 'You could come in for a smear test and go away with a lettuce as well'. Even the fundraising was approached with humour and optimism. For example, they held a 'Don't Do It, Di' dance on the occasion of the royal wedding, as well as an annual fair. Evidently the fund-raising was successful, because when the remaining account was finally disbursed in 1989, they had \$13 000 to donate to an indigenous women's conference and other women's projects. As no-one was paid, they gave themselves permission to be selective in what they did, so there was none of the burn-out that has become characteristic of workers in women's services. Indeed, the process was quite the opposite of burnout. Their work strengthened and nourished them as well as the clients. Rothschild-Whitt (1979b) suggests that economic marginality and an internal support base are two important factors facilitating participatory organisations. The experience at Hindmarsh confirms her observation, and suggests that at times, the price of money may be too high.

Twenty years of feminist activity in Australia have produced a women's services labour force with a remarkable array of skills and experience. In the mid-1970s, most (although not all) of the workers in women's health were new to feminist service provision and to the world of grants and government. Many had worked in nursing or other positions in traditional clinics, hospitals, or social service agencies. Many more had backgrounds in apparently unrelated fields. But for everyone, working in a feminist community organisation was a new experience, and they were involved with the process of creating the procedures and meanings of such organisations. When a group took a new initiative, obtained additional money, or had to replace members who left, they became fully aware of the novelty and vulnerability of their arrangements. Finding new staff with the right political credentials might be important to maintain group cohesion, but centres also developed urgent needs for women who could perform specific tasks like keeping the books, applying for grants, or conducting the kinds of research and data collection on which future funding would be based. In the intervening years, increasing numbers of committed feminists have acquired those skills, so it is not always necessary to sacrifice political acumen to find someone who can keep the sponsors happy.

Another change in the environment of women's health centres which presents them with new challenges is the shrinking pool of volunteer workers on which they have relied. That is not to say that women's health centres no longer rely on unpaid labour. Thousands of unpaid hours are vital for all centres in the development phase, and some centres continue to benefit from the contributions of volunteers. Nor does it mean that the early centres relied entirely or mainly on volunteers, nor that all volunteers were at centres full time. Many of the participants did paid jobs as well as their work for women's health centres.

But volunteers who were free to invest large amounts of time have been vital in the history of women's health centres, and increasingly, unpaid work for health centres is done in addition to rather than instead of a paid job. Very few women can now afford to work as full-time volunteers. This change has been brought about, in part, by the increase in female labour force participation during the period in question. In 1974, just over 40 percent of Australian women over fifteen years of age were in the labour force; a decade later it was nearly 45 percent, and by 1989 more than half of all women were employed or actively looking for work (Women's Bureau, 1983 and 1990). Consequently, proportionally fewer women are available to donate full-time labour to a women's health centre. Several centres survived for months or years with no paid workers, but such strategies are becoming increasingly difficult to sustain.

A deteriorating economy, rising divorce rates, and stricter qualifications for supporting parent and unemployment benefits also limit women's ability to invest themselves in working without pay at women's health centres. During the 1970s and early 1980s, an unknown number of women were supported by husbands or else willingly lived on the dole or a comparatively low pension in order to devote their energies to starting and running women's health centres. This is a practical option for fewer women today. Even women in couple relationships face financial pressures from high interest rates, inflation, underemployment and unemployment, all of which have reduced the number of households that can be maintained by the earnings of one adult. These pressures are compounded for women who become heads of households, particularly lone mothers. Bryson observes that 'women are no longer entitled to support from the state, in lieu of support from a husband, after they stop caring for dependent children' (1987: 112), and the age (of the youngest child) at which women lose entitlement to the supporting parent's benefit has been reduced from 24 to 16 years. At the same time, increased surveillance of all welfare recipients, household-income based means testing and the 'work test' for unemployment benefits rule out access to the dole for many women. Overall welfare dependency has increased during this time (Jones, 1990: 47), but the stringency of welfare regulations apparently has the desired (by government) effect of excluding from welfare recipiency people who are theoretically capable of supporting themselves. Many of the first dozen women's health centres would have collapsed if they had not been maintained by women who lived on the widow's pension or the dole and worked long hours at the centre. It is hard to imagine, for example, where the resources would come from to support the long 'volunteer phase' of a Hindmarsh in the 1990s.

Many of the women who once worked unpaid in the women's movement have been drawn into paid employment in women's services, or in the bureaucracy itself. Perhaps appropriately, significant numbers of women are now formally employed in health and welfare. 'The Social and Community Services Sector is the fastest growing industry sector in Australia and largest in terms of employment' (Women's Bureau, 1988: 5). It also employs more women than any other industry. Several women from the feminist movement have gone into politics. In some ways, feminists going into politics and the bureaucracy constitute an infiltration; a feminist on the inside should be able to oil the wheels for women's services and clients of the state. And indeed some femocrats in women's health units and other locations in the state bureaucracy have sought to do exactly that. Yeatman defines femocrats as 'paid advocates of the interests of women as a gender class' (1990: 61), and argues that their explicit commitment to feminism distinguishes them from career bureaucrats—female as well as male—who have no particular personal or political interest in women's issues. Women's units and the women's policy machinery are clearly responses to feminist advocacy. Femocrats usually choose to seek work in the bureaucracy because they believe they can be more effective advocates for women's interests there. And there is no doubt that women's health policies, as well as other state and federal policies promoting women's interests, have only been developed by the efforts of dedicated women working inside the state.

Nevertheless, like women's health centres, the femocrat's position is inherently conflicted. Femocrats too are caught between the ideologies of the women's movement on the one hand, and the quite different ideology and constraints of the state. Their feminism is a qualification for the job, but working for the state may separate them from the lives and concerns of the women for whom they are supposed to speak, and there are few mechanisms for facilitating their accountability even to other feminists outside the bureaucracy, let alone a wider community of women. (This kind of separation from the community affects all bureaucrats, but it is only a problem for those who seek to advocate on behalf of disadvantaged groups.) Furthermore, routine procedures rarely make allowances for 'special interests', and many of their colleagues (including some superiors in the hierarchy) are unsympathetic. For example, Mary Draper, head of the Victorian Women's Policy Co-ordination Unit during the mid-1980s, was confronted by 'bureaucratic hostility to the idea of the Unit initiating projects and raising community awareness of issues' (Sawer, 1990: 165), all activities that would be considered basic to a feminist program. Thus, the very objectives and commitments that are required for a femocrat's appointment often become liabilities on the job.

The official fiction that all citizens are the same creates special problems for an officer of the bureaucracy who is appointed on the grounds that she can 'represent' women as a group. Femocrats frequently have to argue on both sides: on the one hand, when women are excluded unfairly from rights of citizenship, femocrats advocate equal treatment. On the other hand, treating everyone the same when their material conditions are different compounds disadvantage. In these circumstances, femocrats must advocate respect for difference, rather than defend 'equal' treatment which amounts to treating women like men. Recent feminist writing (eg. Bacchi, 1990) has sought to overcome the apparent necessity to choose *either* sameness *or* difference, but such innovative thinking appears to have made little impact in the public service, where this dilemma is a persistent fact of life. The dilemma is symptomatic of the femocrat's situation, trying to 'operate pragmatically within the existing agenda and at the same time retain idealism, motivation and direction' (Sawer, 1989: 13).

No matter how determined she may be to adhere to her feminist principles, the shift into the bureaucracy inevitably changes a woman's relationship to women's services (such as women's health centres) and women in the community. Unless she is insensitive to her colleagues within the organisation, or indifferent to her own professional future, her interest in women's programs and policies will be challenged and, to some extent, may be diluted over time. She is likely to have several responsibilities, only one of which is advocacy for women's initiatives. She will come to appreciate keenly the dilemmas of policy makers, the politics of funding decisions, and the 'hidden agendas' that influence decision making. Indeed, if she does not develop these insights, her capacity to speak for women will be limited. (However, such experiences and insider knowledge would prove valuable if she moves from a state bureaucracy into women's services.) But at the same time, the femocrat's insider sympathies require her to shift her perspective, distancing her from the very 'interest groups' whose lobbying created her job. Not surprisingly, 'there is enormous pressure. . .to perform miracles, and sections of the women's movement are quick to criticise when they fail' (Smith, 1985: 38–9; see also Lynch, 1984). Anne Summers, who—as a former Head of the Office of the Status of Women—is in a position to know, observes that the women's movement outside the bureaucracy has been scathingly critical of femocrats. 'There has been an almost unwholesome eagerness to find fault with such appointees, to criticize them for what they say, for their silences, even for their clothes' (1986: 60).

In sum, the movement of some feminists from 'the front line states' (McFerren, 1990) of feminist services into the bureaucracy has been a mixed blessing for women's services and for the femocrats themselves. It brings women who are sympathetic and informed into positions where they may be able to act on behalf of women's services. And there is no doubt that they have, at times, been successful in those positions (McLean, Draffen, and Callcott, 1977: 51). But at the same time, the structure and processes of state bureaucracies limit a femocrat's capacity to pursue the objectives that have drawn her into the work. At worst, working inside the state may, particularly in difficult political or economic climates, be mainly a matter of participating in decisions about what feminist services to cut and by how much.

FEMINISM AND THE NEW MANAGERIALISM

Centres must now cope with the 'new managerialism', a development inside the state as well as in the private sector. This approach seeks to conduct relations between government and community groups along a 'free market' model. 'It is not very sympathetic to community-based management; indeed it is not very sympathetic to community health at all' (Legge, 1990: 12). In the health field as elsewhere, the new managerialism requires needs analysis and performance indicators that can be expressed numerically (see Fraser, 1987, for a discussion of the gendered character of the interpretation of need in welfare). 'Governments seek a spurious 'objectivity' through quantitative research' (Meekosha, 1989: 258). While no one would argue with the view that resources should be directed to areas where they will be of most benefit, or that recipients of public funds should use them for the welfare of the community, it is quite another matter to assume that the quantitative measures currently favoured by bureaucracies accurately assess the contribution to public good.

For example, doctors and bureaucrats often claim that women's health centres duplicate services already available from general practitioners, hospital clinics, etc. Therefore, areas of 'need' for a women's health centre are defined by such measures as the distance from the nearest hospital, or the number of GPs per head of population in the region. If women's health centres offer nothing more than 'nice GP services', then such criteria might be appropriate. In that case, women's health centres could be characterised as an expensive luxury, offering mainstream medicine in a more friendly, all-women environment. But most women's health centres have gone 'a bit beyond the pap smear stage', as one worker expressed it. If the work of feminist women's health centres is qualitatively different from, or in some cases even subversive of, mainstream medical care (as I believe it should be and often is), then distance from a hospital is no indicator of whether there is a need for the service. Indeed, it would be only a little perverse to claim that women's health centres are needed even more in areas with many GPs and hospitals.

The new managerialism also favours what are known as 'generic managers', that is, officers who can move quickly and easily from one substantive area to another. When such values prevail, the femocrat's specialist knowledge and commitment cease to be qualifications for the job and become impediments to flexibility and mobility. Femocrats attending a Feminism and the State Workshop (held in Canberra, November 1989) spoke of increasing pressure against being too closely identified with the people for whom programs are implemented (see WEL National Bulletin, November/December 1989, for reports from the Workshop). Apparently the worst insult is to be accused of being 'client driven'. If it is unacceptable within state bureaucracies to advocate for particular groups on the basis of a combination of personal and professional expertise, the position of the femocrats will become even more vexed.

However useful and productive the femocracy may be, the advent of substantial numbers of women working in administrative positions for the state has had the unintended effect of institutionalising divisions in the women's movement. Contemporary feminism has never been a homogeneous, unified movement, and it would not be politically or historically accurate to claim that the employment of women in state bureaucracies has split the movement. But it has given structural expression to underlying divisions, particularly between women who work in women's services as opposed to those in policy and administration. The growth of the femocracy has also created the incorrect appearance that all women working within the bureaucracy are 'liberal' or 'reformist' in their orientation, while all those working outside it are 'socialist' or 'radical'. Those who recommend working in and through the state, who are resigned to some level of dependence on state funding, or who believe that state resources can be hijacked for feminist purposes, are all convinced that women exert greater leverage if feminists inside and outside the state can co-operate, a situation that is proving difficult to promote and sustain.

No systematic study has been conducted of the impact of the division between women inside and outside the state on the effectiveness of women's claims on the state, but from the perspective of the 1990s, getting women into positions of power in the state has had some consequences—for the women themselves, and for the women's movement more generally—that were not anticipated when the first women's advisory positions were created. A symptom of these difficulties is Mary Draper's proposal to establish a group called 'Women Who Don't Want to Be Women's Advisers'. It does not require a conspiracy theory to notice that the separation of women into distinct categories with distinct interests creates an opportunity for enemies of the broad feminist agenda to play women off against each other. Summers sees 'a divided and consequently weakened women's movement [as] one which politicians can more easily ignore' (1986: 60). For the work of women's health centres to thrive, women working inside and outside the state will have to continue to devise practical means of co-operation and mutual support. Their differences are real and consequential and will not disappear. But their objectives overlap enough for them to limit what Florynce Kennedy called 'horizontal hostility' (struggles between groups of women) in order to facilitate the important work in which they are all engaged. 'The main enemy', as Christine Delphy's title reminds us, is not other women but the oppression of women. The more hostile the environment, the more important co-operation and coalition-building become.

Whether in the 1970s or the 1990s, collaboration with the state is hazardous for groups with an oppositional ideology, because the state is characterised by and in turn promotes forms of social relations that tend to undermine community-based organisation. Specifically, Morgan (1981) identifies individualisation, bureaucratisation and professionalisation as three related processes that have diminished the radical potential of the refuge movement. These same processes are continuing dangers to the radical structure and objectives of the women's health movement.

Individualisation refers to the constitution of social issues as personal troubles, reversing C. Wright Mills's classic prescription which calls for the transformation of personal troubles into social issues (1959). Individualism is a powerful concept in the health field because of the long dominance of the strongly individualistic medical model. When issues are processed by the state, the tendency toward individualising increases because of the propensity to categorise people and problems so that the highest level of aggregation is the 'interest group'. Needs are defined as the needs of solitary 'persons', and services are organised to respond to needs that have been isolated from wider social processes. The political, economic and interpersonal contexts of problems are deleted from the analysis and hence from policies and services.

> Social problem management through the capitalist state serves to depoliticize political questions: to incorporate demands through quasimedical models, to individualize and personalize structural problems, and to obscure any class [including sex class] interests inherent in them (Morgan, 1981: 21).

Bureaucratisation was discussed in some detail in Chapter 5, and it is reintroduced in this Chapter through consideration of the pressure toward specialist, hierarchal organisation and the development of work routines designed to generate official records and statistics. Whereas individualisation operates on the definition of the problems that women's health centres seek to re-define and address, bureaucratisation operates at the organisational level, threatening the capacity of women's health centres to sustain means that are congruent with their ends. It remains a major hazard to the pursuit of feminist objectives.

Professionalisation has also been a long-term concern of the women's health movement, and a process toward which the movement has generated an explicitly skeptical orientation (see Chapters 2 and 5). As States more closely monitor and scrutinise women's health centres, centres are required to appoint staff with specified professional qualifications as a condition of the grant. If a centre is seen as an extension of a State health department instead of an independent community-based NGO, it may be expected to take permanent health department employees as staff, people who will be assigned on the basis of professional qualifications and who cannot be assumed to have the politics or the commitments of feminist health centres as priorities. If this concern seems far-fetched, it is sobering to recall that at the time of the final crisis at Hindmarsh, the South Australian Health Commission considered the staff of the Centre to be employees of the Health Commission, and although there were questions about the legality of the move, it succeeded in imposing direct supervision by one of its officers on the activities of the Centre staff.

Although these problems have plagued women's health centres from their inception, they may be of special relevance in the 1990s because of the very accomplishments of the women's health movement. While the centres established during the 1970s and early 1980s were all clearly the results of community initiatives, sometimes against the resistance of the state, women's health has now become more or less accepted as an appropriate concern of most States, and the subject of detailed policies and programs, both State and Federal. The advent of the policies, however, has meant that governments, not women in the community, may increasingly define needs, and nominate the structures and priorities to meet those needs. When governments rather than communities initiate community development, the nature of the enterprise can shift (Dixon, 1989).

This kind of 'reform from above' (Dowse, 1982: 208) is evident in the Victorian experience of the late 1980s in which, after consultations, the health bureaucracy decided on a set of initiatives which were advertised for tender to groups of women in the community. Existing women's services, several of which had been in operation for many years, were uncertain about whether they would continue to be funded if they did not agree to tender for the new services that the Health Department announced, but they believed that the work they were doing was still valuable and at least as important as what women were now 'invited' to undertake. The older groups chose to persevere with their existing services, but they have continued to suffer from funding difficulties. There was also concern that groups would be thrown into competition with one another over scarce resources rather than supporting and encouraging one another's projects. In the event, constructive relations have been built up between the older services and those developed in response to the government's recent initiative, but it has not been smooth sailing. The effect could easily have been to fragment the Victorian women's health movement. Co-operation was facilitated when Nancy Peck moved from the Women's Health Information Resources Collective to become Director of the new Healthsharing Women.

Another example of a very different pattern of foundation can be seen in the Albury-Wodonga Women's Centre. A Women's Health Collective had been meeting during 1985–86, considering the possibility of establishing a co-operative that would build on the services of the existing family planning clinic. The group had decided they did not want a Health Department funded centre because of the constraints that would impose, but staff of the NSW Health Department prepared a submission for a women's health centre and granted the money, although there was no group ready to receive it. I am not aware of any other instance in which money was forthcoming when it was not clear exactly to whom funding had been granted. The original group had chosen not to seek government funding, and no other group had formed with an idea of what they might want from a women's health centre. Consequently many women from the original collective stood aside, wanting no association with this project. Others tried to decide what to do with the money that had become available; still others maintained a more peripheral involvement to keep an eye on developments. A management committee was not established until after the money was received, and more than half of the original committee members were NSW Health Department employees.

In describing the extraordinary beginnings of this Centre, I do not mean to suggest that its work is not effective. They appear to have developed a small, active organisation that maintains good working relations with other agencies in the area and takes the health of local women seriously. Their feminism is spelled out explicitly in their public documents despite their location in a highly conservative community which apparently still regards them with some suspicion. Nevertheless, the process of their foundation is fraught with dangers. If governments take the initiative, they may well determine the priorities and dictate the structures. Groups of women may end up providing cheap social and health services identified by the State as important, instead of organising on the basis of a critical feminist analysis of the needs of women in the community and setting a course of action on that basis. Having put women's health on the political agenda requires vigilance to be sure that it does not become redefined by its new legitimacy: redefined in a way to mobilise votes, conform to bureaucratic procedures, or simplify the lives (and budgets) of officers of State public services. As MacKinnon has said, 'you become what you do not resist' (1990: 5).

THE HAZARDS OF HEALTH

If there are perennial dangers to the women's movement from co-operation with the state, there are also hazards arising from women's involvement in the health field. Chapter 2 explored the way medicine developed as an institution of social control, particularly the control of women. The feminist analysis of these processes is one of the major motivations giving rise to the women's health movement and women's health centres. The impetus to start women's health centres arose from a conviction that doctors had seized control of the female body. Feminist health education and health care were designed to restore to women control over their own bodies and their lives. In the comments that follow, I do not intend to suggest that these were inconsequential interventions, nor do I mean that they have lost their importance. This book is written as an affirmation of women's health centres and their accomplishments. My purpose here is to identify three dangers inherent in the women's health centre project that may frustrate the very aims for which the centres are working. The first danger is that they may be appropriated into the control and surveillance functions of traditional medicine. The second related danger is that the very successes of the women's health movement may expose it to unanticipated consequences such as the commercialisation of womens health services. Finally, there is a danger that the objectives of the women's health movement are formulated in terms that implicitly accept the medical definition of women's bodies instead of developing a theoretical approach that can contest the very concept of the universal female body.

Medical reappropriation

Taking money from the state makes health centres vulnerable to cooptation to the state's agenda. In a more subtle way, working in the health field makes centres vulnerable to taking on the very activities of establishment medicine to which they have objected: social control and surveillance of the population. Some refuges have become keenly aware of the potential for their programs to serve as a cheap means of managing domestic violence and depoliticising the issue (Morgan, 1981). Health centres are also vulnerable to this reappropriation if they become enmeshed in government bureaucracies which, for example, use their records to police welfare fraud, tax evasion, illegal abortions, or drug offences.

The processes of incorporation can develop in even more subtle ways, however. As a women's health centre becomes more institutionalised, and consequently ideological commitment becomes less central in the recruitment of staff, the activities of the centre may come to reproduce the old relations between medical professionals and 'patients' in a new setting instead of changing the nature of the client–professional relationship. This has always been recognised as a problem in the recruitment of doctors, since there are few 'ideologically correct' female medical practitioners. But the problem can develop in relation to other staff as well. Inevitably when the work of women's health centres becomes more a job than a vocation, women will apply to work there because of the hours, the location, or some generalised interest rather than out of an informed commitment to feminism or the political and anti-establishment goals of the feminist health movement.

Unless centres screen for feminist credentials at the point of recruitment, or require appropriate on-the-job training for new staff, the political 'centre of gravity' will inevitably shift. Staff will be hired who have been through the mainstream training and socialisation that produces workers in the industry who define health problems in individual terms, and who regard professional knowledge and skills as the only legitimate sources of solutions to such problems. The Victorian 'Community Development in Health Project' (1990) has proposed several ways of 'reorienting' the values, theoretical and practical skills of health workers. These include time for reflective discussion and documenting case studies, long-term strategic planning, peer support, community accountability, discussions of inequalities in health, and giving high priority to interpersonal skills (Community Development in Health Project, 1990: 84–5). Many women's health centres already pursue similar activities, and others might usefully consider adapting them to their program.

Implementing feminist principles in daily work presents many challenges, even to workers who have a long history of reading, thinking about, and discussing these ideas. Workers who are new to such ideas may find them confusing, irrelevant, and unnecessary complications in a busy work schedule. But without a careful and consistent determination to develop different ways of conceptualising and dealing with health and health problems, inertia is likely to drag the everyday activities of clinical organisations toward medicine's traditional functions: the management of disorder and the containment of protest—the price that individuals and groups have typically had to pay for clinical care.

All fame ...

On his letterhead, mystery writer Arthur Upfield had the inscription: 'All fame and no bloody money'. That motto might well be adopted by many of Australia's women's health centres. Increasingly, their work is being recognised as constructive, significant, even trailblazing. But most of the grants remain meagre. The case of the Multicultural Women's Health Centre in Fremantle is full of ironies that will be familiar to women elsewhere. Approximately 400 women a month now use the services of the Centre (which is described in Chapter 3). Founder and co-ordinator Ronelle Brossard has been nationally recognised for her work with women from non-English-speaking backgrounds. In 1988, she received a *Woman '88* award from the Bicentennial Authority. In 1989, she was Fremantle Citizen of the Year, and in 1990, the Centre was awarded a gold medal by the Public Health Association for its community work with women from non-English-speaking backgrounds. Unfortunately, none of the awards carries a money prize, and despite such acclaim, the Centre still cannot afford a full-time receptionist or nurse, and there is no funding for a health educator. The most recent grant from the Western Australian Health Department was for less than half the amount for which the Centre had applied.

While Australian community health centres struggle to stay afloat, in the United States, women's health (like everything else) has become commodified, and commercial interests have opened attractive clinics which use seminars and health education to recruit paying patients (Worcester and Whatley, 1988). These clinics represent a different kind of recognition: the recognition that women constitute a market that has not yet been fully exploited. At their worst, these initiatives represent 'nothing more than a use of rhetoric from the women's health movement, while serving a purpose in direct contradiction to the goals of the movement' (Whatley, 1988: 132). The possibility that some of these centres may offer improved services to some women presents American women's health activists with a dilemma of how to respond to them, since they are clearly not oriented to the most disadvantaged sectors of the population (women of colour and poor women), and because of fears that the centres will exaggerate medicalisation. At present, there is little evidence of a major movement to such commercial centres in Australia, although a few private fee-for-service women's health centres have been established. The pressure of private medical and hospital interests is never far from the surface in Australia, and a change of government or of health policy could create a more favourable environment for these initiatives. Innovations do not always yield what their advocates intend. Health workers must be vigilant to avoid 'innovation without benefit' (Nuller, 1990: 230).

Whose body? Whose health?

In the struggle over women's health, feminists have put forward the view that medicine is a set of beliefs and practices located socially, politically and economically, and shaped by its locations as much as any other set of beliefs and practices. In advancing this view, a central concept has been the idea of the medical takeover of knowledge and management of women's bodies. Feminist discussions of obstetrics in particular have been informed by the belief that women were gradually excluded from a set of activities (aptly described by Aboriginal women as 'women's business') that had once been women's exclusive domain. The women's health movement has sought to enable women to 'reclaim control' of their bodies and lives.

Politically, the analysis of the medical takeover has been vital because it gave vivid and specific meaning to the notion of medicalisation, and it communicated an understanding of the personal implications of the long-term medicalisation and professionalisation of life, the rise of the expert, and of the gendered character of these processes. On the other hand, there is a weakness in the very analysis that has served so well in organising feminist thinking about the relationship between medicine and women's lives, and in mobilising a vigorous resistance to medical dominance of women's lives. Although doctors and women disagree about who should define, manage and control women's bodies, implicitly they agree that there is an essential, transhistorical female body that has been increasingly accurately revealed by western science (Harcourt, 1987:10). In traditional histories of medicine, women's bodies are depicted as enslaving them to their uncontrolled reproductive processes and malfunctions. The rise of medicine is represented as liberating women through the discoveries and interventions of medical science. Feminist histories, by contrast, concentrate on the sociotechnical capture by male medicine of women's reproductive potential and their corporeal experiences. But they do not dispute the underlying scientific representations of women's bodies, and indeed scientific and medical research is frequently cited as evidence of the factual basis of the feminist (as opposed to the clinical) definition of a condition or its management.

The feminist health movement insists on the legitimacy of women's bodily experience and assigns priority to that experience. Sometimes the movement has argued that medical intervention has distorted what would otherwise be natural (as opposed to social) processes. Childbirth is the prime example. Doctors defined pregnancy and birth as medical emergencies requiring active medical management. We are told that until the progress of modern obstetrics, women were in great peril, and the hazards of birth were exacerbated by dirty, superstitious old midwives. Feminists insist that pregnancy and birth are healthy, natural functions requiring strong, healthy women attended by other women. Medical men intruded into a female domain in an effort to strip women of their most fundamental and uniquely female power. In sum, feminists argue that medicine got it wrong about the essential meaning of the female body. But in the feminist revision, the notion of an essential transhistorical and universal meaning of the female body remains. The revision instates a fundamentally powerful, healthy woman in the place of the fundamentally weak and diseased creature of mainstream science and medicine, but it still relies on a conviction that women's bodies are, ultimately, everywhere and always the same.

As long as the women's health movement subscribes wholeheartedly to the understanding of the body as existing outside history and culture (an understanding it shares with western medical science), we remain vulnerable to struggles over the 'truth' regarding the female body, struggles we may win in some cases but lose in others. In these circumstances, an alternative approach to thinking about the female body would now be welcome, an approach that did not commit feminists to scientific adjudication on every point. Such an approach could acknowledge the discursive constitution of the body, including the sexed body. That is, it could consider that the female body as it is understood 'scientifically' or 'experientially' is not a preexisting, timeless essence which can be accurately depicted or whose spontaneous natural functions can be distorted. Rather, 'the body' as studied or lived is always in the process of being produced socially, culturally and psychically. At times it may be useful to describe the body in terms of organ systems, tissues, and cells; to describe bodily disturbance in terms of infections or injuries; and to manipulate the structure or function of the body through physical or chemical interventions. But the effectiveness of such interventions is not proof that the schemes of scientific anatomy and physiology therefore capture the essence of the body. Like all other knowledge, medicine and the sciences (including anatomy and physiology) are products of social relations. They are knowledges imbued with values and commitments, knowledges whose application has specific social as well as physical consequences. Similarly, at other times, it may be useful to describe the body in terms of other frameworks of understanding, including women's knowledges, feelings, values, and commitments. Bodily interventions based on these knowledges will also have consequences, both social and physical. But

> as a locus of power/knowledge the body is not a possession to be owned or captured by one group or another. There is no true body which can be salvaged once male medical views have been stripped away. The understanding of the body is not separable from the institutions which created it (Harcourt, 1987: 26).

If the women's health movement can elaborate and deploy understandings of the female body that appreciate its ongoing social constitution and its historical specificity, we will be better able to identify the issues we should treat as non-negotiable, and to distinguish them from issues on which compromise is less costly. I believe, however, that our capacity to make such judgments effectively is limited if we rely entirely on an analysis which is based on the simple objective of 'reclaiming control of women's bodies'. While retaining such an analysis, we should be sensitive to its limitations, and should work to develop more complex understandings that can lay the foundations for more effective personal and political action.

THE BODY CONTROLLED?

At the end of such a story, one wants to know what women's health centres have accomplished. Are they, indeed, doing what they set out to do? To answer that question, one would need to investigate issues such as the effect of women's health centres on traditional medicine, on the staff in women's health centres, and on women in the community. It is beyond the scope of this book to inquire into these effects in detail, and it would be a challenging research task to identify the influence of women's health centres, distinguished from other factors contributing to social change. But it is possible to indicate the directions in which one might look for answers, on the basis of the fragments of evidence now available.

Regarding the impact on mainstream health care, there are conflicting patterns. As we saw in Chapter 2, medical resistance to the women's health movement has been vigorous. In the United States, a litigious society, women's health centres were raided by police and workers arrested for practising medicine without a license. A pregnant police officer was sent under cover to infiltrate an American alternative birth collective, resulting in the arrest of lay midwives. In a judgment that heartened women's health activists, the court ruled that 'because pregnancy was not a disease, midwives could not be practicing [sic] medicine without a license' (Ruzek, 1980: 346). Australian women's health workers have also been legally charged, particularly regarding the provision of abortion to minors. Most arrests were never prosecuted or else they resulted in acquittals, but at least one woman (in the US) pleaded guilty, was fined and put on probation (Hornstein, 1974: 35). Nevertheless, the arrests signal the united front that medicine and the state have, at times, mounted against the women's health movement.

The publicity surrounding arrests and court cases may, of course, have informed some women of a service about which they had previously not known, and American trials galvanised the women's health movement. The 1970s wave of prosecutions did not continue, apparently because 'bringing cases to court on charges of practicing [sic] medicine without a license just makes authorities appear foolish and, like many repressive measures, generates movement solidarity'. Apparently in the United States, medical opposition to feminist abortion clinics has remained vigorous, and clinics and clinic staff have been subjected to 'harassment and interference by both medical and legal authorities' (Ruzek, 1980: 342). The sometimes violent harassment of women seeking abortions in the United States has received international publicity. Although such action may be less frequent and less extreme in Australia, women exercising a hard-won legal right are still liable to abuse from right-to-life campaigners. Other women are also punished for trying to take charge of their own health. For example, women planning birth at home who must be transferred to hospital have sometimes found that their admission is delayed, and the hospital often refuses permission for the homebirth attendant to accompany the mother into the hospital. In the late 1970s, the American College of Obstetricians and Gynecologists went so far as to define home birth as 'child abuse'. Some Australian doctors who attend births at home have been subjected to professional sanction, and a few have been prosecuted, even though parents did not complain. Just as this book was going to press, the legality of the Commonwealth's Women's Health Program was being challenged in court. Ironically, the challenge was mounted by an officer of the Department of Community Services and Health, Alex Proudfoot. In his capacity as a private citizen, Proudfoot complained to the Human Rights Commission that the Women's Health Program, and women's health services funded by it, discriminate against men because of the lack of comparable funding for men's services. Commissioner Quentin Bryce refused to investigate the complaint because the Sex Discrimination Act permits such activities under a 'special measures' section. Proudfoot then asked the Federal Court to overturn Bryce's decision (*The Age*, 1 March 1991). At the time of writing the judge ruled that the Commission was required to undertake a full inquiry into the claim that the Women's Health Program is discriminatory.

While powerful resistance continues, there is little doubt that the women's health movement also serves as a catalyst and demonstration project for other forms of health care. Several books have now appeared which discuss how feminist principles can be introduced into mainstream health care settings (for example, Webb, 1986, and Rosser, 1988). An American study found that women were more likely to hold leadership positions in non-traditional than in traditional clinics, and that the influence of these clinics was being felt in mainstream medicine. They cited as examples the increased acceptance of health care teams, health education, and consumer participation in management (Rowland and Schneiderman, 1979). It is likely that similar changes in Australian medical care have similar sources. Universities routinely send medical, nursing, and social work students to observe or do projects or student placements at women's health centres. Some of the same bureaucracies (perhaps even the same bureaucrats) who obstructed the establishment of women's health centres now claim them as accomplishments and examples. An indicator of the proportions of the change can be gauged from Ruzek's observation that, 'Feminist Women's Health Collective representatives. . .found it. . .incongruous that the same public agencies which had been harassing them with threats of arrest were now paying them to fly to Sacramento to provide "expert" opinions' (1978:230).

The self-health movement has drawn heavily on the women's health movement for both information and ways of organising (Wyndham, 1981). In many ways, Australian women's health centres have served as the shock troops of the community health movement. In concert with rape crisis and refuge collectives, they invented the philosophy and many of the structures and procedures that are now more or less generally (if sometimes reluctantly) accepted. They were part of a movement that created the necessity for governments to devise new mechanisms for dealing with community-based organisations. The centres and the States have had to make it up as they went, and not all (either centres *or* governments) have been equally willing to innovate and compromise.

Less is known about the impact on workers of working at a women's health centre. Schlesinger and Bart's study of women working in the Chicago abortion collective 'Jane' found that the majority of the women who participated reported an increased sense of personal competence and an improved self-concept. Despite the fact that many of them were already politicised before they joined the collective, a majority also reported an increased commitment to feminism as a result of their involvement, and the political and personal changes tended to occur in the same women (1982: 145–48).

Although I did not explore it systematically, many of the women with whom I talked volunteered great pride in their accomplishments and a keen awareness of what they had gained from their work. As one doctor put it, 'What we did shows that women can do *anything*'. Doris Hovarth and Silver Moon, who were active during the volunteer phase of Hindmarsh, described the collective's dawning awareness that they actually ran the centre, that they employed the doctors, that they had the power to make decisions that would determine the centre's future, and that they had the responsibility to be competent because women were turning to them for help in serious crises. They flourished in the awareness that they could and did help, and help in ways that empowered other women. Doris said she realised, 'You have to take the power. Nobody is going to give it to you. We were the ones defining what the health care was'. Silver added that through working at Hindmarsh, she learned that 'The patriarchy is there, and you can empower yourself to take the action you need to to get rid of it'. Other workers from other centres described similar personal growth resulting from their involvement. Denele Crozier, Administrator of WHIRCCA and a worker at Liverpool, observed that when people talk about collectives they complain about the problems, but when they are asked what they got out of working in a collective they identify profound gains in such areas as self-identity, sense of personal power, and an extended range of competence. For herself, Denele feels much more able to work in mixed groups, having worked in a feminist collective. It allowed her to develop competence, experience taking responsibility and making decisions, and to become more aware of sexism for what it is.

There have also been casualties, women whose experiences are disillusioning and alienating. Even those who were already 'schooled in collective conflict' sometimes found the battles that broke out in and around women's health centres fiercer than anything they had experienced elsewhere. In a few cases, violent harassment was one weapon of the feminist wars, and there are women who have made lifelong enemies. Even women who remain involved in women's services have scars, and a few have become permanently estranged from the women's movement. Their stories remain largely unrecorded, a painful dark side of feminism. They are paying the price of the movement's achievements. One woman, an optimistic survivor at that, said 'The women's movement has to stop pretending it's nice'.

Least of all is known about how feminist health services are received by the women who attend them as clients. Centres are always busy, which shows that enough women value their services to fill the appointments, but that could be a reflection of the lack of primary care services in the area. Centres have never had the resources to do much systematic research on who comes to them, and no-one has investigated the equally important question of who does not come to them. The consultations leading to the national women's health policy showed a desire among women all over the country for access to women doctors and other health care practitioners. As far as we know, at least most of the clients of women's health centres value the services and education they receive there. The first client at Leichhardt arrived in such a desperate state that they saw her immediately, even though the Centre had not yet opened. Such urgency is not uncommon, and workers report that they often see women who have 'been everywhere' by the time they arrive at a women's health centre. As Chapter 1 showed, the distances some women have travelled to women's health centres also suggest the importance of the services.

There is some evidence that clients of feminist services benefit from going there. Marieskind compared the levels of knowledge of women attending a feminist self-help facility with women attending conventional services, and found that women going to the feminist clinic were much better informed about their bodies and how to manage their own care (1976: 65). An English study of women attending two feminist Well Woman Clinics in Manchester found that clients appreciated the amount of time given to consultations, and the sympathy and understanding they were shown (Foster, 1989: 345). Similarly, women who had stayed at an English women's refuge liked the friendliness and the help and mutual support (Pahl, 1985: 30–1). An evaluation of a women's clinic in California showed that many women mentioned 'the feeling that they have more control over their own health' (Palmer, 1974: 714).

Perhaps the most substantial evidence of women's feelings about the centres is the continuing willingness of women all over the country to lobby for their establishment. While some have suggested that the work of women's health centres is now substantially done, hundreds of women continue to invest thousands of hours to start, organise, and run women's health centres. The number of centres could double as a result of the National Women's Health Program, and the influx of government funding is clearly a response to widespread community support. Government initiatives continue to be heavily subsidised by women's unpaid time and energy. Despite the contradictions discussed in this book, the story of women's health centres is a story of a vigorous and diverse movement that is changing the face of women's health care in Australia. It is said that Australia has more women's health centres per head of population than anywhere else in the world. Virtually all the women I have interviewed feel—whatever their current circumstances and despite continuing difficulties—that women's health centres are part of a fundamental change in basic health care, and that they can claim several important achievements. Except for remote areas, contraception is now nearly universally available. Despite recurring efforts to curtail it, abortion remains legal and available in most states. Much more health information is in the hands of consumers than in the early 1970s. Some doctors are gradually becoming more willing to involve patients in their own care—that is, to act more like consultants to their clients and less like patriarchal authorities. A wider array of alternative therapeutic, illness-prevention and health promotion services are now generally available. The States and the Commonwealth are all finding that they have to take women's health seriously. None of these achievements can be credited to women's health centres alone, but the centres have been significant actors in their accomplishment.

> It may never be possible to say that women have control over their bodies, for bodies do not always behave in predictable or controllable ways, but women will one day be able to say that their bodies are not in the control of anyone else (Greer in Healthsharing Women, 1990: ix).

The future is never secure, but a generation is growing up that simply assumes that it will have access to health services by women, for women: something unimaginable in 1974, when Leichhardt Women's Community Health Centre was born. Women have always voted with their feet for women's health centres. Few centres have had to advertise because they always had more business than they could handle. In the early days, news of the centres was spread by word-of-mouth, newspaper articles, or referrals from agencies or doctors who were unable or unwilling to deal with a woman's needs.

Now women find their way to women's services through another avenue. In the late 1980s, a young woman contacting the Brisbane Women's Health Centre was asked how she found out about the Centre. Apparently mystified by the question, she replied: 'I looked you up in the phone book. Under "W" for *women*'.

Endnotes

1 THE FIRST OF THEIR KIND

1. This group is different from another Melbourne group with a similar name, the Women's Health Resource Collective (later renamed the Women's Health Information Resource Collective), which was opened in 1983 with grant money. The Resource Collective has never sought to provide clinical service.

2. For example, the Women's Archive in Canberra, having started on volunteer labour, ran for more than a year on CEP funds.

2 WOMEN'S HEALTH AND THE WOMEN'S MOVEMENT

1. Although increased use of condoms appears to indicate some increase in men's willingness to share contraceptive responsibility with their partners, I think it can be shown that the contraceptive effects of condoms are a more or less welcome byproduct of AIDS prevention, although condoms are likely to have benefits for women's sexual health apart from preventing unwanted pregnancies and the spread of AIDS. For example, barrier contraceptives have long been known to reduce the transmission of STDs, and it appears that they also reduce the risk of cervical cancer.

2. Ironically, fewer women than men have specialised in obstetrics (Fett, 1971; current data courtesy John Deeble). The nature of the specialist training requirements has effectively excluded anyone who cannot commit themselves to an uninterrupted and extremely demanding schedule during the optimal childbearing years. This is also true of other specialties, but obstetrics and surgery have particularly poor records for attracting women.

3. A partial remedy for medical dominance of childbirth is evident in the establishment of domiciliary birthing services and birthing centres run by midwives. I suspect these developments are results of the combined efforts of feminist and non-feminist pressure groups. The changing 'market' for

obstetric services (i.e., falling birth rate) also puts pressure on professionals to supply the kinds of services clients want.

4. The concept of the 'natural' is problematic, and has generated a literature of its own, exploring the proposition that the very idea of 'nature' is itself a social product which cannot be divorced from its discursive context, and which is infused with a range of diverse and contradictory meanings. 'Deconstructing the natural' has become a project for certain schools of feminist theory. See, for example, Brown and Adams, 1979.

3 THE WOMEN'S HEALTH MOVEMENT AND THE STATE

1. I use the term the state (lower case) to refer to the institution of government in its most general sense, not differentiating any particular branch, level, agency or activity. Where I use the State (upper case), I mean the six States that, in federation with each other and the two Territories, comprise Australia.

2. The impact of the women's health movement on health policy making is the subject of a research project currently being undertaken by Dr Gwen Gray of the ANU Department of Political Science.

Appendix I
People interviewed

Jude Abbs
Pat Ann
Pamela Ashton
Jocelyn Auer
Janet Bacon
Colin Bailey
Barbara Beard
Ronelle Brossard
Chris Brown
Ann Bruce
Vivienne Burke

Mary Callcott
Chris Campbell
Helen Campbell
Sharyn Campbell
Anita Carol
Jenny Chuck
Nola Cooper
Carol Cragg
Denele Crozier
Jane Cruikshank
Areti Devetzidis

Pam Ditton
Jan Donovan
Sara Dowse
Pip Duncan
Sophie Dwyer
Jeannie Edgar
Sue Eslick
Sally Farnes
Lyndall Fowler
Wendy Freeman

Luisa Fuller

Bridget Gardner
Gloria Garton
Helen Garton
Lesley Garton
Christine Giles

Christine Gillespie
Sue Goodwin
Gerri Greenfield
Megan Halbert
Suzanne Hollis
Karin Hoffman
Doris Horvath
Bon Hull
Cheryl Ison
Terri Jackson
Zoy Katzan
Helen Keogh
Sylvia Kinder
Michele Koski

Carol Low
Yoni Luxford
Marg Madder
Marlene McAlear
John McCauley
Linley McGrath
Lynn McKenzie
Barbara McLennan
Pip March
Thea Mendelsohn
Karen Mitchell

Silver Moon
Trish Morgan
Helen Morris
Ea Mulligan

Daina Neveraskas
Liza Newby
Sue Ng
Patricia O'Brien
Sheila O'Neil
Joan O'Reilly
Jo Parrish
Nancy Peck
Fiona Percy
Leeanne Purdom

Lynn Reid
Liz Rivers
Aqua Robbins
Lou Rosenstein
Joan Ross
Lyndall Ryan
Lesley Savage
Sidney Sax
Lea Shaw
Stefania Siedlecky
Beryl Smith
Meg Smith
Rose Sorger
Lorraine Spears
Sally Speed
Onella Stagoll

Bev Stewart
Margaret Stewart
Elizabeth Stroud
Di Surgie

Kath Taperell
Margaret Taylor
Jan Tilden
Vera Tompkinson
Vi Tourle
Carol Treloar
Tranh le Trinh
Anna Vella

Molly Wakeley
Deb Wardle
Paula Watt
Barbara Wertheim
Donelle Wheeler
Jennifer Wilson
Kathy Wilson
Lorann Yen
Annie Zon

Annie
Claire
Daphne
Eloise
Leslie
Lotus
Susie
Toni

Appendix II
Names and addresses of current women's health centres

NEW SOUTH WALES

Albury Wodonga Women's Centre
PO Box 1076
(440B Wilson St)
Albury, NSW 2640
(060) 411–977

Bankstown Women's Health Centre
74 Restwell St
Bankstown NSW 2200
(02) 790–1378

Blacktown Women's and Girls' Health
  Centre
15 + 17 Kildare Road
PO Box 2092, Westpoint
Blacktown, Sydney, NSW 2148
(02) 831–5133

Blue Mountains Women's Health
  Centre
124 Lurline St
Katoomba NSW 2780
(047) 82–5133

Central Coast Community Women's
  Health Centre
(Gosford Women's Health Centre)
PO Box 10
West Gosford NSW 2250
(043) 24–2533/24–2251

Central West Women's Health Centre
PO Box 674
(20 William St)
Bathurst, NSW 2795
(063) 31–4133

Coffs Harbour Women's Health
  Centre
29 Park Beach Road
Coffs Harbour, NSW 2450
(066) 52–8111

Cumberland Women's Health
  Association
PO Box 78
Parramatta, NSW 2150
(71 Grand Ave, Westmead)
(02) 635–3794

Hunter Region Working Women's
  Centre
(Newcastle)
PO Box 38
(Corner Industrial Drive and Avon St)
Mayfield, NSW 2304
(049) 68–2511

Illawarra Women's Community Health
  Centre
PO Box 61
(2/14 Belfast Avenue)
Warilla, NSW 2528
(042) 96–7077

Leichhardt Women's Health Centre
PO Box 240
(55 Thornley St)
Leichhardt, NSW 2040
(02) 560-3011

Lismore and District Women's Health
  Centre
27 McKenzie St
Lismore, NSW 2480
(066) 21-9627

Liverpool Women's Community
  Health Centre
26 Bathurst St (corner Campbell St)
Liverpool, NSW 2170
(02) 601-3555

Moruya Women's Information Centre
PO Box 107
Moruya, NSW 2537
(044) 74-2747

Penrith Women's Health Centre
PO Box 398
(230 Derby St)
Penrith, NSW 2750
(047) 21-8749

Shoalhaven Women's Health Centre
PO Box 314
(59 Osborne St)
Nowra, NSW 2541
(044) 210-730

Sutherland Shire Women's Health +
  Info. Centre
346A The Kingsway
Caringbah, NSW 2229
(02) 525-2058

Wagga Wagga Women's Health Centre
PO Box 258 S
(8 Morrow St)
South Wagga NSW 2650
(069) 21-3333

Waminda S. Coast Aboriginal
  Women's Health
PO Box 978
(47 Berry St)
Nowra NSW 2541
(044) 21-7745

WILMA Women's Health Centre
PO Box 415
(298 Queen St)
Campbelltown, NSW 2560
(046) 272-955

Women's Health in Industry
66 Railway St
Lidcombe, NSW 2141
(02) 646-2400

QUEENSLAND

Brisbane Women's Health Centre
  PO Box 665
(165 Gregory Terrace)
Spring Hill, Q 4004
(07) 839-9962 (008) 017-676

Hervie Bay Women's Health Centre
  PO Box 534
Pialba, Q 4655
(071) 243-280

North Queensland Combined
  Women's Services
Townsville Women's Centre
50 Patrick St
Aitkenvale, Townsville, Q 4814
(077) 75-7555

Rockhampton Women's Health Centre
PO Box 6395
Rockhampton, Q 4700
(079) 226-585

SOUTH AUSTRALIA

Adelaide Hills and Southern Fleuriu
  Peninsula Women's Health Service
c/- Mt Baker Soldier's Memorial
  Hospital
Mt Baker, SA 5251
(08) 391-1104

Adelaide Women's Community Health
  Centre
64 Pennington Terrace
North Adelaide, SA 5006

(08) 267-5366

Dale Street Women's Health Centre
56 Dale St
Port Adelaide, SA 5015
(08) 477-033

Elizabeth Women's Community
  Health Centre
Elizabeth Way
Elizabeth, SA 5112
(08) 252-3711

The Murray Mallee Women's Health
  Service Project
C/- Murray Bridge Soldier's Memorial
Hospital
PO Box 346
Murray Bridge, SA 5253
(085) 328-333

Southern Women's Health and Community Centre
PO Box 429
(88 Dyson Road, Christies Beach)
Noarlunga Centre, SA 5168
(08) 384-9777

The Upper Spencer Gulf Women's
  Health Service
C/- Port Augusta Hospital
Hospital Road
Port Augusta, SA 5700
(086) 410-228

TASMANIA

Hobart Women's Health Centre
PO Box 237
North Hobart, Tas. 7002
(9 Pierce St, Moonah)
(002) 28-0997

Women's Health Line phone service
(008) 001-373 (toll free)
(002) 280-997 (Hobart)

WESTERN AUSTRALIA

Multicultural Women's Health Centre
114 South St
Fremantle, WA 6160
(09) 335-8214

Whitfords Women's Health Service
21 Endeavour Rd
Whitford, WA 6061
(09) 307-6619

Women's Health Care House
100 Aberdeen St
Northbridge, Perth, WA 6000
(09) 227-8122

Women's Health Centre (Goldfields)
PO Box 370,
(12 Dugan St)
Kalgoorlie, WA 6430
(090) 21-8266

VICTORIA

Barwon and South West Region
  Women's Health Service
61 Packington St
Geelong West, Vic. 3220
(052) 232-777

Central Highlands/Wimmera
  Women's Health Service
c/- PO Box 73
Sebastopol, Vic. 3356

Healthsharing Women
318 Little Bourke St
(5th Floor, Information Victoria
  Building)
Melbourne, Vic. 3000
(03) 663-3544

Lodden Campaspe Women's Health
  Service
31 MacKenzie St
Bendigo, Vic. 3550
(054) 430-233

North East Women's Health Service
PO Box 1144
Lalor, Vic 3075

Outer Eastern Women's Health Service
116a Mount Dandenong Road
Ringwood East, Vic. 3135
(03) 879-2199

Wellcoming Women's Health Service
PO Box 1033
Horsham, Vic. 3402

Women in Industry, Contraception
and Health (WICH)
83 Johnston St
Fitzroy, Vic, 3065
(03) 416 3999

Women's Health Service
60 Droop St, corner Geelong Road
Footscray, Vic. 3011
(03) 689-9588

Women's Health Information
Resources Collective
PO Box 187
(563 Nicholson St)
Carlton North 3054
(03) 380-9974 or 387-8702

ACT

ACT Women's Health Service
ACT Board of Health
(06) 245-4111

ACT Women's Information and
Referral Service
ACT Board of Health
(06) 254-2555

Canberra Women's Health Centre
PO Box 1492
Woden, ACT 2606
(3 Dundas Court, Phillip, ACT 2606)

NORTHERN TERRITORY

Aboriginal and Islander
Women's Health Service
Bagot Community Health Centre
Bagot Rd
Ludmilla, NT 0820
(089) 852-930

Congress Alukura Women's Health
Service
13 Mueller St
Alice Springs, NT 0870
(089) 527-552

Darwin Women's Information Centre
Shop 5, Casurina Plaza
Casurina, NT 0810
(089) 277-166

Women's Information Centre
Helm House
Cnr Bath and Gregory Streets
Alice Springs, NT 0870
(089) 515-886

Appendix III
Timeline of events 1973–89

1973
- Women's Commission held on International Women's Day.

- *Control* applies for funding for women's health centre in Leichhardt (Sydney); funding received December.

1974
- Leichhardt Women's Community Health Centre opens (officially on IWD).

- Collingwood Women's Health Centre opens (Melbourne); volunteer service (never funded) provided clinical services until 1975, group work until 1978.

- Women's Health and Community Centre opens (Perth); funded in 1975, funding discontinued September 1976.

1975
- Brisbane Women's House Health Centre (Roma Street) opens; closed 1976 or 1977.

- Hunter Region Working Women's Centre (Mayfield) opens.

- Darwin Women's Health Centre opens; funding withdrawn, closed 1980.

- Liverpool Women's Health Centre opens.

- Hindmarsh Women's Health Centre (Mary Street) opens (officially 1976); funding suspended 1980, but continues to run as volunteer service until 1984.

1976
- Central Coast Women's Health Centre opens (Gosford); volunteer until 1979, when initial funding granted.

1977
- Alice Springs Women's Health Centre opens; funding withdrawn and closed 1980.

- Bankstown Women's Health Centre opens (funded 1985).

- Women's Health Care House (Perth) opens; funded by money previously granted to Perth Women's Health and Community Centre.

- Women in Industry, Contraception and Health (Melbourne) opens.

1978
No centres open

1979
- Wagga Women's Health Centre opens; volunteer until funding received 1984.

1980
- State health authority 'takeover' of Hindmarsh Women's Health Centre; funding suspended.

- Adelaide Women's Community Health Centre opens on funding previously granted to Hindmarsh.

- Funding withdrawn from both NT women's health centres (Darwin and Alice Springs).

1981
- Blue Mountains Women's Health Centre opens (unfunded until 1983/4).

1982
- WHIRCCA established.

- Coffs Harbour Women's Health Centre opens (funded 1986).

- Brisbane Women's Health Centre opens (Woollongabba).

1983
- Elizabeth Women's Health Centre (South Australia) opens.

- Southern Women's Health Centre (South Australia) opens.

- Women's Health Information Resource Collective (Carlton, Melbourne) opens.

1984
- Dale St.Women's Health Centre (Port Adelaide) opens.

- Welling Place privately funded alternative health service replaces Hindmarsh collective; operates until 1986.

- Jilimi Aboriginal Women's Health Centre (Nowra) opens.

- Women's Health in Industry (Lidcombe) opens.

- Illawarra Women's Community Health Centre opens.

1985
- Multicultural Women's Health Centre (Fremantle, WA) opens.

- Shoalhaven Women's Health Centre (Nowra) opens.

1986
- Women's Health Centre Albury-Wodonga opens.

- Central West Women's Health Centre (Bathurst) opens.

1987
- Blacktown Women and Girls Health Centre opens.

- Lismore and District Women's Health Centre opens.

- WILMA (Campbelltown) opens.

- Penrith Women's Health Centre opens.

- Hobart Women's Health Centre opens (limited funding).

- Congress Alukura (Alice Springs) opens.

1988
- Healthsharing Women (Melbourne) opens.

- Women's Health Service (Footscray) opens.

1989
- Commonwealth Women's Health Policy and Women's Health Program launched.

- Barwon Women's Health Centre (Geelong) opens.

- Goldfields (Kalgoorlie) Women's Health Centre opens.

- Lodden Campaspe (Bendigo) Women's Health Centre opens.

- Whitfords (North Perth) Women's Health Service opens.

Bibliography

Aboriginal women (1986) 'The Congress Alukura by the grandmother's law' *Health Issues* August/September: 17–20

Acker, Joan (1990) 'Hierarchies, jobs, bodies: a theory of gendered organizations' *Gender and Society* 4 (2): 139–58

Ahrens, Lois (1980) 'Battered women's refuges: feminist cooperatives vs. social service institutions' *Radical America* 14: 9–15

Albury, Rebecca (1981) 'Women's health—man-made medicine' *Scarlet Woman* 13: 6–11

Allen, Judith (1990) 'Does feminism need a theory of "the state"?' pp. 21–38 in Sophie Watson (ed.), *Playing the State: Australian Feminist Interventions* Sydney: Allen & Unwin

Auer, Jocelyn (1990) 'Encounters with the state: cooptation and reform, a case study from women's health' pp. 207–17 in Sophie Watson (ed.), *Playing the State: Australian Feminist Interventions* Sydney: Allen & Unwin

Auer, Jocelyn and Clare Shuttleworth (1990) 'Women's health: If you don't like it . . . ' *Australian Society* (February): 7–8

Australian Institute of Health (1989) *Achieving Australia's Preventable Cancer Targets: Available Statistics, Data Sources and Requirements*. Statistical Report to the Project Planning Team, National Better Health Program

———(1988) *Australia's Health* Canberra: Australian Government Publishing Service

Bacchi, Carol (1990) *Same Difference* Sydney: Allen & Unwin

Bacon, Wendy and Margo Moore (1978) 'Vaginal infections' pp. 97–103 in *Women's Health in a Changing Society* Conference Proceedings, Vol.2, Commonwealth Department of Health: Australian Government Publishing Service

Baldock, Cora Vellekoop (1990) *Volunteers in Welfare* Sydney: Allen & Unwin

Barfoot, Julia McKinney (1973) 'Free health care for women by women: The Berkeley Women's Health Collective' pp. 89–101 in Anne Kent Rush (ed.), *Getting Clear: Body Work for Women* New York: Random House

Barrett, Michele (1980) *Women's Oppression Today* London: Verso

Barrett, Michele and Helen Roberts (1978) 'Doctors and their patients' pp. 41–52 in Carol Smart and Barry Smart (eds), *Women, Sexuality and Social Control* London: Routledge

Barry, Kathleen (1972) 'The cutting edge: a look at male motivation in obstetrics and gynecology' Pittsburgh: KNOW Press

Bates, Erica and Helen Lapsley (1985) *The Health Machine: The Impact of Medical Technology* Ringwood: Penguin

Bernard, Jessie (1972) *The Future of Marriage* New York: Random House

Black, David et al. (1980) *Inequalities in Health: Report of A Research Working Group* London: Department of Health and Social Security

Boston Women's Health Book Collective

————(1984) *The New Our Bodies, Ourselves* New York: Simon and Schuster

————(1976) *Our Bodies, Ourselves* (Revised and Expanded Second Edition) New York: Simon and Schuster

————(1971) *Our Bodies, Ourselves* New York: Simon and Schuster

Bradnow, Karen, Jim McDonnell, and Vocations for Social Change (1976/1981) *No Bosses Here: A Manual on Working Collectively and Cooperatively* (Second Edition) Boston: Alyson Publications/Philadelphia: New Society Publishers

Broom, Dorothy H. (1989) 'Masculine medicine, feminine illness: gender and health' pp. 212–34 in Gillian Lupton and Jake Najman (eds), *Sociology of Health and Illness: Australian Readings* Melbourne: Macmillan

————(1984a) 'Natural resources: health, reproduction and the gender order' pp. 46–62 in D. H. Broom (ed.), *Unfinished Business: Social Justice for Women in Australia* Sydney: Allen & Unwin

————(1984b) 'Justifying injustice' pp. xiii–xxv in D. H. Broom (ed.), *Unfinished Business: Social Justice for Women in Australia* Sydney: Allen & Unwin

————(1984c) 'The medicalization of childbirth: a new role for the midwife' *Healthright* 4 (1): 10–14

Broom Darroch, Dorothy (1978) *Power and Participation: The Dynamics of Medical Encounters* Unpublished PhD Dissertation, Dept. of Sociology, RSSS, Australian National University

Broverman, I. K., D. M Broverman, F. E. Clarkson, P. S. Rosenkrantz, and S. R. Vogel (1970) 'Sex role stereotypes and clinical judgments of mental health' *Journal of Consulting and Clinical Psychology* 34: 1–7

————(1972) 'Sex role stereotypes: a current appraisal' *Journal of Social Issues* 28: 59–78

Brown, Beverly and Parveen Adams (1979) 'The feminine body and feminist politics' *m/f* No. 3: 35–50

Brown, George W. and T. Harris (1978) *The Social Origins of Depression: A Study of Psychiatric Disorder in Women* London: Tavistock

Brown, Stephanie (1986) 'Action on women's health' *Health Issues* May/June: 12–14

Browne, Karen (1976) 'Reassessing basics' *Quest: A Feminist Quarterly* 2 (Winter): 31–7

Bryson, Lois (1987) 'Comment on Fraser II' *Thesis Eleven* No. 17: 110–13

Bryson, Lois and Martin Mowbray (1986) 'Who cares? Social security, family policy and women' *International Social Security Journal* No. 2: 183–200

Bunch, Charlotte (1987) *Passionate Politics* New York: St Martin's Press

Bunch, Charlotte and Beverly Fisher (1976) 'What future for leadership' *Quest: A Feminist Quarterly* 2 (4): 2–13

Caddick, Alison (1986) 'Feminism and the body' *Arena* 74: 61–88

Caddick, Alison and Rhonda Small (1982) 'Women in Industry: Contraception and Health' *Scarlet Woman* 15: 9–12

Carter, Betty, Gilean Hussen and Lana Abbott (1987) 'Aboriginal women and childbirth—the struggle for the Congress Alukura' *Refractory Girl* No. 30: 14–17

Chesler, Phyllis (1972) *Women and Madness* New York: Avon Books

Commonwealth of Australia (1990) *Breast Cancer Screening in Australia: Future Directions* (Prevention Program Evaluation Series No. 1) Canberra: Australian Institute of Health

Commonwealth Department of Community Services and Health (1989) *National Women's Health Policy: Advancing Women's Health in Australia* Canberra: Australian Government Publishing Service

Commonwealth Department of Health (1985) *Australian Women: A Health Perspective* (A Summary of Statistical Indicators) Canberra: Commonwealth Department of Health

———(1975) 'A community health centre by women, for women: the community health story' *Health: Journal of the Australian Department of Health* 25 (1): 8–12

Community Development in Health Project (1990) *Strengthening Community Health* Northcote, Vic: Victorian Health Promotion Foundation

———(1988) *Community Development in Health: A Resources Collection* Northcote, Vic: Preston/Northcote District Health Council

Cooper, Nola and Merry Spencer (1978) 'Why women's health centres?' pages 149–52 in *Women's Health* in a Changing Society Conference Proceedings Vol. 4. Commonwealth Department of Health: Australian Government Publishing Service

Corea, Gena (1977) *The Hidden Malpractice* New York: Jove/HBJ

Cowan, Belita (1980) 'Ethical problems in government-funded contraceptive research' pp. 37–46 in Helen B. Holmes, Betty B. Hoskins and Michael Gross (eds), *Birth Control and Controlling Birth* Clifton, NJ: Humana Press

Cox, Eva, Fran Hausfeld and Sue Wills (1978) 'Taking the queen's shilling' pp. 121–41 in Colin Bell and Sol Encel (eds), *Inside the Whale* Rushcutters Bay, NSW: Pergamon Australia

Curthoys, Ann (1988) *For and Against Feminism* Sydney: Allen & Unwin

Dale, Jennifer and Peggy Foster (1986) *Feminists and State Welfare* London: Routledge & Kegan Paul

Devesa, Susan S. (1986) 'Cancer mortality, incidence, and patient survival among American women' *Women and Health* 11 (3/4): 7–22

Dixon, Gill, Chris Johnson, Sue Leigh and Nicky Turnbull (1982) 'Feminist perspectives and practice' pp. 59–71 in Gary Craig, Nick Derricourt and Martin Loney (eds), *Community Work and the State* London: Routledge & Kegan Paul

Dixon, Jane (1989) 'The limits and potential of community development for personal and social change' *Community Health Studies* 13 (1): 82–92

Dowse, Sara (1989) 'Keep at it—often and loud' *Australian Society* (February): 8–9

———(1984) 'The bureaucrat as usurer' Chapter 8 in Dorothy H. Broom (ed.), *Unfinished Business: Social Justice for Women in Australia* Sydney: George Allen & Unwin

———(1982) 'The women's movement's fandango with the state: some thoughts on the movement's role in public policy since 1972' *Australian Quarterly* 4: 324–45; reprinted pp. 201–21 in Cora Baldock and Bettina Cass (eds), *Women, Social Welfare and the State in Australia* Sydney: Allen & Unwin

Doyal, Lesley (1983) 'Women, health and the sexual division of labour: a case study of the women's health movement in Britain' *Critical Social Policy* 3 (1): 21–32

———(1981) *The Political Economy of Health* London: Pluto Press

Edwards, Anne (1988) *Regulation and Repression* Sydney: Allen & Unwin

Edwards, Jean (1984) 'Liverpool Women's Health Centre' *New Doctor* 34

Ehrenreich, Barbara and John Ehrenreich (1974) 'Health care and social control' *Social Policy* May/June 26–40

Ehrenreich, Barbara and Dierdre English (1973) *Complaints and Disorders: The Sexual Politics of Sickness* Old Westbury, NY: The Feminist Press

Elston, Mary Ann (1981) 'Medicine as "old husbands' tales": the impact of feminism' pp. 189–211 in Dale Spender (ed.), *Men's Studies Modified: The Impact of Feminism on the Academic Disciplines* New York: Pergamon

Evatt, Elizabeth, Felix Arnott and Anne Deveson (1977) *The Royal Commission on Human Relationships* Final Report Volume 3 Canberra: AGPS

Fatin, Wendy (1990) 'Women in the State' pp. 11–15 in *National Women's Conference 1990 Proceedings* Canberra: Write People

Ferguson, Kathy E. (1984) *The Feminist Case Against Bureaucracy* Philadelphia: Temple University Press

Fett, Ione (1971) 'The Monash University survey of Australian women medical graduates' *Medical Journal of Australia* April 24: 920–22

Flaskas, Carmel and Betty Hounslow (1980) 'Government intervention and right wing attacks on feminist services' *Scarlet Woman* No. 11 (September) : 13–16

Foster, Peggy (1989) 'Improving the doctor/patient relationship: A feminist perspective' *Journal of Social Policy* 18 (3): 337–61

Frankfort, Ellen (1972) *Vaginal Politics* New York: Bantam Books

Franzway, Suzanne, Dianne Court, and R. W. Connell (1989) *Staking a Claim: Feminism, Bureaucracy and the State* Sydney: Allen & Unwin

Fraser, Nancy (1987) 'Women, welfare and the politics of need interpretation' *Thesis Eleven* No. 17 : 88–106

Freeman, Jo (Joreen) (1972) 'The tyranny of structurelessness' *The Second Wave* 2 (1): 20–25 + 42. Also published in 1973 *The Berkeley Journal of Sociology* 17

Freidson, Eliot (1970) *Professional Dominance* Chicago: Aldine

Freudenberger, H. J. (1974) 'Staff burnout' *Journal of Social Issues* 30: 159–65

Frey, Karen A. (1981) 'Middle aged women's experience and perceptions of menopause' *Women and Health* 6: 25–36

Gallop, Jane (1988) *Thinking Through the Body* New York: Columbia University Press

Galper, Miriam and Carolyn Kott Washburne (1976) 'A women's self-help program in action' *Social Policy* 6 (5): 46–52

Game, Ann and Rosemary Pringle (1983) *Gender at Work* Sydney: George Allen & Unwin

Gatens, Moira (1983) 'A critique of the sex/gender distinction' pp. 143–60 in

Judith Allen and Paul Patten (eds), *Beyond Marxism: Interventions after Marx* Leichhardt: Intervention Publications

Glaser, B. and A. Strauss (1964) 'The social loss of dying patients' *American Journal of Nursing* 64: 119–21

Gove, Walter R. (1973) 'Sex, marital status, and mortality' *American Journal of Sociology* 79 (1): 45–67

Gove, Walter R. and Michael Hughes (1979) 'Possible causes of the apparent sex differences in physical health' *American Sociological Review* 44: 125–46

——(1981) 'Beliefs vs. data: more on the illness behavior of men and women' (A reply to Marcus and Seeman) *American Sociological Review* 46: 123–28

Graham, Harvey (pseudonym) (1950) *Eternal Eve* London: Heinemann Medical Books

Haire, Doris (1978) 'The cultural warping of childbirth' in J. Ehrenreich (ed.), *The Cultural Crises of Modern Medicine* New York: Monthly Review Press

Gray, Gwen (1984) 'The termination of Medibank' *Politics* 19: 1–17

Harcourt, Wendy (1987) *Medical Discourse Relating to the Female Body in late 19th Century Melbourne* Unpublished PhD thesis, Department of History, Faculty of Arts, Australian National University

Hartsock, Nancy (1983) *Money Sex and Power* New York: Longman

Healthsharing Women (1990) *The Healthsharing Reader: Women speak about health* Sydney: Pandora

Hole, Judith and Ellen Levine (1971) *The Rebirth of Feminism* New York: Quadrangle Books

Hornstein, Frances (1974) 'An interview on women's health politics' Part I *Quest* 1 (1): 27–36; Part II *Quest* 1 (2): 75–80

Howell, Mary C. (1975) 'A women's health school?' *Social Policy* 6 (2): 50–3

Hull, Bon (1986) 'Why another women's health centre went to the wall' *The Age* (1 August.)

——(1980) *In Our Own Hands—A Women's Health Manual* Melbourne: Hyland House

Illich, Ivan (1975) *Medical Nemesis: The Expropriation of Health* London: Calder

Jackson, Terri, Sally Mitchell and Maria Wright (1989) 'The community development continuum' *Community Health Studies* 13 (1): 66–73

Johnson, John M. (1981) 'Program enterprise and official cooptation in the battered women's shelter movement' *American Behavioral Scientist* 24 (6): 827–42

Johnson, Terrence (1972) *Professions and Power* London: Macmillan

Jones, M. A. (1990) *The Australian Welfare State: Origins, Control and Choices* (Third Edition) Sydney: Allen & Unwin

Kanter, Rosabeth Moss (1975) 'Women and the structure of organizations' Chapter 2 in Marcia Millman and Rosabeth Moss Kanter (eds), *Another Voice: Feminist Perspectives on Social Life and Social Science* New York: Anchor Press

——(1977) *Men and Women of the Corporation* New York: Basic Books

Korenbrot, Carol (1980) 'Value conflicts in biomedical research into future contraceptives' pp. 47–54 in Helen B. Holmes, Betty B. Hoskins and Michael Gross (eds), *Birth Control and Controlling Birth* Clifton, NJ: Humana Press

Koutroulis, Glenda (1990) 'The orifice revisited: portrayal of women in gynaecological texts' *Community Health Studies* 14: 73–84

Lavis, Donald R. (n.d.) 'Oral contraceptives in Melbourne, 1961–71' *Australian Family Formation Project Monograph* No.3. Australian National University: Department of Demography

Legge, David (1990) 'Community based management in community health' Unpublished draft chapter in preparation for a forthcoming collection by the Australian Community Health Association

Leichhardt Women's Community Health Centre (1974) News Release. 22 February. Held in *First Ten Years Collection: The Archives of Sydney Women's Liberation*

Lennane, K. Jean and R. John Lennane (1973) 'Alleged psychogenic disorders in women — a possible manifestation of sexual prejudice' *New England Journal of Medicine* 228 (6): 288–92

Lieven, E. (1981) 'If it's natural, we can't change it' Chapter 12 in Cambridge Women's Studies Group (eds), *Women in Society* London: Virago

Lloyd, Genevieve (1984) *The Man of Reason* London: Methuen

London Edinburgh Weekend Return Group (1979) *In and Against the State* (New expanded edition) London: Pluto Press

Lorber, Judith (1985) 'More women physicians: will it mean more humane health care?' *Social Policy* 16 (1): 50–4

Luker, Kristin (1975) *Taking Chances: Abortion and the Decision Not to Contracept.* Berkeley: University of California Press

Lumley, J. and J. Astbury (1980) *Birth Rites, Birth Rights* Melbourne: Nelson

Lynch, Lesley (1984) 'Bureaucratic feminisms: bossism and beige suits' *Refractory Girl,* 27: 38–44

MacKinnon, Catherine A. (1990) 'Liberalism and the death of feminism' pp. 3–13 in Dorchen Leidholdt and Janice G. Raymond (eds), *The Sexual Liberals and the Attack on Feminism* New York: Pergamon

Mansbridge, Jane J. (1979) 'The agony of inequality' pp. 194–214 in John Case and Rosemary C. R. Taylor (eds), *Co-ops, Communes and Collectives* New York: Pantheon Books

Marieskind, Helen I. (1976) 'Helping oneself to health' *Social Policy* 7 (2): 63–6
———(1975) 'Restructuring ob/gyn' *Social Policy* 6 (2): 48–9

Marieskind, Helen I. and Barbara Ehrenreich (1975) 'Toward socialist medicine: the women's health movement' *Social Policy* 6 (2): 34–42

Marcus, Alfred C. and Teresa E. Seeman (1981a) 'Sex differences in health status: a reexamination of the nurturant role hypothesis' (Comment on Gove and Hughes) *American Sociological Review* 46 : 119–23
———(1981b) 'Sex differences in reports of illness and disability: a preliminary test of the 'fixed role obligations' hypothesis' *Journal of Health and Social Behavior* 22 (June): 174–82

Marshall, J. R. and D. P. Funch (1987) 'Gender and illness behavior among colorectal cancer patients' *Women and Health* 11: 67–82

Marshall, J. R., D. I. Gregorio and D. Walsh (1982) 'Sex differences in illness behavior: care seeking among cancer patients' *Journal of Health and Social Behavior* 23: 197–204

Martin, Emily (1987) *The Woman in the Body: A Cultural Analysis of Reproduction* Boston: Beacon Press

Martin, Patricia Yancey (1990) 'Rethinking feminist organizations' *Gender and Society* 4 (2): 182–206

Masion, Caroly (1978) 'The Women's Community Aid Association Brisbane' pp 154–8 in *Women's Health in a Changing Society* Conference Proceedings Vol. 4 Commonwealth Department of Health: Australian Government Publishing Service

Matthews, Jill Julius (1984) *Good and Mad Women: The historical construction of femininity in twentieth century Australia* Sydney: George Allen & Unwin

McFerren, Ludo (1990) 'Interpretation of a frontline state: Australian women's refuges and the state' pp. 191–205 in Sophie Watson (ed.), *Playing the State: Australian Feminist Interventions* Sydney: Allen & Unwin

McIntosh, Mary (1978) 'The state and the oppression of women' pp. 254–89 in Annette Kuhn and AnneMarie Wolpe (eds), *Feminism and Materialism: Women and Modes of Production* London: Routledge & Kegan Paul

McKenzie, Lyn (1979) 'Melbourne women's health collective: problems with funding' pp 31–42 in Voluntary Associations and Funding Issues Working Party (comp.), *Lost Sleep Over Government Funding: Five Case Studies* Melbourne

McLean, Judy, Gill Draffen and Barbara Callcott (1977) 'The politics of establishing health centres' pp. 45–54 in Department of Prime Minister and Cabinet, *Women and Politics Conference 1975* (Volume 2) Canberra: AGPS

McMichael, A. J. (1985) 'Social class and mortality in Australian males in the 1970s' *Community Health Studies* 9: 220–30

McRea, F.B. (1980) 'The politics of menopause: the "discovery" of a deficiency disease' *Social Problems* 31: 111–23

Meekosha, Helen (1989) 'Research and the state: dilemmas of feminist practice' *Australian Journal of Social Issues* 24 (4): 249–68

Members of the Centre (1978) 'The Leichhardt Women's Community Health Centre' pp. 142–48 in *Women's Health in a Changing Society* Conference Proceedings Vol. 4. Commonwealth Department of Health: Australian Government Publishing Service

Milio, Nancy (1988) *Making Policy: A Mozaic [sic] of Australian Community Health Policy Development* Canberra: Department of Community Services and Health

——(1984) 'The political anatomy of the community health policy in Australia' *Politics* 19: 18–33

Mills, C. Wright (1959) *The Sociological Imagination* Oxford: Oxford University Press

Moir, Hazel (1984) 'Comment on "Women in the Australian labour force" ' pp. 94–100 in D. H. Broom (ed.), *Unfinished Business: Social Justice for Women in Australia* Sydney: Allen & Unwin

Molica, G. J. and N. E. Winn (1974) 'History of the Waikiki Clinic' *Journal of Social Issues* 30: 53–60

Morgan, Patricia (1981) 'From battered wife to program client: the state's shaping of social problems' *Kapitalistate* 9: 17–39

Morgen, Sandra (1986) 'The dynamics of cooptation in a feminist health clinic' *Social Science and Medicine* 23 (2): 201–10

Moore, Henrietta L. (1988) *Feminism and Anthropology* Minneapolis: University of Minnesota Press

Muller, Charlotte F. (1990) *Health Care and Gender* New York: Russell Sage Foundation

Nathanson, Constance A. (1975) 'Illness and the feminine role: a theoretical review' *Social Science and Medicine* 9 (Feb): 57–62

National Hospitals and Health Services Commission (1973) *A Community Health Program for Australia* Report from the National Hospitals and Health Services Commission Interim Committee (June) Canberra: AGPS

Navarro, Vincente (1976) *Medicine Under Capitalism* New York: Prodist

Neugarten, Bernice L., Vivian Wood, Ruth J. Kraines, and Barbara Loomis (1968) 'Women's attitudes toward the menopause' pp. 195–200 in Bernice L. Neugarten (ed.), *Middle Age and Aging: A Reader in Social Psychology* Chicago: University of Chicago Press

Newby, Liza (1988) *National Policy on Women's Health: A Framework for Change* (A Discussion Paper for Community Comment and Response) Canberra: AGPS

Newman, Katherine (1980) 'Incipient bureaucracy: the development of hierarchies in egalitarian organizations' pp. 143–63 in Gerald M. Britan and Ronald Cohen (eds), *Hierarchy and Society: Anthropological Perspectives on Bureaucracy* Philadelphia: Institute for the Study of Human Issues

Oakley, A. (1984) *The Captured Womb: A History of the Care of Pregnant Women* Oxford: Blackwell

———(1980) *Women Confined* Oxford: Martin Robertson

O'Connor, Debra *et al.* (1990) *A Sliver—Not Even a Slice: A Report of a Study on Expenditure on Women and Health Research* Melbourne: Melbourne District Health Council

O'Dea, Thomas F. (1961) 'Five dilemmas in the institutionalization of religion' *Journal for the Scientific Study of Religion* 1 (Oct.): 30–9

Odent, Michel (1984) *Birth Reborn* New York: Pantheon

Otto, Dianne and Eileen Haley (1975) 'Helter shelter: a history of the Adelaide Women's Shelter' *Refractory Girl* No. 9 (Winter): 11–16

Pahl, Jan (1985) 'Refuges for battered women: ideology and action' *Feminist Review* 19 (March): 25–43

Palmer, Beverly B. (1974) 'A model for a community-based women's clinic' *American Journal of Public Health* 64 (7): 713–14

Palmer, George R. and Stephanie D. Short (1989) *Health Care and Public Policy* South Melbourne: Macmillan

Pateman, Carole (1988) *The Sexual Contract* Cambridge: Polity Press

Petterson, Louise (1975) Report prepared for The Leichhardt Women's Community Health Centre. Unpublished report sponsored by International Women's Year National Research Program, Canberra. Held in *First Ten Years Collection: The Archives of Sydney Women's Liberation*

Powell, Susan (1986) 'What's WICH?' *Australian Society* (September): 39

Price, Colette (1972) 'The first self-help clinic' *Woman's World* No. 4, March–May; reprinted pp. 136–40 in 1975 *Redstockings Feminist Revolution* New York: Random House

Reiger, Kerreen (1988) 'Re-organising reproduction or reproducing the organisation?' Paper presented at the Annual Conference of the Sociology Association of Australia and New Zealand, Canberra

Roberts, Keith A. (1984) *Religion in Sociological Perspective* Homewood, Ill.:
Dorsey Press

Rodriguez, Noelie Maria (1988) 'Transcending bureaucracy: feminist politics at a
shelter for battered women' *Gender and Society* 2 (2): 214–27

Rose, Hilary (1986) 'Women and the restructuring of the welfare state' Chapter
6 in Elsa Øyen (ed.), *Comparing Welfare States and their Futures* England:
Gower

Rosenhan, David L. (1973) 'On being sane in insane places' *Science* 179: 250–58

Rosser, Sue V. (1989) 'Re-visioning clinical research: gender and the ethics of
experimental design' *Hypatia* 4 (2): 125–39

———(1988) *Feminism Within the Science and Health Care Professions: Overcoming Resistance* Oxford: Pergamon Press

Roth, Julius A. (1972) 'Some contingencies of the moral evaluation and control
of clientele' *American Journal of Sociology* 77: 839–56

———(1957) 'Ritual and magic in the control of contagion' *American Sociological Review* 22: 310–14

Rothschild, Joyce and Raymond Russell (1986) 'Alternatives to bureaucracy:
democratic participation in the economy' *Annual Review of Sociology* 12:
307–28

Rothschild-Whitt, Joyce (1979a) 'The collectivist organization: an alternative to
rational-bureaucratic models' *American Sociological Review* 44: 509–27

———(1979b) 'Conditions for democracy: making participatory organizations
work' pp. 215–44 in John Case and Rosemary C. R. Taylor (eds), *Co-ops,
Communes and Collectives* New York: Pantheon Books

Rothman, Barbara Katz (1982) *In Labor: Women and Power in the Birthplace*
New York: W.W. Norton

Rowland, Barbara and Lawrence J. Schneiderman (1979) 'Women in alternative
health care: their influence on traditional medicine' *Journal of the American
Medical Association* 241 (7): 719–21

Ruzek, Sheryl Burt (1980) 'Medical response to women's health activities: conflict, accommodation and cooptation' *Sociology of Health Care* 1: 335–45

———(1978) *The Women's Health Movement* New York: Praeger

———(1975) 'Emergent modes of utilization: gynecological self-help' pp.80–4 in
Virginia Olesen (ed.), *Women and Their Health: Research Implications for a
New Era* Springfield, VA: U.S. Department of Health, Education, and Welfare

Sandall, Philippa (1974) 'The Leichhardt story' pp. 88–9 in WEL Said (eds),
From the Gilded Cage Sydney: WEL Publications

Savage, Wendy (1986) *A Savage Enquiry* London: Virago

Sawer, Marian (1990) *Sisters in Suits: Women and Public Policy in Australia*
Sydney: Allen & Unwin

———(1989) 'Feminism and the state workshop' *WEL National Bulletin* 11 (12):
13–14

Sax, Sidney (1980) 'Community health developments in Australia' *Public Health
Reviews* 9 (3–4): 269–305

———(1972) *Medical Care in the Melting Pot* Sydney: Angus and Robertson

Schneider, Joseph W. and Peter Conrad (1980) 'The medical control of deviance:

contests and consequences' pp. 1–53 in Julius A. Roth (ed.), *Research in the Sociology of Health Care* Volume 1, Greenwich, Connecticut: JAI Press

Schlesinger, Melinda Bart and Pauline B. Bart (1982) 'Collective work and self-identity: working in a feminist illegal abortion collective' pp. 139–53 in Frank Lindenfeld and Joyce Rothschild-Whitt (eds), *Workplace Democracy and Social Change* Boston: Porter Sargent Publishers, Inc

Schur, Edwin M. (1984) *Labeling Women Deviant: Gender, Stigma and Social Control* New York: Random House

Schwartzman, Helen B. (1980) 'The bureaucratic context of a community mental health centre' pp. 45–59 in Gerald M. Britan and Ronald Cohen (eds), *Hierarchy and Society: Anthropological Perspectives on Bureaucracy* Philadelphia: Institute for the Study of Human Issues

Scully, Diana (1980) *Men Who Control Women's Health* Boston: Houghton Mifflin

Scully, Diana and Pauline Bart (1973) 'A funny thing happened on the way to the orifice: women in gynecology textbooks' *American Journal of Sociology* 78: 1045–50

Scutt, Jocelynne (1983) *Even in the Best of Homes* Ringwood: Penguin

Seaman, Barbara (1975) 'Pelvic autonomy: four proposals' *Social Policy* 6 (2): 43–7

——(1972) *Free and Female* New York: Fawcett

——(1969) *The Doctors' Case Against the Pill* New York: Avon

Selznick, Philip (1952/1960) *The Organizational Weapon* Glencoe: Free Press

——(1949/1966) *TVA and The Grass Roots* New York: Harper & Row

Shaver, Sheila (1987) 'Comment on Fraser I' *Thesis Eleven* No. 17: 107–10

——(1983) 'Sex and money in the welfare state' pp. 146–63 in Cora V. Baldock and Bettina Cass (eds), *Women, Social Welfare and the State in Australia* Sydney: Allen & Unwin

Shorter, Edward (1983) *A History of Women's Bodies* London: Allen Lane

Sibbison, J. B. (1990) 'Women's health, women's rights' *The Lancet* (July 21): 166

Siedlecky, Stefania and Diana Wyndham (1990) *Populate and Perish: Australian Women's Fight for Birth Control* Sydney: Allen & Unwin

Skrabanek, Petr (1985) 'False premises and false promises of breast cancer screening' *The Lancet* (August 10): 316–20

Smith, Alison (1985) 'Women's refuges: the only resort?' pp. 23–68 in *Public/Private* Don Parry and Peter Botsman (eds), University of New South Wales: Local Consumption Series 6

Smith, Dorothy E. (1974) 'Women's perspective as a radical critique of sociology' *Sociological Inquiry* 44 (1): 7–13

——(1987) *The Everyday World as Problematic: A Feminist Sociology* Boston: Northeastern University Press

Smith, Meg (1984) 'The struggle for women's health centres in NSW' *Refractory Girl* No. 27: 3–6

Sontag, Susan (1977) *Illness as Metaphor* New York: Vintage Books

Standing, Hilary (1980) ' "Sickness is a woman's business?" Reflections on the attribution of illness' pp. 124–38 in Lynda Birke *et al.* (eds), *Alice Through the Microscope: The Power of Science over Women's Lives* London: Virago

Starr, Paul (1982) *The Transformation of American Medicine* New York: Harper & Row

Summers, Anne (1986) 'Mandarins or missionaries: women in the federal bureaucracy' pp. 59–67 in Norma Grieve and Ailsa Burns (eds), *Australian Women: New Feminist Perspectives* Melbourne: Oxford University Press

——(1975) *Damned Whores and God's Police* Harmondsworth: Penguin

Tew, Marjorie (1985) 'Place of birth and perinatal mortality' *Journal of the Royal College of General Practitioners* 35 (August): 390–4

Theberge, Nancy (1987) 'Sport and women's empowerment' *Women's Studies International Forum* 10 (4): 387–93

Thompson, Mary K. and Julia S. Brown (1980) 'Feminine roles and variations in women's illness behaviors' *Pacific Sociological Review* 23: 405

Tierney, Kathleen J. (1982) 'The battered woman movement and the creation of the wife beating problem' *Social Problems* 29: 207–20

Verbrugge, Lois M. and Deborah L. Wingard (1987) 'Sex differentials in health and mortality' *Women and Health* 12: 103–45

Victorian Ministerial Women's Health Working Party (1987) *Why Women's Health? Victorian Women Respond: Report of the Victorian Ministerial Women's Health Working Party* Melbourne: Health Department Victoria

Victorian Women's Health Policy Working Party (1985) *Why Women's Health? Discussion Paper* Melbourne: Health Department Victoria

Waddell, Charles and Pauline Floate (1986) 'Gender and the utilisation of health care services in Perth, Australia' *Sociology of Health and Illness* 8 (2): 170–7

Wallen, Jacqueline, Howard Waitzkin, and John D. Stoeckle (1979) 'Physician stereotypes about female health and illness' *Women and Health* 4 (2): 135–46

Watson, Sophie (ed.), (1990) *Playing the State: Australian Feminist Interventions* Sydney: Allen & Unwin

Webb, Christine (ed.), (1986) *Feminist Practice in Women's Health Care* Chichester: John Wiley & Sons

Weiss, Kay (1977) 'What medical students learn about women' pp. 212–22 in Claudia Dreyfus (ed.), *Seizing Our Bodies: The Politics of Women's Health* New York: Vintage

Whatley, Mariamne H. (1988) 'Beyond compliance: towards a feminist health education' pp. 131–44 in Sue V. Rosser (ed.), *Feminism Within the Science and Health Care Professions: Overcoming Resistance* Oxford: Pergamon Press

WHCH Staff Members (1985) 'Women's Health Care House: an alternative' pp. 162–8 in E. Kerby-Eaton and J. Davies (eds), *Women's Health in a Changing Society* Conference Proceedings Vol. 3. Second National Women's Health Conference, Adelaide

Williams, Fiona (1989) *Social Policy: A Critical Introduction* Cambridge: Polity Press

Wingard, Deborah L. (1984) 'The sex differential in morbidity, mortality, and lifestyle' *Annual Review of Public Health* 5: 433–58

Willis, Evan (1983) *Medical Dominance* Sydney: George Allen & Unwin

Women's Bureau (1983) *Facts on Women at Work in Australia 1982* Canberra: AGPS

——(1988) 'Women in community services' *Women & Work* 10 (1) (March)

——(1990) *Women & Work* 12 (2) (June)

Women's Health Policy Review Committee (1985) *Final Report of the Women's*

Health Policy Review Committee (No. 403) Sydney: Government Printer, NSW

Worcester, Nancy and Mariamne H. Whatley (1988) 'The response of the health care system to the women's health movement: the selling of women's health centres' pp. 117–30 in Sue V. Rosser (ed.), *Feminism Within the Science and Health Care Professions: Overcoming Resistance* Oxford: Pergamon Press

Wyndham, Diana (1981) 'Women and health services—catalysts for change' *New Doctor* (June): 25–8

Yeatman, Anna (1990) *Bureaucrats, Technocrats, Femocrats* Sydney: Allen & Unwin

Zola, Irving K. (1973) 'Pathways to the doctor—from person to patient' *Social Science and Medicine* 7: 677–89

——(1972) 'Medicine as an institution of social control' *Sociological Review* 20: 487–504

Zon, Annie (1982) 'Wimmin's services in Darwin: a summarized herstory' Paper presented at the National Women's Refuge Conference

Index